ROSIE'S GRINGO PALACE

A Novel

by

Irene Tritel

Printed in the United States of America

ISBN: 978-0-9828053-0-5

Text in Trebuchet

Rosie4Tritel@aol.com

What lies behind us and what lies
Before us are tiny matters
Compared to what lies within us.

Ralph Waldo Emerson

ACKNOWLEDGEMENTS

Everyone I have ever had the pleasure, or displeasure, of meeting, has had an impact in my life. Although they may not be mentioned specifically on this page, they are as instrumental to the writing of this novel as those mentioned here.

I feel fortunate that I was able to absorb the heartening encouragement of family and friends, living or deceased, who have deliberately, or unknowingly, pushed me along in this effort. From the Bronx to Palm Springs, from Hollie Davies, editor-in-waiting, to Marvin Goldberg, ex-policeman, from Palm Springs Writers Guild critique group, to Phyllis Greenbach, friend extraordinaire — there is no 'foremost I thank,' or 'lastly I thank,' since all, in their way, have contributed.

. . . AND to William T. Mendenhall, bless his little "keppie" — for putting down the sports page and reading a book that doesn't have spies or detectives in it.

DEDICATION

To the best eggs I ever laid —

Parise, Lori and Michael

PART ONE
THE BRONX, SPRING, 1973

CHAPTER ONE

NOT FOR A MOMENT did Rosie Goldberg Sanchez imagine that the familiar sound of a vacuum could so diversely trigger the start of the day. In some neighborhoods of the Bronx, this being one of them, the sound of a noisy vacuum at five a.m. on a Saturday morning might be cause for justifiable homicide. Rosie didn't know how close she came.

Tony D'Marco, who lived on the ground floor of a nearby tenement building, opened his black gangster eyes and was in an immediate rage that his sleep had been disturbed. He'd been retired many years now, but, still, out of habit, or sheer frustration, he walked barefoot to the closet and reached his long hairy arm to the top shelf for his .45 Colt.

"Where ya goin," his wife asked in the middle of a snore.

"That gumbah, Rosie, is makin a racket wit that damn vacuum — so I'm gonna blow its kneecap off."

She laughed. "What? You got nothin better to do so early in the morning?"

"No," Tony said. "I need the practice. It's been awhile."

Tony's wife pulled back the covers revealing a nightgown that had twisted above her hips. "C'mere." She patted the bed next to her. "I'll give you something better to do."

One thing you could say about Tony; he didn't have a lot of will power.

Rosie's tall, slender body bent forward and backward, up and down, easily matching the flexibility of the hose. Her long dark hair, pulled back in a pony tail, emphasized her angular facial structure, long narrow nose, high cheekbones, large dark eyes and olive complexion. Beads of moisture formed at her hairline and upper lip. Under her arms half circles of sweat outlined her T-shirt.

In a city where the noise level was powerful enough to create a tsunami, you wouldn't think the sound of a vacuum would be jarring enough to interrupt the twilight dreams of some nearby neighbors. Yet, in the sheer silence of dawn, in the half-hour before the city awoke, the sound of the vacuum bolted out the windows of Rosie's small house like lightening, striking various tenement apartments indiscriminately. Tony D'Marco wasn't the only one.

A seven-year-old who had been playing with his tin soldiers the night before dreamt his little army was being attacked. He wet his bed.

A seventy-two-year-old grandfather, whose sexual experiences in the last decade had been rare, thought he was having an orgasm. Disappointed, he farted, turned over, and fell back to sleep.

Seventeen-year-old high school senior, Jimmy Cox, living in a basement apartment nearby, *did* have an orgasm. For a moment he thought the noise came from his penis. *WOW!*

On the sixth floor, a half-drunk father, about to climb into his fifteen-year-old daughter's bed, heard the clamor. Afraid it would wake his wife, he quickly retreated to his bedroom. His daughter cried with relief.

◇◇◇

The street light was still visible through the pulled-down shade in Joey Goldberg's bedroom. He had tried taping the shade to the window frame, but a sliver of light was still visible no matter what he did.

He turned to his left, and glanced at the bedside table where four inch red numbers on a digital clock shouted at him. Five-fifteen! God Almighty, what was that crazy sister of his doing, making such a racket?

He threw the covers over his head but he could still hear the whiz-whirr-sputter-clamor of the vacuum above the otherwise stark silence of the house. Sounded like Rosie was determined to piss off the neighbors.

Joey shivered in the morning chill as he slowly dragged his legs over the edge of the bed. At seventy-eight, after suffering two strokes, he had learned that if he wasn't careful he'd fall flat on his face. Just swinging his legs toward the floor was painful. Sometimes he had to sit there five minutes until all the bones in his body fell into their proper place. He felt the first spurt of urine and then just let go. He didn't worry these days about peeing in bed because Rosie had insisted, after the first few accidents, that he wear Depends. He remembered the argument as if it was yesterday:

"I'm not wearing diapers and that's all there is to it," he'd said.

"They're not diapers."

"I don't care what you call them, I know what they are. It's humiliating."

"I'll tell you what's humiliating," she'd shouted. "It's humiliating, not to mention disgusting, that I have to change your bed every day. This is not a nursing home and I'm not your nurse. And I'm not your mother either – or your girlfriend or your wife."

He had asked her to stop yelling.

"Who's yelling?" Her voice had escalated. "I have enough to do without taking care of some old fart, even if you are my brother."

"I can't wear diapers," he'd blubbered.

"Listen," Rosie had said, hands on hips. "I know this is hard, but you have a choice. Either you wear Depends or you have to change your own bedding every day. Or, you can go to a nursing home."

Rosie had prevailed, one more nail hammered into his independence. Now he was glad because he didn't have to worry about getting up in the middle of the night or getting to the bathroom in the nick of time every morning. It sure did take some getting used to, he thought: peeing in your pants or wearing diapers. Take your pick.

He slid into the flannel slippers, which for years had lain in the identical spot at the side of his double bed. There was a dent in the shape of the slippers on the carpet, just like the concave shape of his body on the right side of the mattress. Joey liked things that were getting on in age, like him. He felt a kinship with such items, as though they were his friends; comforting and loyal, always there and always ready to accommodate him.

Even his room hadn't changed very much. He just wasn't sharing it with siblings anymore. A sepia photograph of his grandparents, in a brown splintered wood frame, hung near the window along with a picture of his parents, taken fifty-eight years ago. Joey was the oldest of five siblings, standing tall next to his father. Rosie was still swaddled in a receiving blanket, held close in her mother's arms.

An oak dresser stood in one corner, ruined by Rosie a few years ago when she painted it green to match the bedspread. A heavy, gilt-framed mirror hung over the dresser on a rope cord with a tassel. There was a night stand on each side of the bed; one with a lamp and the other covered with seventeen bottles of prescription pills.

Joey shuffled down the dim hallway, limping his way toward the living room where he knew Rosie moved chairs and other things around so she could vacuum under them. He kept shuffling along. What was the name of that old Jolson song? *See them shufflin' along. See them da da . . . along. Just take your real pal . . . Go down to the levee, down to the levee.* Well, something like that anyway. He could hear the melody in his head, but nobody would recognize it if he tried to hum it.

He'd lived with Rosie long enough to know exactly the route she took with that vacuum, as though she was driving a car. He could see her plugging the cord in one outlet and then another so she could vacuum in places no one would ever think to look. No one showed more dedication than Rosie when vacuuming.

He finally reached the archway leading into the living room. He observed her slender body moving up and down and sideways as though the vacuum played a tune and she danced to it. Rosie's back was to him and he decided to shadow her around the room and then pounce when she least expected it.

He stole quietly behind her, all one hundred forty pounds of him, wondering how long it would take before she knew he was there. He didn't get very far because, wouldn't you know it, he stumbled over the vacuum cleaner cord and she turned her head slightly as he did so. He hurled himself on to the couch to break his fall, but all Rosie saw was a fast-moving body lurching toward her. Scared out of her wits, she instinctively threw the hose toward the assailant. With the vacuum still running, the hose flew out of control and headed in several directions while the small brush attached to it took its own course. The brush soared to the ceiling like a model airplane and then ricocheted off the wall. Rosie was shrieking; they both ducked as the brush headed toward them, the hose in close pursuit.

"You son of a . . . you son of a . . ." Rosie tried to get the words out but she was gasping for breath as she tried to grab the flailing hose. Finally she managed to pull the plug. Suddenly the room quieted.

Joey was still sprawled on the couch, both hands covering his face with fingers spread apart so he could witness his own demise.

She was on her knees with her butt in the air, holding on to the vacuum cleaner plug as though it would transport her to another time and place. Joey slowly uncovered his face only to find himself looking directly at Rosie's behind as she maintained her stance on all fours. She turned her head slowly.

"You know I'm going to kill you?"

"That's what I figured." Joey started to laugh. He laughed so hard, he thought he'd have a heart attack. Rosie took one look at him and also started laughing. She flopped to her side as Joey fell gently off the couch. The two lay side by side, holding their stomachs, doubled up with laughter, tears streaming from their eyes.

"Stop! Stop laughing," she gasped. "I give up. I swear. I give up. Help me find the damn brush and I'll put the vacuum away. I have no idea where it went."

"I think it's under your ass," he said, trying to control another bout of laughter, struggling for breath.

"Oh, God, you're right. I was wondering what was digging into me." She reached under her buttock and retrieved the brush. "C'mon" she said, groaning as she stood up. "I'll make you a cup of coffee."

"I don't know Rosie. I was thinking of going back to bed but you know how strong your coffee is. One cup and I might be up for two days."

Rosie started toward the kitchen, winding up the vacuum cord and straightening things out. Joey headed back toward his room. "I'll be right there," he said. "I'm going to get my bathrobe. It's freezing in here."

Rosie filled the coffee pot with water and put two heaping scoops of ground decaf in the filter. "I don't know how decaf coffee can keep him awake," she mumbled under her breath. She shouted to Joey. "It's May, for God's sake. How could it be freezing?"

Joey limped back to his room to get his bathrobe. He chuckled as a memory of Rosie as a kid followed him down the narrow hallway past several dozen framed photographs of the family.

◇◇◇

Joey returned to the kitchen and sat down at the small Formica table. He reached for a cube of sugar and put it between his teeth as Rosie poured the coffee.

"You really date yourself when you do that, you know," she commented.

"So-o-o. Who are you going to tell? Everyone I know is already dead."

"Yes, and if you pull another stunt like you did just now in the living room, you're going to join them."

"All right already." Joey sipped the hot coffee carefully, savoring the sweetness of the sugar cube. He suddenly noticed how pensive Rosie had become. Their playful joust in the living room was now replaced with a more somber mood. She wiped a tear with the sleeve of her T-shirt.

"Okay, Rosie, you don't have to cry. I promise I won't pounce on you again."

"Oh, don't be ridiculous! This has nothing to do with you pouncing on me."

He put his arm around her and she automatically leaned into him and found the shoulder she had cried on so many times before. Sometimes he wondered why his shoulder wasn't higher on one side than the other from the weight of her tears.

""My best friend Clara is moving to Los Angeles. We've been teaching at the same high school for twenty years now. I only teach Spanish; she teaches everything. I invited Clara, and her husband, Frank, to dinner tonight." Rosie sniffled. "California is so far from New York; she might just as well be d-e-a-d." Joey wasn't sure how Rosie did it, but the word *dead* was expanded into several syllables so that it sounded like Ella Fitzgerald singing scat. Rosie sighed.

"So?" Joey, asked, his patience waning. "What has that to do with you making a racket and invoking the ire of the neighborhood, not to mention its resident gang members?"

"What gang members? What are you talking about? There are no gang members here." She pulled away from him and reached for the tissue box.

"Why do women deny such things?" he groaned.

"There's nothing to deny. Anyway, I'm getting to it. Give me a break here. It's six o'clock. Where do you have to go? You have a date that I don't know about?"

"Rosie, I'm so glad you've explained why you're vacuuming. I was worried that maybe this was some new obsession of yours." Joey paused, taking a risk. "Or I thought maybe the cleaning lady comes today? You know how you always clean up before she gets here."

"See what I mean? Sarcasm. That's all I get. You never listen to me. I told you a thousand times." She blew on her coffee and took a sip.

"Don't start with me. I always listen. I just don't remember," he said. "Get on with it. By the time you finish I'll be ready for my afternoon nap!"

"Okay. I'll talk fast," she snapped.

He rolled his eyes.

"Clara's retiring. Their kids built a little apartment above the garage and they're pushing their parents to make the move now. The neighborhood is changing and they want somebody around when the kids get home from school."

"How old are the kids?" Joey asked.

"I'm not sure. I think the girl is twelve and the boy is maybe fifteen."

"Sounds like the kids are old enough to take care of themselves."

"Sounds that way to me, too. But it seems there are gangs in the neighborhood now and they're worried about it."

"Okay, now I understand why the house has to be spotless. If there's a hair on the rug it might change your relationship with Clara."

"See. More sarcasm." Rosie started to sniffle again. "I may never see her again."

"A-h-h," Joey said sadly, taking her hand across the table. "Okay, I'm really sorry. But, Rosie, you know nothing's forever."

"I know. But except for you, I don't have anyone except Clara."

"Well, I'm here aren't I? I'm not going anywhere."

"I know, but . . ."

". . . and there's your job."

"I'm tired of my job," she said.

"That's a surprise. What else would you do?"

"I don't know. I want things to be the same as they were when we were kids in the grocery business. I miss it. I miss the gossip, the schmoozing."

"Yep, me too. I remember when you were four, five years old, *Zaida* would sit you on a high stool, like a throne, and you'd hold reign waiting for your royal subjects to come in and tell you how cute you were. Rosie's Palace they called it. Well, we can't go back, that's for sure. Anyway, I think you're forgetting how hard it was."

"I'm not forgetting. But I loved it."

"You're talking crazy. A grocery store!" he pooh-poohed. "You're fifty-eight years old, almost ready to retire from the school district, for God's sake. And with a nice pension, I might add."

"So? Then what?"

"So then, anything. You can sell this old place and travel — start living. What kind of life is this? A ghetto neighborhood in the Bronx, taking care of a sick old man?"

"Joey, don't start. Maybe it's a tough neighborhood, like you say, but we never have any trouble."

"Well, maybe that's because you're a Spanish teacher and speak their language. Anyway, we're not talking about *now*. We're talking about when I'm gone." They fell silent.

"Rosie," he said wearily. "I'm tired of both the house we live in and the house that I, alone, have lived in this past seventy-eight years. I'm looking forward to a new condominium."

"What the hell are you talking about, a new condominium?"

"You know, the one we picked out a few years ago at the mortuary."

"Jesus Christ, will you get off it already?"

"I'm not kidding. The City has been after this property for years. Last I heard they want to develop a small park in-between the tenements."

"Yeah," she said. "A park would be nice." Rosie sighed. She poured another cup of coffee for herself. Joey put his hand over his cup and shook his head, no.

He looked at her. "You know, Rosie, you're still a very attractive woman. There's no reason . . ."

"Stop it," she interrupted him. "I'm not looking, I'm not interested," she said emphatically. "When Ruben died . . ."

"Damn it, Rosie. Ruben died twenty years ago."

"So what?

"Okay, okay! So kill me for bringing it up."

Rosie finished her coffee. "I'm going to set the table for tonight" she said.

Joey rose from the table. "Oy!" *Might as well go back to bed for two, three hours*, he thought. It was only 6:00 a.m.

CHAPTER TWO

ALBERTO AND RAMON ESPARZA, twenty-one-year-old identical twins were returning home after having partied all night. They stumbled off the bus across the street from their tenement building. Ramon laughed as he lost his balance stepping off the curb. Alberto caught him by the back edge of his black T-shirt and pulled him up.

"Shhh, *mi hermano*," Alberto said, also laughing. "You're gonna wake everybody up."

The gutters were shiny from the street sweepers that came around once a week in the middle of the night scooping up debris at curbside. Six-foot wide brush swirls lay on the blacktop like unsuspected eddies in the ocean. The reflection of street lights rippled against the mixture of wet blacktop and cobblestones, creating an imaginary oasis. A pearl gray sky foretold a cloudy day with intermittent showers.

They held on to each other, weaving, their sneakers leaving footprints on the sidewalk from puddles they neglected to sidestep. They walked up six steps and entered the foyer of the old building, never noticing the diamond-shaped marble flooring meticulously set by a stonemason fifty years ago. The diamonds were separated by one-inch decorative squares, most of which had chipped away or come unglued. Ramon tripped on a loose tile. "Damn. Someone's gonna break their head one of these days," he muttered. The flat surface of the floor dovetailed with the side walls of the hallway and continued two feet up, finished off by a wide oak molding strip. Roaches scurried into the cracks of the greenish-brown walls as they felt the vibration of footsteps.

The twins staggered up the marble stairs. Cracked and chipped from age, the marble still showed the subtle black and white grain of the original slab. They hung on to the iron-grill banisters intricately forged by master iron-masters. On the third floor landing Ramon turned around and headed back down.

"Hey, where you goin?"

"Where you think I'm goin? I'm gonna bash in Rosie's door and kill her if she don't shut down that vacuum."

"Oh, for Christ's sake, leave the old broad alone. One look at you and she'll piss her pants or have a heart attack and next thing you know, they'll have you up for murder."

"You know we ain't gonna be able to sleep with that racket."

"C'mon. Whaddya talkin about? Ya know ya ain't gonna kill Rosie. Ya can't have a better friend than her. She ain't gonna be at it all day, right? Forget it. Hell, we gonna sleep all day anyway."

Alberto always worried that Ramon's hot temper could get them in trouble. At times Ramon might have killed someone had Alberto not been there to stop him. With regard to Rosie, any number of neighbors could say that she was *looking for it. Shit . . . ain't no reason to be making that racket when people is tryin to sleep.*

"You're too good, Alberto, you know that? I can see that good oozing right outta ya." He reached over and feigned a jab at his brother, but Alberto shot out and pushed his hand away.

"Watch out now. I'm too tired to be playin with ya."

Alberto quietly turned his key and unlocked their front door. He sighed with relief when he spotted a plastic glass and a half bottle of uncorked red wine on the kitchen counter. "Looks like *Mamacita's* good for the night. Ain't nothing gonna wake her up." The boys headed straight for the refrigerator and dug in to a half package of tortillas and cold leftover chile rellenos, leaving the dirty casserole dish and food remnants on the old Formica table top.

They tiptoed to their bedroom, glancing at their mother's door, holding their fingers to their lips. *Shhh.* The last thing they wanted was a harangue from *Mamacita* Hortencia. They shucked their clothes and piled them on the floor, their mannerisms similar except Alberto was more methodical. He unlaced his sneakers and put them beside his bed while Ramon simply slid them off and threw each underhand toward the wastepaper basket like he would a basketball. They landed near the basket with a thud. Still annoyed at Rosie, he turned to the wall and covered his ears with his flat pillow, but he continued talking, his words slow and heavy. "You ain't forgot we're meeting Simon at *Ramrod* tonight, right?"

"Yeah," Alberto said. "I'm on it. Simon says a hot-shot friend of his from California has been talkin big time about all the money we can make there. Simon wants to go back to California with him, but there's no way his dad will let him."

"Maybe you and me should think about goin," Ramon said, trying to wrap a short blanket around his six-foot-five frame.

"Why should we leave?" Alberto asked. "We got it good. You're working, I'm working . . ."

Ramon interrupted. "Yeah, but don't you ever feel trapped? C'mon, Berto. Look around. Everybody gets old fast in this neighborhood. There ain't nothin to look forward to. I don't want to die here like Pop."

"Listen," Alberto cut in. "I ain't interested in California or anywhere else. Right now I wanna get some shut eye. You gonna let me, or you gonna keep yappin?" He sat on the edge of his narrow bed and massaged his feet. He stretched his long slim body the full length of the iron bed frame until his feet hung over the edge. The mattress was so thin he had put horsehair padding underneath to keep the springs from poking him. He pulled the covers up under his chin, leaving his feet uncovered.

Ramon's eyes closed. Already half asleep, he tried to get the last few words in before he crashed. "Yeah, a little more sweet cream tonight at *Ramrod* and then sleep all day Sunday," he said, remembering the dark-haired beauty he'd spent the evening with. They had both been sweating from dancing the Salsa and he had maneuvered her to a dark corner of the outdoor patio where they continued the dance, even after the music had stopped. Ramon remembered her little cry when he put his hand under her dress.

"Sweet cream?" Alberto rolled his eyes. "I swear Ramon, you're gonna wear it out."

"You know what they say, 'use it or lose it.'"

"I'm particular 'bout my sweet cream. I like it fresh. I like to be the first one to open the carton. Ya know what I mean? Sleep on Sunday? Dream on, bro. Mama could be on her death bed and she'd still drag us to church, unless, of course, you're thinkin you want her to kill you, like she did Pop."

But Ramon didn't hear him because he was already asleep, breathing evenly in a dream world his brother couldn't share.

Before closing his eyes Alberto looked around. The cramped room held their twin beds and an unpainted dresser. The drawers were always open because most of the knobs were lost or broken. One bare window, the panes dotted with paint, looked out on a rusted fire escape. The linoleum flooring was cracked and chipped. Pieces of paint hung from the ceiling. In one corner a leaking water pipe had left a ring of rust-colored stains. A silver radiator, where the twins hung their clothes, sat against a bare wall.

Alberto could smell his pillowcase. A mixture of rancid grease and sweat and a month's worth of morning breath filtered into the bare threads like flour through a sieve. It was almost black, as were the sheets. He put his hands behind his head and looked at the cross which hung on the wall opposite his bed. "There's got to be a better life than this, eh Jesus?" he mumbled. He closed his eyes wondering if Ramon was right and maybe they should go to California.

Alberto's conversation with Ramon brought back unpleasant memories and a glaring newspaper headline:

Woman Suffocates Husband in Sex Act

Three-hundred-twenty-five pound Hortencia Esparza suffocated her one-hundred-twenty-pound husband Jose by having sex with him. Detective Charles McDaniels was called to the early morning scene by neighbors who heard Esparza scream when she discovered her husband was not breathing. Esparza confirmed that she had 'loved her husband to death.' McDaniels told reporters the case was under investigation. "This appears to be an unfortunate accident," he said.

Alberto couldn't recall the entire article. He did remember the morning Detective McDaniels had knocked loudly on their door, announcing that he was with the New York Police Department and to "open up." His mother had stood there, trembling and tearful, as he and his brother hid partially behind her, their small hands clutching her worn flannel robe. She had led the detective to the bed where her husband lay in peaceful repose. A small smile was on his face.

McDaniels had displayed unexpected sensitivity when he shooed the boys off to their room and sat down at the kitchen table with Mrs. Esparza. "Go on boys. I just want to talk to your mama, find out what happened," he'd said. Their scrawny ten-year-old bodies had walked barefoot to the bedroom. McDaniels had looked directly at Esparza, making eye contact in a friendly way. "Why don't you just tell me what happened."

Senora Esparza had sat down heavily. The splintered legs of the chair scraped the linoleum floor and groaned under her weight. "My husband, he was a good man," she'd sniffled. "But, you know, he never work; he sleep all the time and he snore so loud even the neighbors who live two apartments down, complain. I try everything," she'd said. "I warn him. I even go to my friend, she give me special tea to make him stop snoring."

"What do you mean you 'warned' him? What kind of tea," McDaniels asked, alert and suspicious.

"Just tea." Senora Esparza looked at him blankly. "You want to know what kind of tea," she asked. "You would like a cup of tea?" She seemed confused.

"No, no. Just continue. It's okay."

"I like to have, you know" she pointed to her groin, "but we never did it. *Porque?* Because his snoring was so terrible, we couldn't sleep together." She had paused, blowing her nose, tearfully emphasizing half in English and half in Spanish that despite repeated warnings and various remedies, the snoring continued. The detective had taken copious notes which included the fact that Senora Esparza had made love to her husband the previous evening in the hopes that, much like an aspirin would relieve a headache, the shock of having sex with him would abate the snoring.

McDaniels had tried several times to interrupt Senora Esparza when she veered off into explicit sexual details that he did not feel were relevant or appropriate. But Esparza, unaware of his efforts had continued her story unabashed, as though she were talking to her priest or best friend.

"As you can see, even though I am a big woman I am very sexy." Her robe had opened slightly. "And when I get excited . . ."

"It's okay, you don't have to . . ." Detective McDaniel had jumped out of his chair. But Esparza would not be denied the whole truth and nothing but the truth.

"I loved my husband, but he was a small man and in my passion I make a mistake and go on top of him . . ."

"There's no need . . ."

". . . and accidentally I roll over and kill him." This prompted a new flood of tears and sobbing. "He never make a sound after the love-making, not even a short snort like he always do. I think, aha, that is the solution. Sex! But then, in the morning, I see he is not breathing, so I call my neighbor, and she call you." She reached for another napkin. "How will I sleep if I don't hear Jose snoring?" She sighed. "The house will be too quiet now."

Alberto and Ramon rarely talked about their father. No tears were shed when he died because he was an invisible person even before his death, a man who took up space and simply left remnants of himself throughout the household, like cigarette butts, snotty handkerchiefs, dirty socks and razor shavings in the bathroom sink.

◇◇◇

Alberto was right that on Sundays families rose early to go to church. If Rosie had decided to run her vacuum on Sunday instead of Saturday, that would have been perfectly acceptable. Wives and mothers plotted in advance the devious methods they would use to wake their husbands and children for Mass. Sexual favors were a big incentive. "If you go to church with me now, I'll do something special for you later."

Lectures and sermons were heard way before anyone got to church. Preachers couldn't hold a candle to the consistent nagging of an irate and fanatically-religious mother. They were as dedicated as any evangelist. Some neighbors didn't even set their alarm clocks. They just depended on the cacophony of voices that wafted through the air like radio waves from apartment to apartment. "Get your ass out of bed" had a more familiar ring to it than the chiming of church bells.

Sunday dresses were pulled off wire hangers; pendulous breasts, usually unfettered, were confined in triple D Playtex bras; younger girls removed their Mary-Jane patent leather shoes from newspaper wrappings; men searched through their ties for one that wasn't stained. Even the best underwear was chosen because, "God can see everything, even under your dress." Faces were scrubbed, hair braided, nails inspected and, finally, after a fretful morning of parental cajoling and threats, after hundreds of "I don't want tos" and "do I have tos" from the children, families in their Sunday finery marched enmasse to Mass. Neighbors caught up with gossip from the previous Sunday. A feeling of well-being prevailed as it did every Sunday when they thanked God for the little they had and prayed for what they didn't have.

CHAPTER THREE

ALBERTO AND RAMON WERE awakened by the loud mutterings of their mother. She deliberately clanged pots and pans, making as much noise as possible.

"Get up, you bums, it's three o'clock," she shouted from the kitchen. "I don't know why I put up with this. *Que lata*, what a mess. *Esta asqueroso*, disgusting!" she said. The roaches were having a field day. "*Aiee*", she cursed them under her breath.

Since her husband's accidental demise due to her sexual proclivity, Hortencia was now a mere two hundred thirty-three pounds. The stress of Jose's death had somewhat diminished her appetite. She had recently bought a full-figure bra and every time she passed a mirror she would run her hands over her breasts thinking how high and firm they were, how good she looked.

She often thought she would like to remarry, if she could only get rid of those two *vagabundearos*. Henry Cardillo who owned the bakery two blocks away had shown some interest, giving her an extra *pandulce* occasionally and holding her hand longer than necessary when she paid him.

The boys were fully awake now, but continued to languish in bed despite Hortencia's exasperation. They simply ignored her.

"What time is it anyway?" Alberto asked, stretching the full length of his body, pushing his feet a foot past the warm blanket.

"U-m-m. Around three," Ramon yawned.

"Jesus, we slept all day."

"We always sleep all day on weekends," Ramon said. "I'm short about half an hour because of that crazy broad's vacuuming."

"Ramon, knock it off, will ya?" Alberto put his hands behind his head. "You wanna go first?" he asked.

"Okay *hermano*, I'm in the shower," Ramon said as he threw off his blanket.

"Don't use all the hot water."

Hortencia saw Ramon streak through the hallway to the bathroom. He was hopping out of his shorts, one leg at a time, totally unabashed by his mother's presence.

Ay, what a body Hortencia thought. "Don't use all the hot water. Save some for your brother," she yelled.

"Hey, Mamacita, ya got some clean towels?" Ramon asked.

"You want clean towels, go to the laundry," she replied.

Alberto strolled into the kitchen. He walked over to his mom and bestowed a kiss on her cheek. "Hey, beautiful."

"Don't think you can con me with your kisses and bullshit," she said, gently pushing him away, a small smile on her face.

"What's to eat?" He slipped a worn ash-grey tank top over his head as he opened the refrigerator. His shorts were partially open at the fly and he was barefoot.

"Whatever was there, you and Ramon and the *cucarachas* finished it off last night. You want to eat, you buy the food," she said angrily. "I'm tired of cooking and cleaning up after you." It was an old story, one they were told every week over and over again.

"What do you do with the money we give you?" Alberto said casually as he perused the unappealing selection in the fridge. He knew his comment would get a rise out of her.

"What money?" her voice escalated. "What you give me wouldn't even pay for one quesadilla!"

"Ummm, what I wouldn't do for a quesadilla right now" he chided her. "We're still growing boys, Mama. I'm working at the bakery as many hours as Mr. Cardillo gives me. Last week he let me make rolls. I think I ate more rolls than I made," Alberto laughed. "But I'm learnin. It's a good trade and I think I'm gonna like it." He found a shriveled apple in the refrigerator and took a bite of it as he sat down at the small table. "It's better than what Ramon does at the auto shop."

"What Ramon does," she mimicked sarcastically. "Ramon fixes a flat with one hand and puts the other hand under whatever skirt is there, even if it's two blocks away."

Just then Ramon appeared, a threadbare towel wrapped around his waist. "Hey, what's to eat?" His dark hair dripped beads of water on his forehead and he smelled of soap.

"Whatever you find, it's yours," Alberto laughed as he threw the apple core into the trash and walked toward the bathroom. "Mama, how do you keep so beautiful?" Ramon asked.

"Yeah, yeah, you're full of bullshit, just like your brother."

He put an arm around her and pinched her cheek. "I mean it Mama, you're gorgeous."

"You think so?" she said, momentarily buying into his flattery as she ran her hand through her hair.

"Would I lie to you? Alberto and me, we say it all the time, how beautiful you are, and so young to have two such handsome boys."

"Save your breath for your bimbos."

"Mama, how come there's never any food here?" Ramon opened the refrigerator and threw his hands in the air. "What do you do with the money we give you?"

"What money? You're just like your brother. You think I'm getting rich from your pesos? You can't even buy a can of pinto beans. Go out on your own and see how much money it costs." She raised her voice.

"All I know is I'm working my ass off at the body shop. I come home sweaty and stinking from grease . . ."

"Yeah, I'm glad you know it . . ."

". . . Lookin' for something. Anything," he continued. "What the fuck do you do all day? You ever think of cooking anything?"

"Hey, watch your mouth. I cooked yesterday and you and Alberto got home early in the morning and *poof*, whatever I cooked, it was gone. Not one thing left for me except the dirty dishes. I'm not your slave. You want clean . . ."

Ramon interrupted her. "There's never nothin to eat," he complained. "The apartment is disgusting. Even Alberto complained about the filthy sheets."

"So, Alberto complained," she broke in. "What is he? My boss? I have to listen to him? And I have to listen to you with your filthy mouth? You want clean sheets, a home, a cooked meal? Get married! Get out!"

Alberto heard the escalation of voices in the kitchen but was in no hurry to leave the soothing luxury of the shower. He walked into the kitchen a few minutes later as the argument intensified. Naked, except for a faded worn orange towel wrapped around his waist, his slender light-brown body created a different energy in the room, as though the atoms had dispersed, making room only for him.

"Okay, sounds like I missed something."

"Yeah," said Ramon. "You been missing something for a long time *mi hermano*, and you ain't never gonna find it here." He stormed out of the kitchen. Alberto tried to smooth things over. "Whatever he said, Mamacita, he didn't mean it."

Hortencia was quiet. She busied herself at the sink. "It's not that I want you and Ramon to leave, *mi hijo*," she said, sounding tired and confused, her energy drained. "I love you and Ramon very much. It saddens me that you would not do more with your lives than live in this dying neighborhood."

"Mama, where would we go?" Alberto asked. The thought of leaving the Bronx had not occurred to him.

"I don't know. But I know you don't want to live here forever, like your father, like me. *Ay* what dreams we had." She paused. "Maybe you could go back to school," she said, knowing the futility of her words.

"You know I'm not one for school, Mama. I like my job at the bakery."

"Well, it's a good trade. Nothing to be ashamed of. Maybe Mr. Cardillo can give you more hours, more money. Why don't you ask him?"

"You know, Mama, if things get rough you can always go to work."

"Go to work?" she asked incredulously. "What would I do? I never worked in my life. But, maybe I can take a boarder in." Alberto had already planted the seed. "Someone in the neighborhood always needs a place to stay."

"It's never too late Mama," Alberto threw the words over his shoulder as he walked toward the bedroom. Ramon was sulking, tossing his clothes as though he were shooting free-baskets, until they lay in a pile on the floor.

"You're still mad, huh?" Alberto asked.

"Not so mad at Mama as I am at myself. We need to get out of here Alberto. Sometimes I feel like I'm dying."

"Ah-h, forget it, Ramon. Where we gonna go? We got it good here. Ya gotta look on the bright side."

"There ain't no bright side, bro. It's a dead end. This guy who's gonna be at *Ramrod* tonight. Maybe we should listen to what he says.

Ya know he was talkin about how much money we can make in California."

"It's all bullshit, Ramon. If this guy's making so much money, why's he so desperate to tell anybody else about it? There's gotta be a reason. I'll tell you what. We'll think on it. For now, whatd'ya say we go do the laundry? I'm running out of underwear and I'm tired of sleepin on these ratty sheets."

They stripped the beds, gathered their dirty clothes from the floor and corners of the room, grabbed the towels from the bathroom, threw everything into a large pillow case and headed for the laundry. The remainder of the day went by quickly as they busied themselves with necessary activities. Alberto was quiet, focusing on his chores, but Ramon talked incessantly about California.

That evening, dressed in low rider jeans, black T-shirts and kick-ass boots, their dark hair spiked, they left the apartment and headed for *Ramrod*.

By three a.m. the next morning they were on their way to California.

CHAPTER FOUR

CLARA AND FRANK HERMAN had barely left their Manhattan walk-up apartment; they were already anxious about the train ride home from the Bronx.

As they walked down the stairs, Frank extended his arm to his wife of forty-one years. Taking his arm was as natural as opening her eyes in the morning. All Frank's jackets were worn at the elbow where, for years, she had taken his arm. When they were younger he gave his arm to her to keep her from falling. Now she took his arm to keep him from falling.

They had been newlyweds when they moved into this building. In the last few years Frank had suffered the pain of arthritis, and was plagued with high blood pressure and other ailments. But his positive attitude, humor and insatiable curiosity sustained him.

Their apartment was overrun with books of every description. Art and history were among his favorites, but political books abounded and several books of poetry could be found in a remote corner of the living room. Teenagers, besieged with homework assignments, had been known to knock on their door and ask Frank whether he had any information on a particular subject. Although Clara was the teacher, Frank was a natural collector of information that he gladly bestowed on those who needed or requested it.

They slowly walked two short blocks to the subway. The rumble and vibration of each train could be felt as it approached the platform. They stood back cautiously from the edge, Clara clutching her small leather purse tightly under one arm and holding on to Frank with her other. Her daughter, Gloria had sent her a lovely shoulder bag last Christmas, but it lay in a dresser drawer along with other gifts she'd sent that Clara felt were a waste of money.

"I never know what to buy you Mama" Gloria had complained.

"Nothing. Just save your money and send my grandkids to Catholic school," Clara said. "I don't like the idea that they are surrounded by gangs in your neighborhood."

"Where did you hear there were gangs in our neighborhood?"

"I read the papers, Gloria," said Clara. "When you were growing up all we had to worry about was measles and chicken pox and where our next meal was coming from."

"Mama, stop talking about gangs. I'm just glad you and dad are coming," she said, sighing as she hung up. How does she know about gangs, Gloria wondered?

◇◇◇

When Frank and Clara arrived at Rosie's, the street was still rife with children engaged in various activities: skipping rope, skating, playing stick ball and hopscotch. On this warm summer evening, parents sat leisurely on the stoops, conversing with neighbors, reading evening newspapers, absently watching the kids play. Televisions could be seen through the ground floor and basement windows, the echoes of a sporting event resounding from more than one apartment.

The Hermans awkwardly approached Rosie's small house. Frank kept his head down, treading carefully on the uneven pavement to avoid falling. Nobody looked directly at them, but all eyes observed their advance to the front gate.

Rosie's grandparents were married in this house which stood so far back from the street that unless you knew it was there, you wouldn't know it was there. Gnarled vines clung to an old redwood fence providing privacy and protection more secure than a fortress. Occasionally, garbage, toys, and even people were either deliberately, or accidentally, thrown out the tenement windows to the concrete yard below, which separated the tall buildings from the small house. Fortunately the overgrown dense shrubbery precluded even a free-fall body from penetrating it. This was the nature of tenement living where everybody knew everybody's business but nobody invaded anyone's privacy.

Once inside the gate, a narrow garden path lined with tulips and lilacs and other seasonal flowers, enticed you to the front door and reflected the tastes and personalities of its present owners, Rosie and Joey Goldberg, brother and sister.

◇◇◇

Rosie had prepared all day for Clara and Frank's arrival. A beautifully embroidered old tablecloth covered the dining table, enhancing her grandmother's carefully preserved silverware and glasses, used only for special occasions. Tapered candles in crystal candlesticks awaited the touch of a match. Red wine breathed uncorked, ready to be poured. The aroma of brisket, potatoes, and red cabbage emanated from the small kitchen.

Joey had stayed out of Rosie's way throughout the day. Now he was freshly showered, wearing a plaid cotton shirt with a buttoned-down open collar and khaki Dockers. His clothes hung loosely, emphasizing his bony frame. He wore white socks and comfortable loafers. Strands of sparse grey hair were combed to the side, separated by bald spots.

Peering out the front window Rosie saw her guests approaching. She opened the front door and met them halfway. Joey quietly followed behind. Clara and Rosie embraced as Frank reached out to shake Joey's hand. The greetings were a little awkward at first but the two women quickly included the men in their repartee.

"I smell brisket, potatoes, and cabbage, my absolute favorites," said Frank.

Rosie beamed. "Well, it wasn't by accident," she said. "I cheated and asked Clara what you liked."

"Smart girl," answered Frank. He and Joey moved to the small living room as Clara followed Rosie into the kitchen.

"What can I do?" asked Clara.

"Not a thing. Dinner's ready whenever we are." Rosie carried a tray of stuffed mushrooms into the living room,

"I bet this house hasn't changed much since your grandparents bought it." said Clara.

"You're right. Joey and I just made it more comfortable. There was nothing around for miles. My grandfather had a small farm out back."

"You grew up here?" Frank asked.

"Yep, me and Joey and three other siblings," Rosie said. "When our dad died suddenly of a heart attack my mom and five of us kids moved here with my grandparents. Where else could we go?"

"Families were like that in those days. It was a different time," Joey said. "The neighborhood grew up around us and that's when granddad opened a grocery store next to our house. We all worked in that store, right Rosie?"

"We sure did, before school, after school, Saturdays, Sundays. I learned the grocery business inside and out. When Grandpa was ready to retire he asked Joey if he wanted the store or if he thought we should sell it?"

Joey jumped into the conversation. "Hell, no," I told him. "We can't sell it. What would we do?" Joey took another sip of wine. "Rosie'll tell you the rest. I've been talking too much."

"Well, there isn't much more to tell. The store kept us going. Eventually our siblings got married, opened their own businesses and raised their own families. It's all history now." Rosie got up and beckoned them to the dining room. "Tell me about your plans when you get to L. A."

Frank had difficulty getting up from the couch. Clara gave him a hand. He walked slowly to the dining table wondering how he had gotten this old. They deferred some of their conversation until Rosie brought out coffee and homemade apple-peach pie. "I warned you to leave room for dessert," she laughed.

Frank unbuckled his belt. "It's a small price to pay for a slice of that pie."

"Rosie I'm really going to miss you," Clara said. "It's all I've been thinking about."

"Me too," Rosie said.

There was a short lull in the conversation. Joey refilled Clara's wine glass.

"Rosie, I've always wanted to ask you how come you never married after Ruben died. I can't believe someone didn't fall in love with you in all these years," Clara said.

Rosie leaned one elbow on the table while the other held the stem of the wine glass. "I've had a couple of boyfriends," she admitted.

"You never told me about any boyfriends," Joey said indignantly.

"You don't know everything Joey!"

"Oh-oh, I think I might have broached a no-no," Clara said, embarrassed.

"Not at all," Rosie said. " Ruben and I spoke the same language, literally. It never mattered that I was Jewish and he was Mexican, but it took awhile for my family to accept him. He played Mom like a Flamenco guitar. She came to adore him."

"How could you not love Ruben Sanchez?" Clara said. "He was the only science teacher in the system who taught the kids in Spanish, with English thrown in, instead of the other way around. The kids loved it. Two for the price of one, Spanish and Science, all mixed together." Clara went on. "The whole school was whispering when you guys got married. In those days nobody thought a name like Rosie Goldberg went well with Ruben Sanchez. Everyone thought you were pregnant."

"Yeah, even I thought so," Joey laughed.

Clara changed the subject. "Listen, when you visit us in Los Angeles, we'll fix you up with a handsome *Man from La Mancha*."

"Paul Newman would work" said Rosie, smiling.

"I'll see what I can do. First we have to get settled at Gloria's."

"Are you worried you won't be happy in a smaller apartment over a garage?"

"A little, but Gloria swears it's bigger than our present place in Manhattan." She looked at her watch. "Oh, my goodness, it's near ten o'clock. We better start home."

"I'll walk to the station with you. I need the exercise." Rosie said.

Rosie continued to the front gate with the Hermans and spotted Alberto and Ramon walking down the steps of their building. "Hey, Alberto. Ramon," she yelled over. They turned around, surprised, and waited until she caught up. "Where're you two going all spiffed up?" She turned to Frank and Clara and introduced them.

Ramon smiled. "You're looking good, Rosie, considering you must be really tired."

"Why do you say that? Whatd'ya mean?"

"Well, I think you woke up the whole neighborhood this morning," he teased. "I'm gonna have to buy you a silent vacuum or buy the whole neighborhood ear plugs."

"Hey, listen, Ramon," she said, taking him by the arm. "Next time I'm vacuuming at five in the morning, which hopefully won't be in the near future, just knock on the door and I'll fix you a nice breakfast."

"Okay, that's a deal!"

When they reached the station, Clara and Rosie dawdled until they sensed the men getting restless. "I hate goodbyes." Rosie said tearfully. They gave each other one last hug and then Rosie watched as the Herman's and Esparza's descended into the subway.

CHAPTER FIVE

KNOWING THEY WOULD ONLY be going a few stops farther, Alberto and Ramon held on to a pole near the door, swaying with the movement of the train.

"Did you hear what that Miz Herman said?" Ramon asked.

"Yeah, I heard. What of it?"

"California, man. They're going to California."

"Ramon, what do you think?" Alberto asked, ill-tempered. "You think they still got gold in California? That's what you think?"

Ramon sulked. "No, but maybe it's a chance."

"A chance for what?"

"To change our lives; make some real money."

"California ain't gonna change our lives, Ramon. We are who we are."

They stopped talking, each immersed in his own thoughts, until they exited the train. Anyone observing them would know they were brothers because their stride was the same, their shoulders hunched identically, their heads tilted slightly to the left at the same angle. Ramon glanced at his watch, 11:00 p.m. The streets were just cooling off from the day's heat.

Jake Sarkowski, a burly bouncer with a face that would scare a statue, greeted them at the door with his usual, "Hey, good to see ya," even though he didn't really know who they were. They exchanged knuckle and shoulder greetings. Ramon tipped him a couple of bucks.

The place was jumping, the noise level unrelenting. Lip reading and body language were required to carry on a conversation. *Ramrod* had been open over a year and it was a booming success. The owner, Oscar de Luna, who had been a bartender all his life, had lost his wife ten years earlier in a gang-related shooting outside the *COME ON IN* convenience store. He said his dead wife came to him every night in a dream and begged him to open his own business. So that's what he did.

Ramrod drew a mixed crowd, some from nearby office buildings, and others through word of mouth.

Alberto ordered a shot of Jose Cuervo. He waved to de Luna who was busy at the other end of the bar. Ramon, vodka on the rocks in hand, wandered through the crowd, nodding to some and stopping to put his arms around more than one woman. "Hey, baby, you gonna be here awhile?" A raised eyebrow, a sly grin, and a pat on the ass showed his approval. "I'll catch you later." He scouted the room looking for his friend Simon, de Luna's son, anxious to talk to him about his friend from California.

Ramrod had a large patio just outside the back door to accommodate overflow customers. A small group surrounded Simon. Ramon joined them. "Hey, Ramon, just the person I was thinking about," Simon smiled. "Meet Lui Chu. He's the guy I been telling you about that's visiting from California. Used to live around the corner from me."

Ramon held out his hand. "Ramon Esparza."

Chu was a little guy, a head shorter than Ramon. It was difficult to tell his ethnicity. Definitely Chinese with another flavor thrown in. He looked younger than his twenty-six years. Thin and wiry, he exuded a hyper-energy that made people nervous. His right shoulder twitched occasionally as though shrugging off some insect. A fast talker, if you didn't catch his drift right off, he wasn't going to explain it to you. His eyes wandered through the crowd as though looking for someone, or thought someone was looking for him.

"Yeah. Simon told me about you. Says you're a great mechanic. That right?" Lui asked.

"I been at it awhile. I guess I'm good."

"Ya know. I work for a guy who needs a good mechanic. You ever think of coming to Los Angeles? I could get you a job. Good bucks. *Really* good bucks."

"Yeah, I'd love to just blow outta here, but I don't know if I can convince my brother. I'd leave tonight and wouldn't look back."

"What's your brother got to do with it? Ya either leave or ya don't. What's he, your keeper?"

"Nah. But we look out for each other."

"What's he do? He a mechanic too?"

"No, a baker. Makes the best churros you ever ate." Ramon smiled.

"Well, I don know nothin about baking, but I sure can use a good mechanic. You change your mind, I'm leaving around three this morning; driving straight through if I can find another driver. Bring your brother. We can always find something for him to do."

Lui talked it up about Los Angeles. He exaggerated and romanticized every well-known location he could think of: Hollywood, Sunset Strip, Beverly Hills, the Pacific Ocean, Malibu and Santa Monica. Lui captivated his audience. He loved being the center of attention.

"Oh, yeah, it's really somethin. Palm trees everywhere. The air smells like them flowers you buy for your date on prom night. I forget the name of them. . ."

"Gardenias," someone said.

"Yeah, that's them. And ya know, you can run into a movie star any time. I seen lots of 'em. I even seen Steve McQueen once."

Inside, Alberto scanned the crowd, talking to de Luna. A few seats away, a dark haired young woman was arguing with her boyfriend. Her skin-tight green dress pulled against her thighs revealing the outline of her long legs. "Paul, I have to tell you . . ."

"Ya know what?" Paul interrupted her. "You fuckin talk too much, Maureen. Who gives a rat's ass? Just shut the fuck up and have another drink." He squeezed her knee hard. She grimaced.

"I ain't interested. You got it?" He turned toward her, his look ugly, threatening. One hand held his drink, the other lay tight-fisted in his lap.

"Paul, I'm . . ."

"You stupid or something? Or maybe just hard of hearing? I said *shut up*." He motioned to Oscar. "Give this cunt another drink," he yelled down the bar as he removed a fifty dollar bill from his inside bill fold and slammed it on the counter.

Oscar delivered a margarita on the rocks. The cut glass was heavy and cold. Beads of moisture formed on the outside, salt clung to the rim, and a slice of lime floated between the ice cubes.

The woman looked up. Her hair fell back revealing a black and blue eye and swollen lip. Her hazel eyes held steady as she lifted the glass in a deliberate measured movement.

Paul's loud comment to the bartender caused heads to turn at several nearby tables. One man paused in mid-conversation, his stomach muscles tightening. "Somethin's goin down," he said. He stood up, almost knocking the chair over, reached in his pocket, threw a twenty on the table, and yanked his girlfriend's arm, pulling her toward the exit. "Baby, we're outta here."

At the door he muttered to Jake. "Hey, man, I think there's going to be some trouble in there. Some asshole . . ." He didn't finish but just walked off with his girl. Jake shrugged. He was curious, but people were still paying to get in and giving him tips.

Paul continued muttering and cursing. Alberto and Oscar exchanged glances. Alberto, alert, put his drink down, took one foot off the bar rail and planted it firmly on the floor. He kept his eye on the woman. Her lips curled back. Her eyes narrowed. She slowly lifted the glass in her right hand. Paul saw her movement in the mirrored area behind the bar, but did not react swiftly enough. Instead of bringing the glass to her lips, in a sudden unexpected shift, she hurled it at his head. He had turned slightly and the impact caught him above his left ear. The heavy glass shattered leaving a chunk embedded in his skull. Grains of salt and an ice cube glistened in his hair.

A *Credence Clearwater* tape blended with the sound of chairs and tables scraping against the hardwood floor as women screamed and scampered toward the exit. Lui and Ramon, talking quietly on the patio, looked at each other. "Fight," they both said, pushing through the crowd close behind Simon, who had already started toward the bar.

Paul staggered, reeling from the blow. "You bitch. Now I'll take care of you." He reached into his boot and pulled out a switchblade. Maureen leaped off her stool and stepped out of reach, her high heels slipping on the broken glass. He lunged toward her, blood trickling from the wound she had inflicted. Alberto, anticipating Paul's reaction, shot off his bar stool and stepped between them. He shoved the woman aside. "Cool down . . ."

Paul yelled, "Asshole, stay out of this."

"Knock it off!" Alberto yelled.

"Okay, mother fucker, you asked for it! Bring it on." Paul waved the knife back and forth in front of Alberto's face. The crowd drew back. Alberto grabbed a beer bottle and broke it against the edge of a table.

Paul laughed. "That ain't gonna do you no good."

A few men got caught up in the action. "Fight. Fight. Get 'em. Kill 'em."

Simon reached the scene and thought, *Jake's history. How the hell did he let someone get past him with a knife?* "We gotta get this guy down before he hurts someone," he said to Lui.

"Looks like that guy's doing okay," Lui pointed to Alberto.

"That's Ramon's brother."

Alberto held the jagged bottle in front of him. "Hey, man, put the knife down." But Paul could not be persuaded.

"C'mon, c'mon," Paul taunted. "This ain't none of your business, but you want in? I'm willing. C'mon."

Oscar de Luna had come from behind the bar. He tried to wedge himself between the two but they circled around him.

"Hey, enough! Enough!" he shouted.

"This ain't your fight, old man. Get outta the way," Paul shouted.

"Let me handle this," Alberto pushed de Luna aside. Simon, trying to avoid a free-for-all, held the crowd back. Several couples left, unwilling to wait for the outcome, or for the police to arrive.

Ramon and Lui tried to distract Paul while Alberto manipulated him away from the bar, hoping to grab a chair to protect himself. Ramon was ready to step in if he thought his brother couldn't handle this.

Paul stepped forward and back, light on his feet like a dancer, switching the weapon from hand to hand. Alberto had the advantage of height but Paul had the advantage of experience as a street fighter. The switchblade was still superior in range, but the broken beer bottle put them on a more equal footing. Blood and sweat ran down the left side of Paul's head. His shirt looked like a blood-stained map. Shards of glass sparkled at his shoulder.

Several customers had wandered in from the patio to watch the action, their cigarette smoke blending with the stale air of beer, wine and scotch. Broken glass crunched underfoot as Alberto and Paul skirted each other to gain leverage.

Alberto's heart hammered. He had to get the knife. Although the loss of blood weakened Paul, he was still formidable. Women clambered over each other to get out, but their escorts were in no hurry to miss a fight. "I'll be there in a minute baby. Wait for me outside." A few men took bets and egged the fighters on.

"Get 'im, get 'im," they shadow-boxed for emphasis. They didn't care who won. Above the deafening noise level a CD by Andy Summers of *The Police* could be heard.

Suddenly Paul made a quick move with the knife but Alberto sidestepped and caught Paul's side with the edge of the beer bottle. Paul backed off, holding his side, a surprised look on his face. Alberto hoped the fight was over, but Paul, blood running down his side, said, "You got lucky; now it's my turn."

They circled cautiously, each waiting for the other to make a move. There was a lot of blood on the floor and as Alberto evaded a blow he slipped and fell backward. Paul quickly moved in, but Alberto grabbed his leg and he fell hard to the floor, grunting. They rolled over, Paul landing on top. "Now you *spic* bastard, die!" Spit formed at the corners of his mouth. His face distorted in a snarl. The adrenalin release was so satisfying and pleasurable he thought he would thank Maureen later for giving him the opportunity to kill someone. *This ain't nothing to do with winning a fight, asshole. This is about respect.*

Alberto's jagged beer bottle had been knocked out of his hand, giving Paul the advantage. He brought the knife down toward Alberto. Despite his injury he was strong, motivated by hatred. One quick thrust would kill Alberto. Ramon made a move to jump in. Distracted, Paul turned his head and loosened his grip. Alberto felt Paul's focus shift. He grabbed the man's wrist and twisted, redirecting the knife upward toward Paul's ribs. Paul fell over, screaming and writhing.

"Son-of-a-bitch."

Alberto jumped up and moved back.

Paul pulled the switchblade from his side and held it threateningly, ready to continue the fight. But Simon stepped in and grabbed it as his father reached for a bar towel to put pressure on the wound.

"Hold still asshole, unless you want to die," de Luna barked. "Someone call an ambulance."

"I'm outta here," Lui whispered to Ramon. "No way I'm gonna get involved with the cops."

"You still planning on leaving at three?"

"I'm planning on leaving right now! You coming with me?"

"I don't know." Ramon started toward Alberto who was so stunned, he wasn't even moving.

"You got any money?" Lui asked.

"None to speak of."

"You're gonna need around three bills. You'll make it back in a day once we get to L.A. But to get there we'll need some bread."

"Bread we got. Money we ain't got on such short notice," said Ramon. "But maybe. . ." He thought for a few seconds. "Listen, if you drive us uptown, I think I know where I can get the money. If I do, you'll have a couple of traveling companions. If not, then you're on your way solo. Whatd'ya say?"

"I'll meet you out back. The cops'll be here any second."

Ramon grabbed Alberto and half carried, half pulled him toward the back door. Alberto didn't resist. The sirens were close.

"What happened to the girl?" Alberto asked, dazed.

"What girl?"

"The guy I was fighting with had a girl with him. That's what started the whole thing."

"We don't know about no girl," said Ramon.

On the way out Ramon caught Simon's eye. "The guy with the knife . . . he gonna be okay?"

"Yeah. Thanks man, for getting my dad out of the way."

"No problem. Anyone asks, you don't know who we are, right?"

"Right!"

CHAPTER SIX

AFTER SAYING GOODBYE TO Clara and Frank Herman, Rosie walked slowly back to the house. The air was cool and moist. The smell of concrete mingled with rare patches of grass. People still sat in doorways and on stoops, although the children had been put to bed long before. Everybody knew her. There was no reason to be fearful.

"Rosie, how are you?" someone called out.

"What are you doing up so late?" another voice asked.

"Walking my invisible dog," Rosie laughed.

She had walked this street so many times, the concrete remembered her footsteps. An overwhelming sadness enveloped her. It wasn't just the loss of Clara. Pushing sixty, still teaching at the same high school, still living in the same small house where she was born, still living with the memory of Ruben, she grieved for the loss of her youth and the mundane life she had led. She reached their small house and unlatched the iron gate. The old hinges cried out. Joey had left the porch light on; a small lamp also shone through the window. Not quite ready to go in, Rosie rocked gently on the wicker swing and closed her eyes.

"Ruben, wherefore art thou, my Ruben?" she whispered, looking skyward. She only thought of him once in awhile, but now his memory awakened her loneliness, her longing for him, for someone, for anyone. She wanted to be held, kissed, caressed, and told how beautiful she was. The desires she had suppressed for so long came to the surface. Her tears started slowly, almost one at a time; first for Ruben, then for the loss of her best friend Clara, for Joey who was so ill, for her dead siblings, for the wars, the chaos in the world. But mostly her tears were for herself. She reached into her pants pocket for a tissue, but then remembered it was in shreds, discarded in the nearest trash bin after leaving Clara at the station. She would either have to wipe her nose on the sleeve of her blouse, or go in for a tissue. Wouldn't you know it, she thought. For want of a tissue, a sadness has passed. Can't even have a good uninterrupted cry these days!

She pulled herself up from the wicker swing and walked into the kitchen relieved that Joey had cleaned up.

Rosie got ready for bed, adhering to her usual nightly ritual. Shivering slightly in the cool summer night, she crawled into bed and pulled a light summer blanket over her. She stretched her body with a sigh of relief and relished the thought of a new day, a late Sunday morning cup of coffee and the New York Times crossword puzzle.

As her eyes closed she remembered her earlier conversation with Joey. Would she have the guts to take his advice, sell this place, travel, retire, fall in love again? Yeah! Right! The house was worth quite a bit of money now. They had been approached several times by the City, but both agreed that with Joey's declining health they were better off staying put.

It was 2:00 a.m. before she dozed off. Despite her exhaustion, or maybe because of it, she slept fitfully.

◇◇◇

As Lui brought his car to the alley, Ramon continued to drag Alberto through the back of the bar, still asking about the girl. "Maureen, I think her name is," he mumbled. "That guy's one mean son-of-a-bitch."

"Hey, bro, we can't be thinking about no girl. We're leaving for California tonight."

"Whaddya mean, 'leaving for California?'"

"Listen, Lui here is taking off for L. A. right now, and we need to go with him. That fight in the bar . . . we don't wanna get in no trouble with the cops. You may have fuckin' stabbed a guy."

"I don't think so, Hermano. I don't 'member." His lip was swelling and he couldn't speak clearly. "Things happen in a fight. He was gonna kill that girl. I didn't have a choice," Alberto said.

"Yeah, I know. But who's gonna believe it? Listen, Lui's taking us home to get some money. We need three big ones, and then we're taking off for L. A. Tonight! Lui says there'll be a good job waiting for me. We'll pay back the money soon as we get there." Ramon talked fast so that he could skip over questions he knew Alberto would ask as they continued through the narrow back passageway of the bar toward the alley.

"Hold on, Ramon." Alberto pulled back, trying to clear his head. "What do you mean 'pay back the money'? Pay it back to who? Mama ain't got no money."

"Not Mama."

"Then who?"

"Rosie!"

"Jesus, Ramon. It don't make no sense, what you're sayin'. Leave our jobs? Just pick up? No goodbyes? No looking back?"

"Yeah. That's what I want, *hermano*. No looking back, only looking ahead." They staggered out the back door of *Ramrod* into the cool air, Alberto limping and leaning heavily on Ramon. Lui's headlights came toward them. They heard the police sirens screaming nearby.

In the shadows behind a dumpster, a small figure emerged, stilettos clicking as she tottered toward them.

"There she is," Alberto pointed. "Maureen."

She ran over to Alberto. "Thank you, thank you." She tried to embrace him, but Ramon blocked her. He only wanted to get his brother in the car.

"I heard you talking. Take me with you," Maureen pleaded. "You know he'll kill me. I have no place to go."

"Get in the car," Ramon yelled to Alberto as he shoved him into the back seat.

"No. Not without her." Ramon knew how stubborn Alberto was, and this was no time to argue.

Lui had his foot on the pedal, ready to shift into drive. "I don't care who gets in this car, but it better be right now or I'm gone."

Maureen didn't wait for another invitation. She jumped in before anyone could object. Ramon gave Alberto a final shove and followed him, his hand simultaneously reaching to shut the door as he pulled his leg in at the last moment. Lui was out of there, tires squealing, tailpipe smoking, adrenalin pumping, and sweat dripping down the side of his face. In his rear view mirror he watched the police cars arrive as he pulled away. Close, real close, he thought, a small smile on his face. Lui loved a challenge. "Where to?" he asked. Ramon gave him directions. Within twenty minutes they were in front of Rosie's house.

Lui and Ramon ignored Maureen, as though, if they denied her presence, she wouldn't be there. *I ain't gonna deal with this now*, thought Lui. Maureen curled up and tried to make herself invisible. She figured if they hadn't already kicked her out, they weren't going to.

Ramon was betting his brother wouldn't let him go to Los Angeles by himself. Usually it was Alberto who made major decisions, but this time Ramon would press his advantage. Maureen!

◇◇◇

Rosie didn't hear the car drive up, but she heard the squeaky gate when Ramon opened it. She lay still for a moment, reached for her robe at the end of the bed, put her slippers on and walked out to the hallway, still not certain she hadn't imagined the sound. A moment later there was a soft knock on the front door.

"Miss Rosie. Are you there?" Ramon asked.

She recognized his voice, but stalled for time. "Who is it?"

"It's me . . . Ramon. I know it's late, but I gotta talk to ya. It's serious."

"Just a minute." She walked to the living room window, parted the blinds slightly and peered out. She slowly undid the lock and opened the door. Ramon slid in.

"For God's sake, Ramon . . . what the hell's going on?" She spoke in a loud whisper, not wanting to wake Joey.

"Miss Rosie, Alberto got into a fight tonight. I think he's in trouble. We need to get away for a few days, let things cool down." He hesitated. "You know how 'Berto always takes care of me, but now I need to take care of him." He told Rosie what happened but exaggerated the circumstances, deliberately leading Rosie to believe that this was a case of life and death. "I gotta do right by Alberto." He appealed to her sense of loyalty.

"Well, damn it Ramon, it's two in the morning. What do you want me to do?" She threw up her hands and then hesitated. "He didn't kill anybody, did he?" she asked as an afterthought.

"No, nothin' like that."

"Did you rob someone?"

Ramon took a moment to answer. Then, he blurted out, "Miss Rosie, we need three hundred dollars right away."

"Three hundred dollars!" she shrieked. "Well, I guess you didn't rob anyone, unless it was a homeless person," she added sarcastically. "Ramon, you think I'm a bank or something? Where am I going to get that kind of money at this hour?"

"Rosie, c'mon. I swear to you. I swear on anything you want, I'll pay you back in a week."

"But, Ramon . . ."

"Rosie, dammit, don't ask so many questions. Just do this one thing for us and we'll be in your debt forever. Please."

Rosie looked into Ramon's eyes, saw the desperation and tried to assess the situation, to analyze it, to give it some reality. But she was so tired.

'You're sure nobody killed anyone?"

"No, honest, Rosie."

"What about your Mama? Aren't you going to leave her a note or something?"

"There ain't no time. You do it for us. Tell her we'll be in touch."

She looked closely at Ramon. He seemed uneasy and apprehensive, pacing — three steps right, three steps left. "Where's Alberto? He okay?" she asked

"Yeah." He saw her waver.

"Wait here a minute." She walked to the back of the house, looking over her shoulder to make sure he wasn't behind her. She opened the door of a seldom-used storage closet and withdrew a shoebox, counting out three, one hundred dollar bills.

Back in the living room she held out her hand to Ramon. "Here," she said. "You know this is totally irrational, not to mention ridiculous. I hope I'm not abetting a crime."

They looked at each other, neither of them speaking, Ramon not really comprehending why Rosie had given him the money, and Rosie not really comprehending why she had done it.

"Rosie, you're a good woman. There ain't many around, that's for sure," Ramon said. Awkwardly, he went to hug her, and as he did so he experienced something he had rarely felt before. Affection, love. It was only a momentary feeling, one he could not identify at the time. It reached into his gut like a shot of tequila.

He walked out the door, a smile of relief and triumph on his face. He held the three bills in front of him and waved them at Lui who was peering out the window anxiously. As far as Ramon was concerned, they were practically in California.

CHAPTER SEVEN

LUI HUNG HIS HEAD out the car window anxiously awaiting Ramon's return. When he saw him dangling the hundred dollar bills, his estimate of Ramon rose one hundred percent. "Goddamn, I'll be a son-of-a-bitch. I didn't think you could pull it off."

Ramon jumped into the passenger seat with Lui. "I'm jazzed," he said.

Maureen shriveled herself like a snail, folding her legs beneath her and digging her body into a corner of the back seat. She shivered with anxiety, fearing that Paul might be looking for her this very minute. She pulled her jacket over her shoulders and closed her eyes.

"Maureen, you got something?" Alberto nudged her. "I feel like I just wrestled a bear."

Rummaging through her purse, she found a small packet, opened it and passed the pills into Alberto's outstretched hand. He didn't ask what they were. He just swallowed them, threw his jacket behind his head, and rested it against the window. Within five minutes he was breathing deeply. Maureen tried to stay awake, but her head kept falling to her chest.

Several hours passed. Lui and Ramon smoked and kept up a conversation, mostly about California. As the sun rose and flooded the car with daylight, Alberto stirred. His mouth was dry and he'd have given anything for a cold beer. Maureen was asleep, her mouth slightly ajar, breathing softly and curled up against the door. She had taken off her high heels and her feet pushed against his thigh. He had a momentary impulse to run his hand up her leg.

Alberto tried to recapture the events of the previous evening. The only thing he remembered clearly was Maureen lifting the margarita glass and smashing Paul in the head with it. Everything else was blurred.

Ramon was driving, Lui asleep in the passenger seat. He looked in the rear view mirror and noticed that his brother was awake.

"Welcome to the world, bro." Ramon gave him a big smile.

Alberto was dead silent, looking out the window. Ramon recognized the silence as a warning and the smile left his face. His hands tightened on the steering wheel; he figured it was best to keep his mouth shut.

"Where the hell are we?"

"Scranton," Ramon said softly.

"You want to tell me again why the fuck we're on our way to Los Angeles?" Alberto asked. Ramon was quiet.

"I asked you a question and you better have a good answer." Alberto moved forward and grabbed the back of the driver's seat.

"You almost killed a guy, is why . . ."

"Bullshit! I didn't almost kill nobody. Someone comes at you with a knife, you're gonna to protect yourself."

"Yeah, well ya know, you coulda kept outta the whole thing. It wasn't none of your damn business."

"What the hell are you talking about? This guy was about to kill a woman and you're saying nobody shoulda stopped him?"

"Well, yeah, but it could have been somebody else . . ."

"Look," Alberto said leaning back. "Do me a favor will ya. Don't talk to me. Because I don't really want to be here. Ya know what I mean? I feel like I been hijacked and I'd just as soon be back in the Bronx. Going to Los Angeles was your dream, not mine." He sat back, his elbow on the window ledge, his head leaning in his hand. "Just stop at a goddamn gas station 'cause I'm about to piss out the window."

Maureen listened to the argument with closed eyes. This is all my fault, she thought.

"Yeah. Next gas station I see we'll stop, get something to eat, a cup o' coffee – and then you can drive, and princess there," he pointed to Maureen, "she can keep you company up front. You'll feel better once you get a cup of . . ."

"Don't tell me when I'll feel better, asshole."

"Okay, I get the message. You wanna go back? You like that life? You wanna just live with Mama forever – have her tell us when to wash behind our ears?" Ramon asked, one arm in motion, the other on the

wheel. He took the offensive. "I can drop you off at a bus station and
. . ." He knew this was a risky strategy because if Alberto said *okay* he
wasn't sure what he would do, continue on, or go back to the Bronx
with him. Silence.

"You know what the trouble with you is, bro? You think too damn
much," Ramon finally said.

"Yeah, well one of us gotta think. It's better than havin your
brain stuck in first gear like it's goin up a mountain all the time." But
as they squabbled back and forth Alberto thought, *maybe Ramon is
right. I'd probably live there the rest of my life, sharing a bedroom,
working a dead-end job. One thing I gotta give Ramon. He's got moxey.
What the hell — no way I can let him go to Los Angeles by himself
anyway. We ain't never been separated before.* He tried to put his
anger aside. "Are we following a map, or am I just going to wing it?"

"Oh," Ramon chided him, breathing a silent sigh of relief.
"Where'd you learn to read a map? We ain't ever been nowhere."

"There's lots of things I can do, you don't know about." He
changed the subject. "So what did Rosie say when you woke her this
morning? How come she opened the door for you?"

"She knew it was me. I guess she figured it was a real
emergency."

"And what did you tell her? I mean, what story did you make up
for her to give you three hundred dollars? It must've been good."

Ramon laughed. "Well, I just told her you killed somebody and we
had to get out of town. You know Rosie always had a soft spot for you."

"Very funny!"

"I swore we'd pay her back. I only said that you got in a fight and
might be in trouble with the police. I didn't mention we were going to
Los Angeles."

"Jesus!"

Maureen opened her eyes. Her legs were cramped and one foot
was totally asleep. She struggled to sit up straight and searched for her
high-heeled shoes, one under the passenger seat.

"Good morning, beautiful," Alberto said.

Maureen just nodded. She looked out the window and saw various
signs indicating they were in Scranton. Her purse lay beside her and she

wondered whether any of them had thought to rifle through it while she slept. She'd find out once she got to a bathroom.

She thought about the previous evening and remembered how Paul had humiliated her by telling the bartender to 'bring this cunt a drink'. Something had snapped in her. It was that one word that did it. She wondered how she could have allowed herself to get so low. Like Ramon, she recognized this as an opportunity for a new start.

When the fight started, Paul had removed his jacket and thrown it to the floor. While he and Alberto moved around the room for position, Maureen picked up the jacket and removed the billfold. No one was paying attention to her as all eyes were focused on the two men. Paul's billfold contained a stack of hundreds which Maureen quickly removed and put in her purse, returning the billfold to his jacket. The minute she smashed that margarita glass against his head she knew she'd have to leave, or be killed.

By now they were all awake, their minds focused on one thing; the nearest bathroom and that first jolt of caffeine. Maureen was quiet, fearful they would change their minds about taking her with them; she didn't want to risk antagonizing anyone.

Ramon finally pulled into a major station where there was a market and a coffee shop.

"Okay, so what's it gonna be?" he asked, looking at Lui. "Bacon and eggs or coffee and chewing gum?"

"Well, I'd just as soon move on if everyone's agreed," Lui said. "So I'll just settle for coffee and chewing gum."

They all got out, stretching and moaning. The men headed for the restroom. Maureen was embarrassed because she still wore a pale green skin tight dress which came to mid-thigh and was low-cut. It was stained from the spill of the margarita and it smelled of liquor and smoke. Her shoes were killing her and she hobbled as she walked tentatively into the market toward the ladies room. Her long hair was tangled and her mascara had run. Her body ached. If Lui hadn't stopped the car she was certain she would die from all the cigarettes he and Ramon had lit up. She inhaled deeply, her lungs sucking in the oxygen, like a vacuum cleaner.

The ladies room was occupied. *Wouldn't you know it?* As she waited, leaning against the wall, crossing her legs, she glanced around the store, her eyes scanning the sparse array of clothing. She heard the toilet flush, the water from the sink, and then the paper towel dispenser. Another minute and she'd be in there. A heavy-set woman exited. "It's all yours darlin'," she said, raising her eyebrows as she looked at Maureen's tight-fitting dress and bruised face.

Maureen locked the door quickly behind her. She barely pulled her pants down in time. She removed her torn panty hose and threw them on the floor. Still sitting on the toilet, she looked in her purse to make sure the money was still there. She had no idea how much there was. One hundred, two hundred, she kept counting the hundreds as if she were dealing out cards. Twenty-two! Jesus! Over two grand! She'd never seen that much money. She stood up, adjusted everything and finally looked in the mirror. Dark circles rimmed her eyes; the bruise on her lip was scabbing. She squirted soap on her hands, worked up some lather, and washed her face. She found an old rubber band in her purse and pulled her hair back in a pony tail. *Now, if I can only find something to wear.*

The men were scanning the aisles for cigarettes and other items. The green dress caught Ramon's eye but he couldn't put it together that she looked different because her hair was tied back and she wasn't wearing makeup. Maureen wondered if they had thought of leaving her but she wasn't as concerned about it now that she had some money. At least she could buy a ticket to somewhere or even stay in Scranton.

The market had one small rack of cheap clothing, mostly T-shirts sporting a Scranton logo, as though she'd really want the world to know that's where she'd been. She bought a dark green shirt that said PENNSYLVANIA STATE UNIVERSITY, a pair of grey knit elastic waist shorts, flat plastic beach shoes, and a "Phillies" baseball cap. A toothbrush and toothpaste were added to the purchase.

Lui and Ramon leaned against a brick wall outside, drinking coffee and smoking. Lui was on his cell phone to someone named Charlie.

"Yeah, Charlie, I got the man for you." He took a drag out of his cigarette. "Yeah, he's got a brother too. No, his brother ain't gonna help us. He's a baker." He listened and then laughed. "That's a good one, Charlie. The brother bakes bread and we're going to be rolling in dough. Yeah, I like that one." He laughed heartily. "We're on our way.

In Scranton. Yeah, it's a shit hole alright. It ain't like Santa Monica, that's for sure."

"That was Charlie," he said to Ramon as he hung up. "He's anxious to meet you."

In the market Alberto spotted Maureen at the cashier's counter. "You about ready?" he asked. He tried not to notice her bruises which were more obvious now. "You need some money?"

"No, thanks. I have a few bucks. Look, I need another few minutes," she said. "I have to change out of these clothes."

"Don't worry about it. Take your time. Get yourself something to eat when you've changed. I'll take care of it."

She gave him a grateful look. In the ladies room, she changed into her new clothes and threw everything else in the trash. In a T-shirt, shorts and baseball cap, she looked like a teenager.

Alberto watched from a distance as she exited the ladies room and headed for the coffee urns. She poured a cup of coffee, black, raising her eyebrows slightly in pleasure at the first sip. Instead of Danish she selected a hot dog and, depressing the mustard dispenser, she formed a long straight line in the center.

Very precise. Careful. Alberto's brain stored this small insight into Maureen's character.

She suddenly looked up, saw him, and gave him a big smile wincing slightly because of her lip. It was unexpected and it unnerved him. This was a Maureen no one had seen in a long time. Something indefinable had changed, and it wasn't just her appearance.

Alberto paid for her food and they exited the market. Lui and Ramon were taken aback at Maureen's new look, but were too tired and anxious to get going to say anything. They got into the back seat as Alberto and Maureen got into the front. He took the map off the dashboard and looked for their next stop, already marked by Lui.

Ramon and Lui fidgeted in the back until they got comfortable. Ramon had his back to the window, his long legs pulled to the side. Lui slouched down, his jacket behind his head, his short legs stretched under the front passenger seat and his visor down over his eyes.

When they were out of the city, Alberto was the first to speak. "So, Maureen, is this the new you, or the old you?"

"Both," she said. "It's the new me, back to the old me. Does that make sense?"

"I don't know," he said. "I'm too young to have an old me."

"How old are you?" she asked.

"Going on twenty-two."

She gave him a sidewise glance. "When are you going on twenty-two?"

"Oh, about a year or so," he laughed. "What about you?"

"I'm ancient . . . going on twenty-five."

"Jesus! You look like a kid. I'd never have guessed you were that old."

She laughed.

"I didn't mean it . . ."

"That's okay, I know what you mean."

"So, how'd you get hooked up with that scumbag, Paul?"

"I don't know. How does anyone get hooked up with anyone? You're in a certain place at a certain time, and bingo, your whole life changes. He was a way out."

"A way out of what?"

"A way out of the rat race, I guess," she said wistfully. "But you can't get out of the rat race if you're depending on a rat to get you out."

"What did you expect?"

"I don't know. I guess I thought he'd support me until I made it through college. I finally did get the degree but I don't know if it was worth it. I was so used to being abused; I didn't even recognize it anymore. Paul was noxious, like turning on the gas oven and doing yourself in. You know what I mean? He was such a failure himself, he couldn't stand to see anyone else succeed. I was his prisoner and he was my warden, you know the usual macho bullshit. I didn't have the guts to leave until last night when it suddenly occurred to me I wasn't Maureen anymore. I was no one." She looked over at him. "I want to be someone, Ramon. I want to be respected, to feel good about myself like when I was in school when, against all odds, I stayed on top of my class. I swear I don't know what motivated me back then. I think it was the only way I could prove I was worth something."

"So what happened last night?"

"My God! Was it only last night? I feel like a millennium has passed."

"A millennium," he echoed.

She looked over, saw the perplexed look on his face and realized he wasn't familiar with the word. ". . . Like a thousand years," she said. "I don't know what got into me last night. Something snapped. It was that word. That 'c' word. I thought, *now* or *never*. If he kills me, so be it. Either way, to leave him or stay with him would be a death sentence." She looked at Alberto. "But then, my Prince Valiant stepped in to defend me from the dragon," she smiled.

"Prince Valiant," he echoed.

"Yeah. He's the hero in the comic strip that always saves the girl."

She closed her eyes and drifted off. Alberto's thoughts lingered over Maureen's story. Her 'Prince Valiant' she had said. He smiled. He had done the right thing when he defended her against Paul. *Wow! Four years of college!* He had never spoken to anyone who had a college degree.

CHAPTER EIGHT

AT THE AIRPORT CLARA clutched her old purse with one hand and Frank with the other. She wore tan polyester pants with a permanent crease down the center, and a print cotton blouse, both size sixteen. Her dark brown cable knit cardigan was unevenly buttoned; one of the buttons hung by a thread.

An inexperienced traveler, Clara had difficulty opening and closing the folding door of the lavatory on the plane. Squinting, she'd had to search for her glasses to figure out how the latch worked. *OCCUPIED — UNOCCUPIED*. The flush scared her when it whooshed down the waste.

Their daughter, Gloria, and son-in-law Martin, met them at the gate. They exchanged glances as Gloria's parents neared.

"You think we made a mistake bringing them here?" Gloria asked her husband.

"I don't know. I hope not. Your Dad's really aged. Maybe the trip was too much for him."

They stopped talking as Clara and Frank approached, smiling and holding their arms out to embrace their children. When Gloria hugged her father, she realized how frail he was; his breathing was labored. He reluctantly agreed to a wheelchair.

"Where are the children?" Clara asked looking around.

"They hardly ever come with us anymore," Gloria said. "God forbid they should give up an hour with their friends."

"They couldn't come to meet their grandparents?" Frank asked.

"Oh, you know how kids are," she apologized. "They'll be there when we get home. They couldn't resist my homemade enchiladas."

"Grandparents they can resist, but enchiladas, no!" muttered Frank.

Suddenly Gloria was aware that the generation gap between her parents and children would be difficult, if not impossible, to breach.

Martin left the three of them at the curb as he brought his car around. They wound their way out of the airport into traffic on Century Boulevard.

"How old are the kids now?" Frank asked.

"Marty's fifteen but he's already five eight. And Hannah - well, you'll see," Gloria laughed.

"Fifteen," Frank mused. His shoulders slumped. *I don't know if Clara and I can handle a fifteen-year old.* Gloria had made it all sound so good. She'd waged a campaign, like a general, writing and calling often, always reminding them they were getting older and needed to live closer. Frank felt his chest tighten.

Martin honked his horn as they pulled into the one-car driveway. Martin, Jr., a lanky clone of his Dad, walked out, letting the screen door bang hard behind him. He was barefoot and wore frayed cut-off jeans and a white T-shirt. *Thank God it doesn't have writing on it like THERE IS NO GOD,* Frank thought. He quietly appraised his grandson. In the boy you could already see the man.

Hannah followed behind her brother. "Dammit Marty, you don't have to slam the door in my face." He totally ignored her and flew down the porch steps to help his grandfather out of the car. Mandatory hugs and kisses were bestowed all the way around. They tried to ignore the awkwardness which a three-year absence had forged.

"Come in, come in," Gloria shooed them all.

Frank wandered off and looked around the living room trying to remember if anything had changed. Several family photos were on the mantel. He focused on one taken of him and Clara some twenty years ago. The photo had been taken on a beautiful spring afternoon at the Bronx Zoo.

She'd said, "Take your camera. Sometimes the monkeys are outrageous. You know, they do all sorts of crude things." She'd looked at him mischievously.

"Clara, behave yourself," he had admonished, stifling a small smile.

They had asked a passerby to take their picture and it turned out to be one of the few good photos they had of the both of them.

If there were other changes, Frank didn't really notice. He wasn't sure what he was looking for; maybe a book he hadn't read, or a comfort level he hadn't yet felt. He wandered out to the back patio and lay down on a striped canvas lounge chair, exhausted from the trip. He stretched his legs and folded his arms lightly on his chest.

Clara and Gloria busied themselves in the kitchen, gossiping about mutual friends and family. Hannah joined them.

It was dusk. Frank finally felt his body relax. He smiled as he heard Clara and Gloria giggling through the kitchen window. A TV newscaster was reporting the events of the day. Frank only half listened. The world was changing. Last year Nixon actually made a visit to communist China. The Supreme Court's ruling on Roe vs. Wade seized the headlines. Protests had erupted throughout the country, some for and some against. The governor of Alabama had been shot at a political rally.

The air smelled of lemon blossoms; the trees cast their shadows as the last vestige of sunlight fell below the horizon. Frank's left arm slid off his chest and hung to his side. An exquisite peace enveloped him and his spirits soared. *Clara . . . my love . . .* "

◇◇◇

Only a week had passed since Clara and Frank had left for Los Angeles. Buried in paperwork at the high school Rosie didn't have time to miss her. The students and faculty were on edge, dealing with finals, graduation, prom, and upcoming vacations.

Summer had finally won its subtle battle over the cool rainy days of spring. It hit with fervor, casting a combination of clouds and humidity along with unbearable ninety-two degree temperatures. WHEREVER HARDWARE on Tremont Avenue experienced a frenzy of sales for cooling fans of all sizes. Customers rooted themselves in front of the fans until they cooled off, and then either moved on, or bought one in whatever size was available. Rosie cursed nylon stockings. Her clothes clung to her as she rushed to meetings with guidance counselors, parents and co-workers.

Heading home, she merged with other passengers on the train from Manhattan to the Bronx. She held tightly to a strap, her legs balanced to the lurch of the train at each stop. She could smell the musty odor of her own perspiration.

She walked the half-mile from the station to her small house carrying her black pumps in a tote bag. She had laced up a pair of Nike's the moment she left the school grounds. Joey was waiting for her at the door. He looked smaller and smaller every day, like a shriveled apple hanging on to its core.

"Hi, handsome," she greeted him.

"Rosie . . ."

"What's wrong?" She could tell from his face it was really bad news.

He hung his head and didn't look at her. "I don't know how to tell you."

"What? What is it?"

Joey just stood there, unable to speak.

"Joey," Rosie raised her voice. "For God's sake . . ."

He stumbled on his words. "I-- It's Clara's husband, Frank."

"Frank?" Rosie's voice faded. "He's hurt?"

Joey shook his head.

"Dead?"

Joey nodded.

She put one hand over her heart and held on to the porch railing with the other before sitting down. Joey sat on the bench opposite her, his hands clasped tightly in his lap. "I wish there was something I could do," he said.

"Isn't it ironic?" Rosie pinched the bridge of her nose. "All these years they resisted leaving New York. Finally they decide to move to Los Angeles, and what does God do in his infinite wisdom? He decides now would be a good time for Frank to move even further! Just move away forever." She was speaking to herself more than to Joey as her body rocked back and forth. "'Just go Frank,'" God says, "'Don't look back, don't worry about a thing. Just go.'" She waved her hands in front of her, as though shooing Frank away.

Joey stood up and limped into the small kitchen. His hip hurt as he reached under the counter and pulled out a bottle of Jim Beam, still three-quarters full, which someone had brought them three years ago. Against doctor's orders he poured himself and Rosie a hefty drink and took it out to the front porch. She reached for it without hesitation.

"You know," she said. "If you weren't my brother, I'd marry you."

"Ditto," he said. They clicked glasses.

"To Frank," they said in unison, sipping for awhile in silence. Joey savored the warmth of the liquor, but grimaced with each swallow.

"Who called to tell us?" Rosie asked.

"Gloria's husband."

"Did Martin say how it happened?"

"Frank just went out to take a nap." Joey's voice broke and he couldn't continue. "It's not a bad way to go." He took a tissue out of his pocket and blew his nose.

"Take your time," Rosie said. "There's no rush. Telling it fast or slow isn't going to change the ending."

"You don't realize how little time you have left until something like this happens," Joey said. "I mean, we just saw Frank last week, and now . . ." he paused, his voice fading. "And he's not the only one we've lost this past year."

"I know."

They sat for awhile as the night sky darkened. The sounds of children playing in the street diminished. From the tenements the aroma of ethnic foods — beans and rice, green peppers, chorizo, mingled with the humidity of the overhead clouds.

Rosie stood up. She brought the glass to her lips, the last drop of liquor coursing its way through the ice cubes as they clicked one more time against her teeth. She said, "Well, I can't put this off forever. Guess I better call Clara."

CHAPTER NINE

LUI AND RAMON SLEPT fitfully in the back seat of the '63 Impala, a red four-door hard-top with dual exhausts and only sixty-seven thousand miles on it. She purred like a newborn kitten sucking on its mother's nipples. Alberto asked Lui if he owned the car legally.

"What the hell ya talkin' about?" Lui had said.

"Well, I'm just thinking if we're stopped by the cops it won't look too good, three men and a woman driving a car with California license plates. Ya know what I mean?"

"You think I'm driving a stolen vehicle across country? Jesus! Ya gotta gimme more credit than that, man." Lui turned his head away.

Alberto had been suspicious of Lui from day one and figured him for a con. But Ramon was so gung-ho about California, it never occurred to him that Lui might be full of hot air.

As they pulled out of Scranton Alberto lit up a joint.

"Don't you think that's a little risky?" Maureen had asked.

"Yeah, but it'll make the trip so much easier," he laughed. He rolled the window down a few inches. "You interested?"

"Okay, what the hell." She took the joint from him and held it between her thumb and forefinger as she inhaled. "A little harsh," she said coughing and then felt the impact of the marijuana as it raced to her brain. They passed the joint back and forth.

"Did I remember you saying Cleveland was your home town?"

"Yes, don't get me started on Cleveland. I have a lot of memories, some good, some bad. For me, Cleveland is like leftover scraps of dried egg on a plate. I have some unfinished business there that needs to be cleaned up."

"Whatd'ya mean?"

"I'd like to stay there overnight." She looked to the back seat to make sure Lui and Ramon were asleep. "You think you can convince those two gorillas to give me a few hours to do what I have to do?"

"What do you have to do?"

"I have to see a woman about a scar."

"A woman about a . . . ?"

"Yeah. That's what I said, a woman about a scar."

"Maureen, I gottta tell ya," Alberto said, "I have looked you over from the top of your lovely head to the bottom of your pointy painted toes, and there ain't no scar I could see. Who's the woman?"

"My mother," Maureen gave a harsh laugh. The marijuana was having its effect. She leaned her head back, started talking and then couldn't stop. It was like striking oil: a gusher, *here she comes, let 'er rip*! Her eyes clouded over as she went back in time. "When I was thirteen a boy walked me home from school and offered to carry my books. We were both shy but managed to make small talk about our homework assignment, and what subjects we both liked. I was so excited, I couldn't wait to get home and call my girlfriend. When we arrived I saw my mother peering out the window, watching us. The minute I saw her face I knew I was in for it.

"She was in one of her 'mean' moods. I could always tell but I was usually crafty enough to stay clear. Not this time. As I walked in the door she slapped my face hard. My books fell to the floor. I lost my balance and fell backward over the banister.

"What'd I do," I screamed. "What'd I do?"

"'You're just a little slut, that's what,'" she yelled.

"I tried to pull away from her but she pushed me into the bedroom on to the bed. I was peeing in my pants, gasping for breath. She was beyond angry; like a maniac. I really thought she was going to kill me. A cigarette dangled from her mouth the whole time, the ashes getting longer and then falling, longer and then falling." Maureen had stopped talking.

"So what happened?" Alberto looked over at her.

"She put the cigarette out on my thigh," Maureen said, her voice low. "That's what happened. End of story."

"Jesus!" Alberto said. "Where I come from you gotta be worried about your father, not your mother."

"She always hated me."

"Hated you? I never heard of a mother hating their kid."

"Believe me, Alberto. She hated me." Maureen reached into her purse for a tissue. "I remember what she said when she walked out of the room; something about having a little reminder the rest of my life and thinking twice before running around with boys.

"I didn't know what she was talking about, 'running around with boys.' I lay there, in terrible pain, afraid to move. I watched as my mother left the room, a small smile of satisfaction on her face, as though she was getting even with someone, or taking revenge on a past wound of her own. That was the worst part - the smile on her face.

"When I awoke it was dark. The house was quiet, eerie; I didn't even hear the T.V. I went into the bathroom afraid to look at the black hole in my thigh, it was hurting so bad. I saw myself in the mirror, flushed, eyes swollen. It wasn't me. It was somebody else. I wasn't thirteen anymore.

"I looked for something to put on the wound. All I found was Vaseline and a band aid. It festered for a month until it scabbed. I avoided my friends and was depressed for weeks. My grades fell so low I thought I'd be in sixth grade forever."

Maureen couldn't speak for a few minutes, the pain of that memory still lingering after all these years.

"Sweet Jesus!" Alberto muttered. "Wasn't there someone you could tell?"

"Not really. There was a neighbor, a Mrs. Patterson. She knew what my life was like. More than once she'd phone if she thought things were really getting out of hand, like a loud argument or too much screaming. I think I had a grandmother somewhere, but I only remember her vaguely, like a ghost. It could have been my imagination or wishful thinking." Maureen shifted her legs, blew her nose and wiped her eyes again.

"That's one hell of a story, Maureen. And then you met up with Paul and got more of the same," Alberto summarized.

"Something like that." She reached into her purse and withdrew a stick of gum. "Want some?" she asked.

"Yeah," he said. "A cold beer would be better, but I'll settle."

She removed the foil and handed him the gum. "You want me to drive awhile?"

"Nah. I like driving." They savored the first burst of flavor. "So, it must've been tough living with her after that," Alberto said.

"It was always tough living with her. I was scared all the time. She was small-minded and mean."

"What about your dad?"

"I don't remember him at all. I was told he died shortly after I was born, but I don't know who told me that. I used to think my Mom hated me because maybe I was the cause of his dying."

Both of them were quiet for several minutes. She couldn't believe she had run off at the mouth like that. "You ever hear a mother doing that to a kid?" Maureen asked.

"Maybe. But I never knew anyone it happened to." He hesitated. "You ever hear of a mother killing a father by having sex with him?"

Maureen tilted her head toward him. "No way," she said. The somber mood was broken by Alberto's comment. They both got hysterical with laughter. The joint burned his fingers as he took a last hit and flipped the 'roach' out the window. The tears were rolling down Maureen's face and Alberto was doubled over, hanging on to the steering wheel for support."

"You're kidding, right?" She was gasping for breath, holding her stomach. "Oh, my God, oh my God," she shrieked. "You mean you have a story worse than mine?" She could hardly get the words out.

"No, I wish I was kidding, but I'm not," he said between spasms.

Their laughter finally subsided as they pulled into Youngstown.

"I'll tell you the whole story one of these days."

"So what do you think?" Maureen was more serious now. "You think you can buy me some time in Cleveland?" she looked back to see if Lui and Ramon were still asleep. "Alberto, you know what it's like, all these years thinking about what this woman did to me? It's like a fly that keeps buzzing around until you kill it. I gotta kill it."

"Yeah, I guess so, but don't go getting radical on me. I'll do what I can," he said. "You know where this piece of work lives?"

"Well, I knew where she lived when I left. If she's not there, I'll just have to go into therapy for the rest of my life, or wind up with someone like Paul again."

"So, what do you think you're going to say when you see her?" Alberto asked.

"I'm not going to say anything," Maureen said. "I'm just going to kill her."

◇◇◇

Alberto was aching to stretch his legs. *If I don't get out of this car soon, I'm going to be crippled.* He massaged his left knee. As they approached Youngstown he slowed to the thirty-five mile per hour speed limit.

Lui and Ramon were stirring in the back seat. "Well, well, me sleeping beauties, what say ye?" Alberto assumed a pirate's voice.

Neither of them said anything.

"Not too talkative this morning?" Alberto smiled. "Sorry if the accommodations were less than what you're used to."

"Shut up," Lui grumbled as he peered out the window, trying to determine where they were.

Youngstown wasn't exciting by any standard, but it was a good sized city. It had seen its heyday as a steel town in the fifties, but now, twenty three years later, jobs were difficult to come by and the deterioration was obvious.

"The first breakfast place I come to, I'm gonna stop; bacon and eggs, pancakes, home fries, a cup of coffee, and whatever else they have. Whatd'ya think?" Alberto said. Taking their silence for a 'yes', he kept his eye out for a coffee shop. His stomach was growling. A huge sign caught his eye *BREAKFAST SPECIAL ALL DAY $1.50.*

"Here we go," he said, pulling in to pot-holed parking lot. "How bad can you fuck up breakfast?"

They took their time getting out of the car, stretching and moaning like old men, holding their backs, turning their heads to loosen neck muscles. They all looked the way they felt — grouchy and grungy, dog tired, and in desperate need of a shower and a good night's sleep. They made quite a picture: three men in dirty jeans and two days' stubble, and a young woman in grey shorts and a Pennsylvania T-shirt. Ramon followed the other three languidly, observing their quickened steps toward the smell of bacon and coffee. Maureen held the door for him.

"Ain't we a picture?" he grinned. She smiled.

The proprietor, also the chef, saw the four of them enter and select a table. In his early forties, clean shaven with a double chin and thinning hair his mouth opened and he couldn't seem to close it. His pants were held up by clip-on royal blue suspenders and his large stomach protruded beneath a white cook's apron. He looked easily ten years older than he was.

"Jesus," he said under his breath as he approached them. "There ain't no menus. Everything's on that chalk board over there." He nodded his head toward the counter. Only two other tables were occupied, one with two women in their sixties, and one with a young man and woman, probably in their twenties. They all averted their eyes, trying not to look at the foursome, but it was impossible. The locals were a suspicious lot, wary and not welcoming of strangers. Although travelers passed through often, they rarely saw a woman dressed as Maureen, short shorts, well built, accompanied by two Chicanos and one Chinese Hawaiian who looked homeless.

You should have seen me in my tight green dress yesterday Maureen chuckled to herself. The young man couldn't take his eyes off her. Maureen provocatively crossed her long legs. Ramon noticed and it brought a small smile to his face. *Yeah, baby you're g-o-o-d. Show 'em what ya got.*

"What can I get you?" The owner deliberately blocked the young man's view.

"Well, first thing," Lui said, "is coffee all around. And water."

"The waitress don't come in 'til four, so I'll take care of you, best I can," he apologized.

Ramon lit a cigarette. "As long as the chow's good we don't care who serves it."

"No rush," said Maureen, aware of the owner's discomfort.

Lui was savoring the uneasiness of the other customers. He didn't think they'd ever seen a Chinese Hawaiian. He was tempted to order breakfast in pidgin English, 'geev 'um wha' he want," or "howzit goin' brah."

The owner made two trips with the coffees and water and then took their orders.

"What's your name?" asked Alberto, just making conversation.

"Burt. Burt O'Malley."

"Don't tell me you're an Irishman?" Maureen smiled.

"Well, yeah. We used to have a lot of Irish in this city. Irish and German mostly, but that was a few years back when everybody was workin' steel."

"Bet you don't have any Chinese Hawaiians," Lui said with an odd smile that was malicious or genuine, hard to tell which.

"Nope, can't say as we do."

"Bet you don't have many spics either," Ramon said.

"Oh, yeah. We got lots of Mexi . . . I mean, whatever." He avoided eye contact.

"Mr. O'Malley, don't pay any mind to these guys. You and I know the only ones that matter are the Irish," Maureen said, with a slight brogue and twinkling eye. Burt visibly relaxed, a small smile on his lips.

She continued, "I'm going to have that breakfast special you got advertised in your window for a dollar fifty. I want the works, whatever it comes with, plus sourdough toast with lots of butter, and don't stop filling up on the coffee."

"Ditto on that, but add a stack of pancakes," said Ramon. "What the hell, for a dollar fifty I can pretend I'm a rich man." He tilted his chair back to stretch his long legs.

Alberto and Lui ordered the same. They made light conversation as they waited for the food, mostly discussing their next stop, Cleveland. Maureen was uneasy, drawing into herself. The food arrived and was surprisingly good, and Burt kept filling the coffee cups.

As they finished their meal, Maureen excused herself from the table and went to the restroom, but on the way she stopped to talk quietly to Burt. She asked him to add up the order and give her the check.

Lui's eyes narrowed as he watched her reach into her purse for the money. *Be interesting to know how much money that broad has with her.* He hadn't thought to ask Maureen to share expenses. But now Lui wondered whether he should broach the subject. Not that they would throw her out if she didn't have it, but his motto was *if you don't ask, you don't get.* Gas was expensive. It had gone up to a dollar a gallon, and there was a shortage. When Maureen returned to the table, he said, "I noticed you paid the breakfast tab. I'm thinkin' maybe you can put in your hundred fifty, like the rest of us, for expenses and stuff?"

Maureen wondered if Lui knew how much money she had with her; whether he had looked in her purse at an off moment. But then she figured she was probably being paranoid.

"Okay. Fair's fair," she said, reaching into her wallet. "You want a credit card or cash?" Maureen joked as she handed Lui a hundred dollar bill and two twenties.

"I figure the extra ten paid for breakfast," she said.

Lui slid the money into his jeans.

"What time you figure we'll get to Cleveland?" Alberto asked.

"I don't know," Lui said. "Maybe a couple hours, around four. I was thinking maybe we'd give ourselves a break, stop overnight and push on early tomorrow. Whatd'ya think?"

"Great idea," Maureen said before anyone could object. "I'll get my own room," she hurriedly added. "Also — I have a favor to ask," she blurted out, looking at Lui.

Surprised, he waited.

"I need to borrow your car for a few hours after we've booked in somewhere." She held her head down, waiting for the answer.

"Hey, I don't loan nobody my car," Lui said. "It's like my kid."

"C'mon, Lui," Maureen pleaded. "I only need a couple of hours. Honest. I'll be real careful. Please."

Alberto spoke up. "Oh, for God's sake, Lui, let her have the car for a couple hours. What's she gonna do, go to L.A. without us?"

"How the hell do I know?"

The twins stared him down, holding out their hands, palms up. "C'mon, give the girl a break. We're family, ain't we?" Ramon put his arm around Lui's shoulder. Lui shrugged him off. "Okay, okay, but you don't bring her back," he pointed his finger at Maureen, "I'm gonna file a stolen vehicle report."

She stifled a smile, but kept a straight face. "I always knew you were a good guy. I never did believe what everyone said about you."

Lui looked up quickly. "Whatd'ya mean, 'what everyone said?'"

Maureen started to laugh. "Gotcha," she said, as she gave him a big hug.

CHAPTER TEN

ROSIE PUT HER EMPTY Jim Beam glass on the kitchen counter and looked at her watch. Seven p.m. That would make it four in Los Angeles. Clara would probably be there. She reached in a top kitchen drawer for her telephone book and thumbed to the number.

A man's voice answered.

"Hello, Martin?"

"Marty," he said. "Not Martin. You want my dad?"

"Martin Junior?" Rosie asked, surprised. "My God, you sound just like your dad. This is Rosie Sanchez — your grandmother's friend from the Bronx?"

"Oh-h, hold on. I'll get my grandma." He set the phone down. Rosie heard blurred voices in the background and finally Clara came on.

"Rosie," Clara started to cry. "I'm so glad to hear from you," she said between sniffles.

"Clara . . . I don't know what to say. Joey and I are so saddened by this terrible news, we can hardly believe it."

"I can't believe it either. My Frank . . . Gone! Yesterday he was complaining about leaving his beloved books behind, and now, gone! It's so stupid, the things we worry about."

"Clara, darling, I wish there was something I could do."

Clara didn't hear her. She just rambled on and Rosie did not interrupt.

"I'm telling you, Rosie, he was more in love with those goddamn books than he was with me!" Clara walked out the back door, holding the phone in one hand, untwisting the long cord behind her. She pulled a used tissue out of her skirt pocket, blew her nose and sat down heavily on a patio chair. The pillow was cold and slightly damp. "Finally, I'd had it. I wasn't going to argue with him anymore. I just had every last one of them shipped here. Cost a pretty penny too!" She started to laugh. Rosie couldn't tell whether it was a nervous cackle, an angry howl, or a sorrowful cry. "Can you imagine? An entire storeroom full of books that no one's going to read, ever again. Wherever you are, Frank," she raised her fist to a cloudy sky, "I hope you enjoy your goddamn books!"

Rosie didn't say anything.

"I'm coming totally unglued, Rosie. I have no idea how I can be of any help to Gloria without Frank being here."

"So what? You went out there to help them and now they have to help you? What's the big deal? You're family. I mean, the kids sound old enough to take care of themselves."

"Well, that's true. It's just to make sure they come home from school and don't get involved with the wrong crowd; do their homework . . . that sort of thing."

"I hate to say this Clara, but someone's got their head up their ass if they think an old lady can handle teenagers."

"I'm not exactly ancient, you know," Clara retorted, miffed.

"Yeah, but I think you're forgetting your last few years at the high school; how vile kids can be. If you are, I can still remind you," Rosie said sarcastically. "They do what they want, not what they're asked to. You sure you have the strength for this?"

"I don't know," Clara said. "We were going to have a family gathering but Frank's death put everything on hold."

"Have you had a chance to scout the neighborhood yet?" Rosie asked.

"Only from the car as Martin drove us to their house. It doesn't look so different from the one we came from; mostly Latino like us with the usual small businesses . . . a pharmacy, laundry, bicycle shop, a record store." She paused. "Some things seemed a little off."

"Like what?" asked Rosie.

"Like a lot of kids hanging out at the music store when they should have been in school. But I'm trying not to be judgmental," Clara paused. "I don't suppose you could come out for a week or so?" Clara asked, sniffling.

"Oh, sweetie, I'd be there on the next plane if not for Joey. He's much too fragile."

"I didn't think so, but there's no harm asking."

Rosie put her empty glass in the dishwasher. "When's the funeral?"

"There'll be a Mass tomorrow and the burial the next day."

"Listen, Clara, try to be strong. We'll be praying for you." Rosie hung up.

She walked out to the porch. Joey still nursed the last of his drink. *He's probably been bitten by a hundred mosquitoes. They could draw blood better than any R.N.,* Rosie thought.

"You hungry?" she asked.

"Starving," Joey said.

"You know I'm not cooking, right?"

"Right!"

"How about you and me getting a burrito at El Gallito?"

"You're on!" he said, pouring the ice cubes into the rose bush and slipping into his shoes.

CHAPTER ELEVEN

THE POLICE ARRIVED AT *Ramrod* just after Lui Chu pulled his Impala away from the scene. They quickly established that Paul Brody had provoked a fight, pulled a knife on his opponent, and inadvertently stabbed himself in the process. Nobody seemed able or willing to identify the other fighter. Brody, abrasive and drunk, was taken by ambulance to Bronx Hospital and released several hours later. The police were happy to chalk it up to one more bar fight.

When Paul couldn't find Maureen in the hospital lobby, he pushed his way to the front of a long line and asked the intake nurse whether anyone had asked about him, in particular a blue-eyed brunette. "Sir," she said, looking him dead in the eye and waving her pen. "Look around you. Yo'all see these people waitin' to be taken care of? They been here since five this morning - and so have I. So don't push your luck." *In other words, don't mess with me asshole,* she thought. "You think I'd remember?"

"Never mind, bitch," Paul said, heading for the exit. *Maureen probably took a cab home,* but he wondered where she'd have gotten the money. He felt for the billfold in his inside jacket pocket. Whew! He was relieved it was there. Twenty-two hundred big ones for Maggio, aka *Streetbank,* for a loan he took two weeks ago. *Streetbank* was not a person you could put off. He'd break your legs in two minutes and then add two minutes of overtime to your bill.

Paul was feeling so sorry for himself he looked like he could sit down on the curb and cry. *What a life,* he thought. *Lose a bet and then borrow money to pay it back. The interest was more than the goddamn loan. On and on, never ahead. And now this fucking gash.* He hailed a cab and grimaced as he got into it. He reached into his pocket for a couple of pain pills which the doctor had given him, *something called Vico something.* He couldn't even read the label. *Someone is going to pay for this, that's for sure! Wait'll I get my hands on that bitch.*

He gave the driver his address and settled back, closing his eyes, pressing one hand lightly over the bandaged area to make sure it was all intact. It felt sticky. As they approached his apartment he again reached for his billfold, this time removing it to pull out a one hundred dollar bill. It was empty. "JESUS!" he yelled, searching his other pockets. *Nothing! Nada!* It didn't occur to him that Maureen might have taken the money. First he thought someone at the hospital; then he thought someone at the bar. The cab driver became uneasy as Paul muttered and cursed under his breath. "Someone stole my money," he said. The cab driver, having heard this more than once, pulled over.

"Hey, what're you doing?"

"Pal, you don't pay, I don't drive. Get out!"

"You son-of-a-bitch," Paul said. "I'm a sick man, for God's sake. You just picked me up at the hospital."

"Like I said . . ." the cabbie opened his door and started to get out.

"Wait a minute . . ." Paul stalled. "I got some friends over at *Ramrod*. It's just down the street. Ya know where it is?"

"Yeah, I know where it is."

"I can get the money there."

"Ya better . . ."

"Don't worry, you'll be paid."

The cabbie waited outside *Ramrod* as Paul went in. It was early afternoon, the day after the fight, and only the owner, Oscar de Luna, was there, getting ready for this evening's crowd, stacking glasses, filling ice bins, making sure there was enough beer. He was surprised when he heard footsteps. By the time he looked up, Paul was in his face, grabbing him by the shirt and putting his fist against de Luna's throat.

"I need some money, old man; the money you guys stole from me last night."

"What're you talking about?" de Luna gasped. Paul dragged him to the cash register. "Open it," he shouted.

De Luna did as he was told and Paul removed about five hundred dollars, the 'float' for the evening's business.

"This ain't gonna do it. Where's the money you took from my jacket?"

"What jacket? I swear, we didn't take no money from you. We were busy trying to break up the fight. We were worried about the damage," he sputtered. "There was no time. Your girlfriend . . ."

De Luna's face reddened. He suddenly felt weak and dizzy. He knew his blood pressure had gone off the charts.

"Yeah." *My girlfriend!* "I only got one more question for you, old man. What's the name of the son-of-a-bitch I was fighting with? I seen your kid talking to 'im."

"I don't know," de Luna fell to his knees, sweating and gasping for breath. Paul held him up by his shirt, and was now pulling his head back. "Either you tell me, or one of your sons will," he spewed his anger in de Luna's face.

"Alberto . . . Esparza - Bronx," De Luna wheezed.

The cab driver got tired of waiting. As he walked in the door he saw Paul kick de Luna in the ribs and let him fall to the floor, unconscious. Paul raised his hand, showing the cabbie the money. He grabbed him roughly by the arm and pushed him outside. "C'mon. Let's go."

"Hey buddy, no hands, huh?" the cabbie said.

"Just move it." Paul's wound was open and bleeding and he was having trouble breathing. They drove to his apartment. He paid the driver and walked up two flights of stairs, only one thing on his mind — Maureen!

Maureen's clothes and personal items were there; it did not occur to him that she wasn't returning. He needed to rest. *She'll be back. Where could she go?* He wasn't thinking straight. *What was it the bartender had said? His girlfriend picked up the jacket? No way! She'd be too scared to take the money. But where was she? Esparza. Alberto Esparza.* Paul fell on the bed. *Later,* he thought. *I'll deal with it later.*

He awoke several hours later, his head clear and the wound not throbbing. He showered carefully and applied a new bandage which had been given him at the hospital. He looked up Alberto Esparza in the phone directory. No luck — but Ramon Esparza was listed. He remembered hearing that name called out during the fight. He'd take a chance. He wanted his two grand.

Paul walked slowly to the corner to hail a cab. As he left, the police pulled up in front of the building, their guns drawn. They signaled each other silently, up to the second floor, apartment two thirteen. Too late.

The headlines caught everybody's attention the next day:

BAR OWNER FOUND DEAD IN LOCAL BAR.

◇◇◇

Paul gave the cabbie directions to the Esparza apartment in the East Bronx. He got out of the cab painfully, cautious of his wound, and told the driver to wait. As usual, three or four men and women were gathered around the stoop gossiping. When the cab pulled up the conversation ceased. Everyone became anxious, on edge. The men looked at each other, their instincts heightened by a foreboding of imminent danger.

Paul limped over. "What apartment does Esparza live in?" he asked. "You know, the kid with the brother?" He tried to maintain a friendly manner, but the smile on his face belied the threat in his voice.

Two men nodded, not answering directly. The women shrunk back instinctively, almost hiding behind one another. In one moment the group had gone from pleasantries to apprehension and silence.

"So what apartment am I looking for, amigos?" Paul asked.

No one answered. Paul drew closer, the smile fading. "I don't want to ask again."

One man moved forward, his face weathered, his black mustache and sideburns sliced with gray. A bead of sweat curled down his back. "We don' want no trouble," he said as he took the cigarette out of his mouth and threw it on the ground, expelling the last puff of smoke. He bent his head slightly and stamped out the lit butt on the concrete.

As the man brought his head back up, Paul gave him a short hard punch to the midriff and pulled him close. The man grunted doubling over. The other men moved in, frightened but ready to come to their neighbor's assistance. One woman cried out softly. The women rose as one and moved quickly to a small corner of the stoop, cowering.

"I don't want no trouble either. I just want a number!" Paul said.

The man looked at his neighbors as if asking permission. Several nodded. "Third floor, on the right," he whispered. "I don' know the number."

"See!" Paul released the man who stumbled backward. "I knew we could settle this friendly-like," he said with a smirk. "No harm done, right?" He walked into the building and headed for the third floor, holding his side again.

The neighbors gathered around each other.

"We need to call the cops," Connie from the basement apartment said.

"Are you loco? What we gonna tell them? Someone punched Manuel in the stomach because he wouldn't give them an apartment number?"

"You know the cops. They wouldn't show up 'til tomorrow anyway," another said.

"Listen, the guy's looking for Ramon or Alberto, right? Well, they aren't there anyway."

"How do you know?" Connie asked.

"Because Henry at the bakery asked me this morning if I knew where Alberto was and I said I didn't know and that he should call Hortencia. Maybe she would know where her son is."

They all considered this information.

"So if that's the case there's nothing Hortencia can tell the gringo," Connie said smiling. "*Nada!*"

Paul walked up the three flights of stairs, stopping at each level to catch his breath. He fingered a small knife in his jacket pocket, his mind testing how fast he could withdraw it, open it, and slit somebody's throat. *Maybe ten seconds,* he thought. *Gotta get it down to five!*

He remembered the fight with Alberto. *Son-of-a-bitch, made me stab myself. I ain't takin' no chances this time.* He flexed his fingers over the knife again and again. He reached the apartment. The hallway was alive with the simmering smell of tomatoes, onions and green peppers. The aroma of cilantro and cumin trickled through the hinges and cracks of the door frame. His nostrils flared and he was reminded of how hungry he was. He knew of a good steakhouse on Second Avenue. But first he would get his money.

Hortencia had left the door unlocked because she was expecting Henry Cardillo at eight o'clock. When Paul knocked before the hour she thought *A-h-h, he must be anxious.* "Come in," she called. Hortencia looked quite beautiful, despite her abundant figure. Her dark hair coiled around her head in a long thick braid. She wore a flowered blouse which showed ample cleavage, and a long skirt, elastic at the waist. Her sandals were from Mexico; she only wore them on special occasions to avoid wearing them out.

Paul opened the door and almost knocked Hortencia over. She drew back quickly, almost losing her balance. "Who . . . who are you? What do you want?" she raised her voice. She tried to sidestep Paul and head for the open door, but he quickly closed it behind him, grabbing her arm and twisting it behind her. She cried out. "What do you want?"

"I want my money." His eyes darted around the room.

"What money?" she screamed. "You think I have money?" She couldn't believe someone was trying to rob her. "What're you crazy? You must be crazy to think I have money!" Hortencia thought Paul's intention was to rape her, but now he was asking for money. If she wasn't so frightened she would have laughed in his face.

Paul's eyes darted anxiously around the room, expecting one of the twins to appear.

"It's not *your* money I want. It's *my* money I want." He moved her toward the bedroom, looking around as he held her in front of him. Confident, finally, that no one else was there, he struck Hortencia a hard blow to the jaw and knocked her to the floor. She was stunned and began to whimper. Her lip started to bleed and she had this ridiculous thought; she didn't know if she should be more worried about her life or getting blood on the carpet. Paul immediately straddled her and withdrew his knife. *God, how he loved this! This was perfect; almost as good as punching out Maureen!*

"I want my money. Twenty-two-hundred big ones." He put his knife against her throat.

"Twenty-two . . . ? Senor, you are making a big mistake." She slurred her words through her swelling lip. "Listen, please," she begged. "I never seen twenty-two hundred dollars in my whole life. I'm worried how to pay my rent and you are asking me for . . ."

"If I don't get my money bitch, you won't have to worry about paying your rent. You'll have to worry about paying for your funeral."

His instinct told him she was probably telling the truth. Not that it mattered. He might slit her throat anyway. "Well, if you don't have it, I'll just have to wait here until your sons show up and find their mother dead."

"My sons?" Hortencia cried. "What have they to do with this? I haven't seen those bums for two days. I thought maybe I'm lucky and they won't come home. They're not dead, are they?" Hortencia asked, suddenly contrite.

"No, but they will be if I don't get my money," Paul snarled.

"I don' know 'bout no money. I don' think they have so much money because . . ." she paused. "Senor, you think you can get off me?" Her leg was folded under her and was cramping. "It is very uncomfortable . . ."

"Too fucking bad," Paul said, but he did raise his body slightly allowing her to straighten her leg.

Paul hated most people but there was an innocence about Hortencia that appealed to him; somewhere within him there was still an element of humanity that had rarely been touched. He immediately stifled the feeling and would not let it surface. *You stupid bitch,* he thought. *You're not even smart enough to know I could kill you and never look back.* The thought of killing Hortencia aroused him. He suddenly was very aware of her voluptuous body beneath him. *Maybe another time,* he thought.

"Like I say, I don' think my boys have any money because the lady who live in tha' small house next door, she come to me . . ."

"What lady?"

"Rosie."

"Lady . . ." Paul interrupted, putting pressure on her arm.

"Okay, okay, my boys ask her for three hundred dollars and she give it to them. So that's why I don' think they have so much money."

"You say this Rosie lives next door?" he asked, suddenly alert.

"Si. In the little house."

"She lives there alone?" Paul asked.

"No, she look after her *hermano.* He's old, sick."

Paul got up and started toward the door. Hortencia struggled to her feet.

"Look what you done to me," she said, looking in the hallway mirror, straightening her skirt and blouse. "I get all pretty for my friend, and now - big lip."

Paul walked slowly down the stairs, his side throbbing. He met Mr. Cardillo coming up. "Boy, you're in for a treat," he said spitefully. "Apartment 303, right? That was the best fuck I ever had."

Mr. Cardillo stepped back, a bewildered look on his face. *What the hell is he talking about?* He rushed up the last flight of stairs, certain Hortencia had been raped. The door was slightly ajar. He entered cautiously, calling her name.

Hortencia came out of the bathroom and fell into his arms. Her lip was swollen, her leg ached and she was limping.

"This crazy man . . ."

"I know. I saw him on the staircase. Are you okay?"

"Yes, yes. But Henry, we have to call the police. Right away! I think he's going to Rosie's house." She told Henry what happened.

"You didn't leave anything out?" he asked, remembering what Paul had said about 'the best . . . ' He didn't even want to think about it. He picked up the phone and called the police.

"Henry, my dinner," Hortencia complained.

"Forget the dinner," he said. *Women!* Henry thought. *She was almost killed; maybe she was raped and doesn't want to tell me. And what does she think about? Dinner!*

CHAPTER TWELVE

ROSIE AND JOEY TOOK their time walking back from El Galleto. They rounded the corner, still discussing the premature death of Frank which had been the topic of conversation all evening; the suddenness of it, and how you have to live each day because you never knew what would happen tomorrow.

It was still early evening, balmy, a hint of cool breeze winding its way through the tenement canyons. Rosie wasn't quite ready to face the long evening. "Do you mind if we stop at More Used Books?" she asked Joey. The book store was only a few blocks away and Rosie hadn't been there for a while. She loved to spend an hour or so visiting with the owner, Patty More, browsing through the dusty shelves of hard and soft covered books of every description.

"No, go ahead," he said. "I'll just head on home."

They parted, Joey waving as he continued on. He took his time, his right knee hurting, his breathing a little uneven. He had been leaning on Rosie, but now he was on his own and he could tell the difference. *Should have taken my cane*, he thought. *Oh, well, just a couple more blocks.*

Paul was waiting for him.

Joey opened the gate and walked up the path toward the front door, his head down, searching his pockets for the key. He did not notice Paul who was partially hidden by the large oak tree that shadowed the porch. As the door squeaked open, Paul leaped forward and pushed him into the house, kicking the door shut behind him. Once again, Paul had his knife handy.

"Where's that little sister of yours?" Paul snarled.

Joey was so frightened, he couldn't speak. He thought his heart had stopped. His mouth was dry; he was gasping, choking from fear. He felt himself grow faint, his legs giving way. Paul made a move to grab him, but suddenly Joey was dead weight. He slipped out of Paul's grasp and fell to the floor banging his head against the corner of the kitchen counter. The spurt of blood was immediate. Paul's wound was also bleeding, the floor slippery as their blood mingled.

"Answer me or I'll slit your fucking throat," Paul hovered over Joey, holding his side with one hand and his knife with the other. But Joey could no longer answer.

Frustrated and weak Paul couldn't think clearly and his eyesight was blurring. He heard the familiar shrill sounds of police sirens. *Get out! Get out now!* He pulled himself up and stumbled toward the door. He managed to stagger down the porch steps to the path. Suddenly he was confronted by the three men he had spoken with earlier. They had heard the police sirens. They weren't going to let Paul leave.

"Where you goin' senor?" asked Manuel, the man whom Paul had punched in the stomach. He was more emboldened now that he knew the police would be there momentarily.

"Outta my way," Paul lunged at him and lost his balance. The other two men closed in. The sirens were upon them, just outside. Car doors were slamming and the neighbors could be heard giving the police directions. Hortencia and Henry Cardillo had come downstairs. She pushed ahead leading the police to Rosie's house, moving her arms frantically, her full breasts bouncing precipitously above the line of her low-cut blouse. She was jabbering excitedly in Spanish and English. Two policemen followed her cautiously. When they saw Manuel and his friends surrounding Paul, who was still wielding his knife, they immediately called for additional assistance. Someone mentioned that they had seen Joey return home. A policeman entered the house. He called for an ambulance.

◇◇◇

Patty More lifted her head from the dusty antique desk sitting smack in the middle of the room surrounded by book cases, the tinkle of the front door bell alerting her that there was a customer.

"So what haven't I read yet?" Rosie asked, smiling.

Patty walked toward her, squinting through her near-sighted eyes. She put her glasses on top of her grey hair. "ROSIE!" she shrieked. "Where ya been? I haven't seen you in ages." Patty gave her a tight bear hug and they both walked to the back of the store, arms around each other, where an old couch and a couple of easy chairs sat on a worn Persian rug. A fireplace raised its brick façade in the near corner, waiting to welcome readers at the first call of winter.

Rosie remembered when Patty and her now deceased husband, George, had opened the book shop, some twenty years ago. No one thought the neighborhood could support a book shop, but, in truth, neither Patty nor her husband needed the income. It was just something they wanted to do in their retirement.

"So how come you've been such a stranger?" Patty asked. They stopped speaking and looked up for a moment when they heard the raucous sounds of police sirens and an ambulance.

"Oh, you know how it is. I'm working like a demon, trying to finalize the school schedule for next semester, wondering how I'm going to get through this summer's heat and humidity, hoping some major calamity doesn't befall Joey, and on and on. A dear friend of mine just lost her husband; totally unexpected."

"Well, I certainly know how that is," Patty said sadly.

"Yes, I know you do. That's why Joey and I decided to have dinner out tonight. We were trying not to think about it. But it just doesn't go away, does it?"

"Well, in time," said Patty.

"How are you managing with the store since George's death? I mean, isn't it too hard for you, being on your own?"

"It was difficult at the beginning but I'm only open noon to five, Tuesday through Saturday. I just love doing this. Have you thought of quitting that awful teacher's job?"

"Are you kidding? I think about it all the time. Joey is always on me to quit. I come home exhausted, irritable, bitching about the kids, the politics, the curriculum . . . you name it! But what would I do? I'm almost sixty, but I don't feel ready to retire."

"Well, sixty is young, to me. I'm heading for seventy and I'm still going strong. Haven't you ever dreamed of owning your own business, or doing something you'd absolutely love?" Patty asked.

"Yes, but you'll burst out laughing when I tell you."

"What?"

Rosie hesitated. "I've always wanted to own a grocery store like my granddad did."

"A grocery store!" Patty screamed. She did burst out laughing.

"See, I told you so," Rosie also laughed.

"Why a grocery store?"

"I don't know. I grew up learning the business. I just loved talking to the customers, ordering goods, doing the books," Rosie said pensively. "Joey practically took the store over once Grandpa died. That store took care of our entire family. I never minded working there after school and on weekends."

"So, what's stopping you?"

"Well, for starters, all the humongous markets that are springing up all over the place. I don't think I could compete. Besides, the only way I could do it would be to sell the house and take an early retirement. Anyway, I can't do it while Joey is still with me."

Patty thought for a few minutes before responding. "You know, you wouldn't exactly have to compete with those mausoleums. They need to make huge profits to survive. You wouldn't have to make that kind of money to maintain your style of living."

"What style of living?" Rosie said sarcastically.

"That's what I mean, Rosie. I don't make much money in this little book store, but at least no one's looking over my shoulder, telling me what to do. When I go home at night, I've usually got a smile on my face. As long as the shop can sustain itself, I'm okay with it; you know, pay the rent and buy the books."

"It's an idea, but I don't think I'm ready."

The two women continued talking, catching up on old times until Rosie said, "Well, gotta get home. Joey is waiting for me, probably snoring up a storm. It's a toss-up which gets louder, the TV or Joey's snoring." Patty walked her to the door and they hugged a warm goodbye.

"Don't wait so long to visit," Patty admonished.

Rosie walked the few blocks to her home. As she turned the corner, several neighbors approached her.

"Rosie, what happened? We saw police cars near your house and an ambulance too."

Rosie's heart started to palpitate. Her steps quickened and she began to run. *JOEY!* As she approached her house Hortencia and Mr. Cardillo were waiting for her.

"Joey!" Rosie screamed. "Is it Joey? Where is he?" She was trembling.

"Si, si, Rosie. They took him. The ambulance *a la infermidad.*" Hortencia was jabbering in English and Spanish.

"What hospital? Is he alive?" Rosie was crying. "Oh my God. Please God, let him be alive. Please God," she kept mumbling.

Mr. Cardillo tried to remain calm, but he, too, was very nervous. "Rosie," he said, taking her by the shoulders and looking her in the eyes. "Joey was alive. They took him to Bronx Hospital. Paul wanted his money . . . "

"Paul? Who's Paul? What money?" Rosie was totally confused.

"Don't worry. The police have him. Hortencia and me – we were waiting for you. I'll drive you to the hospital and explain everything."

Mr. Cardillo's bakery truck was waiting. The three of them tried to fit in front, but because of her weight, Hortencia had trouble lifting her body into the truck. Henry went behind her, put his hands on her buttocks and counted 'one, two, three' ugh! It was like trying to push a piano through a doorway. After several tries, she finally made it, breathing heavily from the exertion. But that left no room for Rosie. "You know, Henry, you have to buy another car, or keep a ladder in this one."

She looked in the back where there were racks of bread and Danish. She thought fleetingly maybe she could sit back there. The Danish looked mouth-watering and she would help herself to one or two. *Yes. Two pieces of Danish and a shot of Tequila.* That would ease her anxiety. She wanted to go with them but she could see the futility of trying to fit the three of them into the front seat. She and Rosie looked at each other; Hortencia, with a great sigh, graciously offered her hand to Rosie, who helped her from the truck. Neither said anything; words were not necessary. As they drove off, Hortencia shouted to Henry, "come back, no matter how late."

Henry dropped Rosie in front of the hospital as he went to park. She ran in, frantically approaching the administration desk. "I'm Rosie

Sanchez, I mean Rosie Goldberg. You brought my brother in, Joey? Joey Goldberg?" Rosie asked questioningly.

"Oh, yes. Joseph Goldberg," she hesitated as she looked at her intake chart. "He's in room two twenty one. If you wait a moment I'll have someone show you . . ."

But Rosie didn't wait. She ran to the elevator, pacing as she watched the floor stop indicator. Her heart was beating wildly, her head beginning to throb. She moved aside to let two people out. Rosie got in and pushed the second floor button. As she exited, the floor nurse tried to help her, but she just ran to room two- twenty- one, glancing at the room numbers as she passed them. "Joey, please be alive," she prayed. "Please, God. Let Joey be alive."

CHAPTER THIRTEEN

THE FOUR TRAVELERS LEFT the coffee shop. Alberto loosened his belt a notch, and Ramon patted his stomach with a satisfied grin. Lui lit up a cigarette. Maureen followed absent-mindedly a few steps behind the twins. "I'll drive," Lui said sliding into the front seat.

Maureen noticed a newspaper stand a few feet away. "Wait a sec," she said. "I want to see what's going on in the world." She searched her purse for the correct coins and deposited them into the slot. She wanted something that would keep her mind off their next destination: Cleveland.

"I'll sit in back with Maureen," Ramon opened the door for her. "She and Alberto was talkin' the whole time we were asleep, Lui. I'm thinking maybe I missed something interesting." Ramon smiled at her and she shrugged her shoulders as she manipulated her long legs into the back seat. She slid over to make room for him.

Ramon treated her differently than he did other women. Usually Ramon only had to snap his fingers and women would fall all over him. He was the one in charge, in control. Maureen was not the kind of woman he usually made a play for. She was too smart. He was more comfortable with women who came on to *him* so he was sure of his ground. Enough of them did, so he hadn't needed to learn the art of subtlety. If someone was interested in him, fine. If not, that was okay. He wasn't looking for a permanent relationship, just to get laid. Maureen was a challenge. First of all she was gorgeous. And second of all, she was savvy. He was aware of the smoothness of her legs as he settled into the back seat. He imagined running his hands along her thigh reaching a point where she would either say "no, no" or "yes, yes," and "pretty please."

Lui let out a heavy sigh and loosened his belt. "I'm stuffed," he said as he pulled out of the parking lot. Everyone was quiet for a time.

"So, Lui," Alberto said. "What kind of job you got waitin' for Ramon?"

"Auto mechanic," Lui hesitated and gave him a sidewise glance.

"That's all? Auto mechanic?"

"Yeah. What'd ya think?"

"So how come he can make so much money? Ramon was working as an auto mechanic in the Bronx. He never made the kind of money you been talkin' about." He paused. "You sure it's legit?"

"It has its risks, but Ramon's job . . ."

"What kind of risks?" Alberto asked.

Ramon spoke up before Lui could answer. He was distracted by Maureen's legs, but he was also listening to the conversation up front. "Hey, hey! If you're going to talk about my new job, I think I should be in on it. So don't be whispering." He was a little put off with Alberto's interference. "You don' have to be askin' questions for me. I can ask my own questions."

"Yeah? Well how come you haven't asked any yet?" Alberto shot back. "How do we know there's even a job waitin' for you?"

Lui continued. "It ain't no secret. Don't worry about this. The guy I work for owns a legitimate business . . . a shop where they do all kinds of repairs on automobiles; body work, engines. Name's Charlie Mello. Been in business twenty years; very reputable."

"Yeah?" Alberto asked. "So what do you do for him?"

"Me?" Lui laughed. "I scout for mechanics - guys who know cars."

"So what're you saying? They can't find no mechanics in Los Angeles? You have to look for them in New York?"

"Not the kind Charlie needs." Lui shrugged. "Anyway, I wasn't exactly looking for mechanics. I was takin' a few days off, visiting my good friend, Simon, getting a smell of the old neighborhood."

It started to rain. Lui put the windshield wipers on low. "I bet it rains all the way to Cleveland," he said.

"Anyway," he continued. "my old landlady was happy to see me. I owed her a few bucks from three years ago and I paid her off, with interest. Ramon and me, we got to talkin' out back at de Luna's and he wanted to know more about L.A., so I told him about Charlie Mello's place. And then, boom! You got yourself into a fight with the princess's boyfriend." Lui glanced back and gave Maureen a thumbs up.

"It ain't my fault that the four of us became traveling companions. I was ready to go solo."

Alberto knew Lui was right but he wasn't sure whether to thank him, or ream him out. "Yeah. So what'dya want me to do? Give you a medal?" he said sarcastically.

"Well, a little appreciation would be . . ." He stopped in mid-sentence as Maureen cried out.

"Oh-h no! Oh, my God," she moaned, covering her eyes. The newspaper dropped in her lap. "Jesus!" she said.

"What?" Ramon shouted. He turned toward her. "You scared the shit out of me. What is it?"

"This article on page eight. It's about Paul. That son-of-a-bitch broke into some woman's apartment. Hortencia somebody."

"Hortencia? Give me that paper." Ramon grabbed the paper from Maureen. "That's my mother! Jesus God Almighty! If anything happened to her."

"You called Mom since we left?" Alberto asked, alarmed.

"No. I thought we'd call when we got to Cleveland."

"You mean all this time we're gone and you didn't call her? What the hell's the matter with you?"

"Hey, don't come down on me, bro. I didn't see you pick up any phone neither. I told Rosie to tell her we wouldn't be home."

"Okay, okay. What's the paper say?"

"Here, you read it," Ramon handed the paper to Alberto knowing he couldn't read it fast enough to satisfy Alberto.

MELEE IN EAST BRONX ENDS IN DEADLY BRAWL

Police are investigating the death of Oscar de Luna, owner of Ramrod in the lower East Bronx. Suspect Paul Brody was taken into custody on suspicion of murder. Brody had instigated a fight at the bar the previous evening where he suffered a self-inflicted knife wound. A cab driver told police he drove Brody to the bar and waited for him at the curb. When Brody did not reappear, the driver entered the bar and saw Brody kick de Luna who already appeared to be dead.

"Jesus!" said Lui. "Oscar dead! I can't believe it. Yesterday we were partying and today he's dead? Maureen, who the hell is this guy? A hit man or something?"

Maureen was crying. "It's all my fault; all my fault," she repeated.

Alberto, read on.

> Brody had brandished a knife and forced the cab driver to an apartment in the East Bronx where he accosted Hortencia Esparza and demanded two thousand two hundred dollars which Brody claimed had been stolen from him the previous night during a fight with Esparza's son, Alberto Esparza. Mrs. Esparza directed Brody to the residence of Rosie Sanchez, a neighbor, whom Mrs. Esparza thought might have the money, or know of its whereabouts.

"Jeez!" Ramon said. "This guys a real piece of work. How could you have been with a guy like that?" he asked Maureen.

"I don't know. I don't know," she moaned.

"There's more," said Alberto as he continued reading:

> Homicide Detective, Marvin Johnston, told reporters that witnesses saw Brody go to Sanchez's home where he accosted Sanchez's elderly brother, Joseph Goldberg. According to Goldberg, who was semi-conscious when police arrived, Brody dragged him into the house and threatened him with a knife, demanding money. A fight ensued. Goldberg said he fell to the floor and hit his head on the corner of the kitchen counter. The detective said both Goldberg and Brody were bleeding profusely, Goldberg from his head injury, and Brody from a stab wound accidentally self-inflicted the previous evening at *Ramrod*. Police credited the neighbors with thwarting Brody's escape. Goldberg was taken to Bronx Hospital.

Alberto handed the paper back to Maureen. No one spoke. Each of them wondered how they had contributed to this web of circumstances, their cumulative guilt rising to the surface. Lui broke the silence.

"Okay. So who's got the money?"

"Never mind about the money," Alberto said. "We have to call Mama – find out if she's okay."

But the money was on their minds. They looked at each other suspiciously.

"Hey, don't look at me. If I had the money I wouldn't have gone to Rosie," Ramon said.

Maureen's stomach knotted. "I've got the money," she said defensively. "I deserve to have it. I gave that scumbag three miserable years during which time I feared for my life, never knowing if at any moment he would take it into his head to kill me.

"I never had enough money to leave him and maybe I didn't have the guts. So when you were fighting," she looked at Alberto, "I picked up Paul's jacket and took the money out of his billfold. I knew I'd have to disappear or he'd kill me. When I heard you guys say you were going to Los Angeles, I thought maybe my luck had finally changed. I was ecstatic. I finally had some money and I was going far away; so far that Paul wouldn't find me. And now it seems like he'll never find me. I don't think he'll get out of prison in my lifetime."

Maureen's large blue eyes were clouded with unspilled tears. "I had a terrible childhood and I plan to close that chapter of my life when we get to Cleveland." She looked at them defiantly. "I need this money to start over again, and nobody's taking it away from me." She waited anxiously for their response. "You want to leave me at the next stop, go ahead. But I'm keeping the money." A minute or two went by.

"Yeah, hey, far as I'm concerned, the money is yours, Maureen." Alberto was the first to speak. "Right, Lui?"

Alberto addressed Lui specifically because he could tell from Lui's downcast eyes that he was fighting with his inner conscience; Lui did not answer immediately. Two thousand and some dollars was a lot of money and he was wondering how he could manipulate the situation to his advantage. *Maybe this isn't the time to push on this. Let her have the money for now. I can always find a way to get it later.*

"Yeah. I guess so," Lui said. But he couldn't quite let it drop. "Maybe you can pay for a couple more meals, huh?"

Maureen looked at Ramon who had not yet spoken. "Whatd'ya say, pal?" Maureen squeezed his hand and gave him a big smile.

"Yeah, yeah. I'm in if everybody else is," he said, a small smile on his face.

Maureen's relief was palpable. Her shoulders relaxed and she let out a small breath. She had cleared the air and they all felt good; almost euphoric.

Suddenly Alberto sat up with a jolt. "Hey, Lui, stop at the next station. We have to call Mama - find out what happened and if she's okay."

Lui pulled in to a station at the first opportunity and immediately headed for the men's restroom, lighting a cigarette as he walked, holding the lighter against the wind and taking a deep drag.

Hortencia's phone rang two, three, four times before she picked it up. Once seated on her couch, she had difficulty getting up to answer it. She even had to allow a goodly amount of time if she needed to go to the bathroom. "*Bueno,*" she said.

"Mama!" Alberto shouted. "*Esta Alberto.*"

"So?" she asked. "You think after all these years I don' know my own son's voice? I could die, nobody would know, or care, or call. Not even a phone call. Two sons an' nobody call."

"Mama . . ." Alberto tried to interrupt. But Hortencia was on a roll.

"I was almost killed. A man hit me and hold a knife at my throat." She did not pause. "He wants money. 'What money?' I ask him. He says he had a fight with you. 'What fight?' I ask him. I don' know nothing 'bout no fight. I don' know nothing 'bout no money."

"Mama . . ."

"I send him to Rosie. Now I'm sorry I send him to Rosie. But I am frightened. I think maybe Rosie know about money. But look wha' happened to Joey. All my fault . . ."

"Mama, it's nobody's fault."

"But where are my sons? Supposed to protect their Mama! Where are you? Where is Ramon?"

"Me and Ramon . . ." He did not want to tell her where they were. He didn't know if the police would be questioning her about their whereabouts. *The less she knows, the better off we'll be.* "Mama, Ramon and me, we're okay. We decided to take a few days to investigate a job offer for Ramon."

"What kind of job?" She broke her train of thought and went on to another matter. "Mr. Cardillo - he is very mad with you - that you did not come to work . . ."

"I know. I really feel bad about that. Tell Mr. Cardillo I'm sorry; that I appreciate he gave me a job in the bakery." Alberto was afraid to ask the next question. "Mama - how is Rosie's brother, Joey?"

"We don' know. Mr. Cardillo, he drive Ms. Rosie to the hospital. She is there every minute. Joey, he is still alive, but it is bad. Mr. Cardillo - he has been very kind to me, and to Ms. Rosie."

"Mama. I'm glad you're okay. You want to say hello to Ramon?"

"Why not? What else have I got to do than to talk to my handsome *hijo*, even though he is a bum?"

Ramon had been listening to Alberto's conversation and now he took the phone. "Mama - it's good to hear your voice. I'm glad you're okay. Me and 'Berto, we was worried."

"Good! I'm glad you worry about your Mama sometimes. You are okay, *mi hijo*?" Hortencia had a catch in her voice. "I miss you." She paused. "But Mr. Cardillo, he takes good care of me. Tell me, Ramon, it is a good job you are going to get?"

"I hope so Mama. We'll call again soon. Tell Rosie we're sorry for her trouble and that we hope Joey will be okay." Before saying goodbye, Ramon said, "And Mama. You don't have to tell anybody we called, or that we won't be home for a while."

"*Porque?* I ask the police if you are in trouble. 'No' they say."

"Well," Ramon thought up a reasonable excuse. "We don't want everybody to know you're alone." He was surprised and relieved that they were not wanted by the police.

"Oh, *Hijo*, that makes sense."

"Oh, one last thing, Mama. Are you still as beautiful as two days ago?"

"How can I be beautiful with my big lip and black eye?"

"Mamacita, to me you will always be beautiful," Ramon said

"Bullshit! Always with the bullshit," but he could tell she was smiling. "I give you and Alberto kisses," and she hung up.

CHAPTER FOURTEEN

ALTHOUGH CLEVELAND WAS LESS than an hour away it took Maureen over ten years to get there. As they got closer her body reacted to the thought of seeing her mother again. Her neck muscles tightened sending an electrical charge to her head like a light bulb shorting out. Her foot tapped involuntarily and she crossed and uncrossed her legs to stem the movement. She stared out the window seeking some recognition of the past. But there was nothing. Everything had changed. *No homecoming parade, Maureen. No welcome mat! No red carpet!*

Maureen tried, but was unable to ignore the toxic memories of her mother's brutality; the bruises, the hairline crack in her glasses when her mother knocked them off with a hard slap, the cigarette burn on her leg, the pain in her ribs where her mother had punched her for any reason, or for no reason. The abuse did not abate during Maureen's teen years and, in fact, her mother's venom became more intense as she saw the child become a woman.

Have I always been alone? Maureen wondered. *Was there never anyone else - a father, an aunt, a minister, a God?* Her blue eyes clouded over. *No wonder I fell into the arms of that asshole Paul. Looking for love in all the wrong places, wasn't I?*

Alberto noticed her silence. He tapped her on the shoulder. "Hey, kid, everything alright?

"I'm not sure. I'm just trying to figure out how I got to where I am."

"Where are you?"

"That's the thing, Alberto. I don't know. I can't remember me at all." She closed her eyes again.

For two years prior to her graduation Maureen had secreted a small amount of money, some pilfered from her mother's purse, some earned in part-time jobs. With a sharp knife she cut a section of pages out of an old textbook, leaving a hollow area where she kept the money. The book was on a bookshelf in her room along with other textbooks which she knew her mother would never look at.

She had impeccable spelling skills and could type almost as fast as you could talk. Most of her after school jobs was in law firms as a front desk receptionist. However, as she picked up legal jargon, she was called upon to type briefs and other legal documents. The pay was good and she loved the environment. *This is what I want to be. A lawyer!*

A day or two before graduation Maureen waited for an opportune time, packed a few items in a small suitcase, took it to the bus station and left it in a locker. A bus for New York was leaving Friday afternoon, allowing her enough time to finish her valedictorian speech and arrive in time for the five o'clock departure. She did not reveal her plans to anyone and imagined her mother would simply shrug her shoulders and say 'good riddance.'

Her eyes closed and she thought back to her high school graduation. Through sheer willpower she had maintained the highest grades at Mayview High School and was proud to be selected valedictorian. There was no one with whom she could share the achievement, not even a close friend. She recalled now, ten years later, that she had worked diligently on her speech, seeking help and advice from several supportive teachers. She remembered parts of her speech as though it was yesterday:

> . . . *You — and I — have spent the last four years together, some with ease and others with difficulty. Despite the turmoil of external pressures, both personally, and within the world at large, we have had one aspiring goal - to graduate and bring honor to ourselves, to our teachers, and to our families who have attempted to prepare us for the future.* She hesitated, looking at her notes, then continued. *And are we prepared for the future? NO! We are not.* One day I'm confident and the next day I'm not. I'm scared, she thought.
>
> *Within the confines of Mayview High School, we were protected, as in a cocoon. We had no need to*

disturb the orderly relationships between student and teacher, no need to define ourselves through greed and power, no need to assert our control over others.

Now, however, we are faced with a different set of parameters. Who could have foreseen the assassination of our President and the escalation of violence in our country and throughout the world? This presents a daunting challenge to this graduating class. No longer will we be able to sit on the side lines while others make decisions for us. We must become part of the decision-making process. We must use our youth and energy and reason, not only for our own purposes, but to secure the peace and integrity of our country.

Although you and I move forward individually, I pray that together we will have the wherewithal and conviction to direct our country to its destined place in history.

The applause from the graduating class had been overwhelming and heart-warming. Maureen shook hands with everyone as she stepped from the podium. She had her money with her. Her suitcase was at the bus terminal. It would be almost ten years before she returned.

◊◊◊

They were approaching Cleveland, its sky line undistinguished from other large cities. The rain had stopped but the early evening sky still held the threat of more.

"D'ya want to stop anyplace in particular?" Lui asked, directing his question more to Maureen than to the others.

"If I remember correctly, there's a Best Inn and a gas station about ten miles down the road. And there's a coffee shop right next door. The name may be different now but I'll recognize it if it's still there."

Lui drove on through stop and go early evening work traffic. He was uncomplaining but a little uptight because Maureen had mentioned again that she wanted his car that evening.

"There it is, there it is" Maureen shouted. "A different name but still the same old dump." Lui pulled off the road and maneuvered the car into the registration area.

"You sure you want to stay in this place?" Lui asked, rolling his eyes. "It ain't exactly the Ritz." He observed the pot-holed parking lot and the rundown cars.

"I know," Maureen said. "But it's not Ritz prices either."

"So, uh, ya gonna meet an old boyfriend or something, Maureen?" Lui was curious as hell. "Ya know, maybe you should tell us where you're goin' so I'll know where to pick up my car if anything happens." He smiled but his tone was serious. "Just in case, not that I expect anything to happen, but like I say, just in case."

Alberto was anxious; he remembered Maureen's story about her mother and he thought *maybe, just maybe* she would kill her. He didn't want to start off this new life being an accessory to murder. As Lui and Ramon walked into the office to make arrangements, Alberto took Maureen aside.

"Listen! You ain't really gonna do your Mom in, are ya?"

"I don't know, Alberto. I've hated her for so long it's hard to tell what I'm capable of."

"Well, think about this, Maureen. Like you said before, this is a good time to start fresh. You don't want no murder rap on your sheet." He put his arm around her shoulder. "Ya know what I mean?"

"Yes," she whispered, giving him a grateful look. "I know what you mean."

"You know for sure your mama is still living in the same apartment?"

"No, she's not. I called the neighbor who lived next door, Mrs. Patterson. She said, "Maureen dear, it's been so long. No, your mama don't live here no more . . . someplace on Barnes Street. Just look it up, dear. So nice to hear from you."

"I know where Barnes Street is but I have no idea why she's living there."

Lui came out of the office with three key cards . . . a room for him, one for Ramon and Alberto, and a room for Maureen. She held out her hand for the room key and the car keys. Lui reluctantly parted with both. She wasted no time but immediately got into the Impala and drove off, waving her arm and saying, "adios amigos." All three wondered if they would ever see her again. Lui ran after the car and warned her again that if she didn't bring it back he would call the police.

Maureen drove a couple of miles down the road to a familiar department store and bought a pair of tight-fitting black jeans, a black and white striped T-shirt, and black easy-on tennis shoes. A black leather hobo handbag, a pair of gold earrings and a drop-dead studded leather belt completed the ensemble. She then drove back to the motel, showered, put on some make-up and changed into her new clothes. Despite the informal attire she looked beautiful, successful and confident. She felt ready to face her mother again and hoped it would be for the last time.

Maureen found the house. Her heart sprung out like a jack-in-the-box. She felt the beginnings of a vicious headache. The old fears returned like used coins newly cleansed in acid wash. Bile rose in her throat.

The shade was pulled down at the front window but a faint light shone opaquely against the darkened porch. *Why do I feel compelled to do this,* she wondered? *Because I know I won't be able to go forward unless I first go backward,* she answered. She opened the car door and sat there for several minutes, paralyzed, until she found the courage to walk up the path to the small front porch. She knocked tentatively on the door. A television could be heard within and, finally, footsteps. Maureen braced herself.

"Who is it?" a woman's voice asked. Maureen was silent, frozen. The porch light came on. Again the woman asked, "Who is it?" When Maureen still did not answer, a shadowed figure could be seen at the front window peering out the side of the shade. Seeing Maureen the woman came back to the front door and opened it. She was not Maureen's mother.

"Are you lost? Are you looking for someone?"

Maureen peered at the woman. She was tall, stately. There was a sense of familiarity about her which Maureen could not define. Her hair was white, pulled back loosely at the nape of her neck. She wore a print housedress that zippered up the front, and a long-sleeved dark blue cotton cardigan from which her bony wrists protruded, as though the sweater had been a hand-me-down. They looked at each other for a long time, neither saying a word, each recognizing in the other familial features - blue eyes, high brow, a certain bearing and mannerism.

"Maureen." It was not a question. The woman breathed in, almost a gasp. The door opened wider and Maureen walked in.

She felt as though she'd been here before, a memory so vague she dismissed it. And yet, she recognized the placement of furniture, the location of the kitchen, the scent of furniture polish on old wood, and the mingling of odors emanating from the outdated wallpaper and paint. Above all, there was a new odor that was not familiar — an underlying hint of medications and menthol, and urine.

"Who are you?" Maureen whispered, knowing the answer before it was given.

"Your grandmother," she said.

CHAPTER FIFTEEN

DAYBREAK FILTERED THROUGH THE shade in Joey's room. Just as he couldn't avoid the unnatural glow of the street lamp at night, so he couldn't avoid the natural approach of dawn.

He was lying on his back, afraid to move his head because it hurt so much when he did. He opened his eyes and stared straight ahead, at the ceiling. *God, this house is old*, he thought, looking at the splintered molding, the chipped ivory-colored paint. *We should have sold this place long ago. Ach! Too many memories! Too late!*

The house was quiet; the hustle of street noise had not yet begun. He heard a slight rustle and moved his head carefully toward the sound. There was Rosie, fast asleep in the lounge chair he had reluctantly purchased a couple of years ago so that he could watch television in his own room and turn up the volume as loud as he needed to. She was snuggled in an old blanket he hadn't seen for years; *probably dug it out of the top shelf of the closet. Chair sure is coming in handy these days*, he thought, *with Rosie sleeping in it since I got home from the hospital. Poor Rosie. Stuck for years with a sick old fart of a brother . . . could've had a life if not for me. And now - since that altercation with that son-of-a-bitch, Paul . . . crazy bastard — the burden on Rosie is even worse. I still can't figure out what the hell he wanted; talked about twenty-two hundred dollars being stolen from him. Man was really off the wall, but definitely a threat to Rosie . . . couldn't let that happen, could I? I'm dying. She knows but she won't let me talk to her about it.*

Rosie stirred and slowly opened her eyes. She stretched. "Oh God, my aching bones. I'll never be the same." She looked over at Joey, surprised he was awake. "Maybe we *both* should have gone to a rehab center. I bet they'd let us share a room and give us a good rate. You know, two for the price of one."

"Rosie, I don't know how you barely open one eye, and already you're talking. I think you start talking before you wake up." She looked at him through half-closed eyes.

He stared back at her. "What are you looking at, you gorgeous creature?" he rasped.

It took her a minute to respond. "Well," she looked around the room. "There's no one else here, so you must mean me. How discerning of you," she chided, "to recognize beauty despite the dark circles under my eyes, the grey strands in my uncombed hair, and the stunning flannel nightgown I wear for these special occasions, compliments of Mom who died twenty years ago." Rosie said.

Joey laughed, or tried to. He thought perhaps this was the time to mention, casually, of course, that he knew he was dying. He was silent for several minutes, his silence gathering momentum until Rosie could feel their unspoken conversation would be turning more serious.

"Listen, Rosie . . . "

"Don't start, Joey. Don't say it."

"Rosie, you have to listen to me. Please. Or I'll sulk all day."

She started to laugh. "You always sulk all day. What kind of threat is that? Did it ever occur to you that I don't care if you sulk all day?"

"Rosie, whether I live another hundred years or die tomorrow, there are certain things you have to know."

"A hundred years is out of the question. There's no way I could put up with you that long," she said.

"Will you listen, for God's sake - just once. Stop being snide and listen." Joey hesitated, getting his thoughts together. "For starters, I want you to start making arrangements to sell this house."

"What?" She pulled the blanket up under her chin. "Are you crazy? I've lived here all my life. Where would I go?"

"Rosie, you have to sell this house. Get an attorney and make arrangements."

"I won't do any such . . ."

"Yes, you will - TODAY! I can't continue to live this 'half life' much longer. You must accept the reality of it. It would really make me happy if I could leave peacefully, knowing you've been taken care of."

"Joey, I can't talk about this." She started to cry and dabbed at her eyes with the sleeves of her nightgown.

"Besides the value of the house," Joey ignored her tears, "there's other money you need to know about."

"Other money?" she cried, and sat up straighter leaning toward him. "Now you're talking! Now I'm listening!" she said jokingly with a lump in her throat. She fussed with the blanket again. "What other money?" she finally asked.

"I have a nest egg . . ."

"What do you mean 'a nest egg'? You have an exotic bird somewhere that laid an egg and it's worth a lot of money? Or what?"

"Rosie, if you can't be serious I'm either going to kill you, or kill myself. I'm too weak to argue." He leaned back and heaved a big sigh, his energy waning.

"Okay, you leave me no choice but to listen to your jabbering . . . on one condition."

"Anything," Joey said wearily.

"First I need to make us a cup of coffee. I can't handle your whining without caffeine." She maneuvered out of the lounge chair, first one leg, then the other, her knees clicking into place, complaining to herself the whole time. "Ugh! That's the worst chair to get in and out of. Be right back," she said as she headed for the bathroom, and then the kitchen.

Joey could hear her puttering around, the tap water filling the coffee pot, the refrigerator door banging shut, the shaking of the coffee can, the clink of the spoon. He sighed, leaned back against the pillow and waited patiently, picturing Rosie's every step. She returned with a standing tray: two mugs of coffee, some crackers and sliced cheese, and a small crystal dish containing strawberry jam.

She helped him get his feet over the side of the bed, put a blanket around his legs and set up the tray right beside him. His head ached with the slightest movement, but he didn't tell her. He knew he finally had her attention.

"There," she said. "That's your exercise for the day." She pulled up a straight chair and they sat facing each other.

"Rosie. I know you don't want to hear this, but I beg you. Please listen. The only reason I don't want to die is . . ."

" . . . Joey, don't."

"Rosie, you promised. You're making this very difficult for me."

"Okay, but can you say it fast so we get it over with?"

"It'll take as much time as it takes. Don't rush me. I've wanted to tell you this for the last ten years and now you want me to say it in ten seconds," he chastised her. "Rosie, people die every day and they never get to say what they want to, mostly because their loved ones won't let them. I need to say some things to you. I *need* to," he emphasized. "Do you understand?"

"Yes, I do. But, Joey, I already know what you're going to say."

"It doesn't matter whether you know it or not. This is *my* need, not yours."

"Okay, I'll shut up." She made a sign to zip her mouth shut.

"Thank God! First of all, no words or deeds, or anything can repay you for taking care of me all these years; for giving up your life for me."

She reached over and squeezed his hand.

"You may not have looked upon it as a sacrifice, but in my heart I feel you could have remarried after Ruben's death had it not been for me." Joey paused, his breath shallow. Rosie tried to interrupt but he held up his hand, warning her not to speak. He took a sip of coffee. She spread a cracker with strawberry jam and left it on the plate for him.

Joey continued: "Several years ago I made a killing in the stock market. I didn't tell you because I wasn't sure if it would be a great investment – or if I would lose my shirt. I was afraid that if I lost the money you'd be harping on me for the rest of my life."

"That's a fact." Rosie leaned forward as she strained to hear his words.

Joey hesitated. "Well, it was a hit, with a capital *H*. I made a lot of money. When the stock reached a certain point I pulled out and put the money in an interest-bearing CD. And that's where it's been this past ten years."

"You mean all these years, instead of worrying about the price of smoked salmon, I could have been buying caviar? This is inexcusable, unconscionable," she suddenly smiled. "Joey, you little devil! Just how much money are we talking about?" She spelled out the word and almost whispered it, as though someone was listening who shouldn't have been. "I mean, enough to buy a good bottle of wine – or Ripple?"

"A lot, Rosie. Really a lot! The money is in a trust, all in your name. Open the file drawer there in the corner and look for a brown folder under . . ." he left off. "Oy, vey" he said, an expression she hadn't heard him use in years. He blinked his eyes shut. "I forgot where I filed it."

"If it's somewhere in the file cabinet, we may never find it. We'll have to hire a search team." She walked toward the cabinet and opened one drawer after another. "Look at this mess." The drawers were crammed with magazines, old documents, photographs, greeting cards, and years of haphazard filing.

"Okay, okay. Give me a minute," he said. She waited. "Look under 'I'."

"Why would it be under 'I'?"

"Investment, maybe?" Joey suggested meekly.

"There's no brown folder under 'I'," Rosie said. "Are you sure you're not hallucinating?"

"Okay, look under 'R' for Rosie, 'T' for Trust, 'M' for money, 'S' for stock."

"You're sure the folder is brown? Your eyesight, among other things, hasn't been so good lately."

"Don't rub it in. I'm thinking, I'm thinking. Give me some time here. I'm a sick man."

"I can't believe this," Rosie muttered as she looked through the file drawer under all the letters he had mentioned.

Several minutes went by. Rosie stood with hands on hips, waiting.

"I know! I know!" he shouted. "It's under 'B'. That's where it is, under 'B'."

"Under 'B'," she repeated. "Why would it be filed under 'B'?"

"For Bonanza. 'B' for Bonanza!" he whooped, suddenly coughing and wheezing and trying to catch his breath.

Rosie left off looking for the file and immediately went to his side. "Enough excitement for today," she said, moving the breakfast tray aside and positioning his legs under the covers. "I'll find it, darling. You just rest." She gave him a sip of water and the coughing spasm abated.

"Rosie," Joey's voice was barely audible. He closed his eyes. "Promise me. Call our attorney this morning. Tell him to bring the necessary papers to transfer the deed to you. Also, Rosie, I want you to sell this house. Travel. Go see your friend Clara in Los Angeles. Go on a cruise. Find a wonderful man and get married again. Between the money in the trust, the money you get for this house, and your pension from thirty years in the school system - you can live well for the rest of your life and never have to worry. You have to get out of the Bronx, Rosie. When I'm gone there will be nothing to stop you - nothing and no one to hold you here."

As Joey fell into a deep sleep, Rosie looked for the brown folder under 'B'. There it was. An indistinct brown envelope labeled BONANZA which she might never have found had he not told her about it. Still in her faded nightgown, her hair unkempt, the unpleasant residue of over-brewed coffee on her breath, Rosie carried the two inch thick file to the dining room where she pulled out a chair and set the folder on the table before her. She flipped it open and started to read the trust document.

"Oh my God," she uttered. "OH MY GOD!"

CHAPTER SIXTEEN

MAUREEN STOOD THERE, UNABLE to speak. Her grandmother opened the door wider and stepped aside to let her in.

"Where's my mother?" Maureen asked, looking around. Her grandmother hesitated and waved toward a wheel chair in the center of the living room.

The room was in disarray. A table with medications sat at the end of the dark corduroy couch, the armrest threadbare. One worn seat cushion held the imprint of an invisible body. "Who's here?" Maureen heard her mother's voice - irritable, petulant, as harsh as she remembered it. When there was no answer her mother turned the wheelchair around.

Maureen just stared. Baggy cotton pants emphasized her mother's thin frame. Long boney fingers with sharp knuckles held to the arms of the wheelchair. Harsh parenthesis brackets surrounded a forbidding mouth. Prominent cheek bones sought release from the thin covering of skin. Ilsa moved her head forward and peered through squinted eyes, not immediately recognizing her daughter after a ten year absence. "YOU!" she exclaimed. "Why did you come back? I thought you'd be dead by now."

"Isn't that a coincidence?" Maureen said, her voice edgy. "I thought the same. But here you are, just as kind and sweet as ever."

Ilsa grunted. "Don't waste your sarcasm on me. I never had no reason to be kind and sweet. Ask your grandmother. She knows."

"Knows what?" Maureen looked to her grandmother.

"Nothing," Eileen said. "She's just ranting again about the past. She has nothing to do but dwell on things that never happened."

"What do you mean, 'things that never happened'? I'm not adopted or something, am I?"

"No, no. Don't worry 'bout nothing like that," her grandmother said.

"I wouldn't be worried. I'd be grateful. It would explain so many things," Maureen said.

"Some things can't be explained." Ilsa shouted.

"Shut up," Eileen interrupted her. "Not another word," she warned.

Ilsa clamped her mouth shut, her lips forming a thin line.

"How did this happen?" Maureen looked at her grandmother for an answer.

"You don't have to talk around me, I'm sitting right here and I'm not deaf. You can ask me direct," Ilsa said.

"I've never been able to ask you anything, direct or otherwise, so why would I start now?"

"Well, since you're not asking, I'll tell you anyway. It's none of your goddamned business. Why don't you just go back to where you've been," her mother's voice heightened. "Get out!" she screamed. "You ruined my life."

"What do you mean, *I ruined your life*?" Maureen shot back. She tightened her fists and walked toward the wheelchair. Her grandmother tensed, prepared to intervene.

"Let's not talk about who ruined whose life. I still have the scars," Maureen's temper flared.

Her mother answered. "There are scars that scab over. And then there are scars you can't see that never heal. They just stay with you 'til you die."

"So which kind was yours?" Maureen cried, not listening for the answer. "I could kill you right now and never look back."

"Then do it! Why don't you do it? That would be the one good thing you've ever done for me!"

Maureen shook with anger as she paced back and forth from the wheelchair to the doorway.

"Why did you hate me so much?" Maureen asked.

Her mother's tone softened. "Maybe it wasn't you I hated so much. Maybe it was me I hated so much." She spoke the words more to herself, but Maureen heard them. "I didn't have the courage to kill me so I tried to kill the closest thing to me, the thing that was the biggest part of me - you!"

Maureen was confused. "You're saying I was the biggest part of you?"

"Don't flatter yourself. I didn't say you were the *best* part. Only the biggest."

"I don't understand any of this." Maureen felt exhausted, empty. She leaned against the wall and sank to the floor holding her head in her hands. *What the hell is going on here?* Her mother was trying to tell her something. Maureen reached for it but it eluded her.

Ilsa's eyes clouded over with a window of memory. "When you have nothing to do but sit in this chair, it also leaves you with nothing to do but think. I've been blaming you all these years, but maybe it wasn't only you."

"Well, finally you got one thing straight," Eileen said sarcastically. "Your life was ruined way before Maureen was born."

"Yes. And you watched, didn't you? You saw it happening but you did nothing. So you keep out of this," Ilsa barked.

Eileen gave her daughter a threatening look. "I didn't see nothing *happening*. Don't forget who's wiping your ass these days, and cooking your dinners too," she reminded her.

Ilsa tried to propel her wheelchair toward Eileen, but the wheels got caught on the buckled carpeting. "Goddamn carpeting," she muttered.

Maureen's head was pounding. The argument between her mother and grandmother was reminiscent of the arguments she had had with her mother; angry, vicious, hateful! She wanted to disregard her mother's innuendos but they were now airborne and difficult to ignore. She tried to add it all up in an orderly fashion, like a calculator one, two, three plus four, five, six equals. She asked her grandmother again, "What happened?"

"Some kid, practicing his left turn for his driver's license, ran into her. Next thing you know she's in a wheelchair, partially paralyzed. She gave them her name and they managed to track me down. Ironic, isn't it? For years we lived in the same house but avoided each other at all costs - and yet, here we are, together, 'til death do us part."

Maureen got up from the floor and walked to the window. "Did we live with you when I was born?"

"For awhile," Eileen said.

"Was my grandfather around?"

"Yes. Why do you ask?"

"I don't know. It just seems strange, I don't remember him at all," Maureen said. "How old was I when we left?"

"I'll tell you how old you were," Ilsa shouted. "Old enough for him to . . ."

Eileen walked to the wheelchair and gave her daughter a warning look as she answered Maureen. "You didn't know your grandfather because your mother was jealous as hell he'd love you more than he loved her. She made sure he kept his distance."

"That's not the reason," Ilsa screamed. "And you know it!"

"I don't know nothing, and neither do you," Eileen's voice escalated again.

"Okay. I give up!" Maureen shouted. "Either tell me what you're trying to say or I'm outta here. This was a big mistake. I don't know what I was expecting. Maybe it was to spit in my mother's face. Maybe it was to see whether there was something there I hadn't seen when I was a kid, like a smile, an apology, a reason. But nothing's changed. It sounds like she got what she gave." Maureen started to put her jacket on.

There was no answer from either mother or grandmother. Afraid Maureen would leave, her grandmother moved away from the wheelchair, took Maureen's arm and led her into the small kitchen, pulling out a chair. "Look, I'm sorry about all this. Please don't go. At least have a cup of tea with me," she said.

"Something stronger would be a blessing just about now." Maureen sat down tentatively, afraid her mother would charge through the doorway at any moment.

Seeing her discomfort, Eileen reassured her. "Don't worry. She can't get the wheelchair into the kitchen. It won't fit through these old doors. We're supposed to get a handyman out here to remove the door frame, but I haven't gotten around to it yet," she smiled with satisfaction. "This is the only place in the house where she can't follow me. Here and the upstairs bedroom."

Eileen rummaged through a lower cabinet as she spoke. "Aha! I knew there was some cognac hidden somewhere. Here it is," she said as she pushed aside other long-forgotten items.

"When I asked you before 'what happened,' I wasn't only referring to the accident," Maureen said.

"What were you referring to?"

"Well, my mother seems to be telling me something, but I'm not sure what it is."

"The ranting of an old lady, that's what it is. When you listen to that gibberish every day as I do you stop paying attention."

Maureen looked around the kitchen noticing the chipped drawers, the need of paint. "No one ever spoke to me about my father. Did you ever meet him?"

"No, I never met him. When she was almost seventeen Ilsa met your father at a small club I never heard of, somewhere downtown. She and a girlfriend went there to listen to some jazz. She took a shine to the sax player and she never came home that night or the next."

Their conversation was interrupted by Ilsa who finally got her wheelchair past the bulge in the carpet. The effort had caused beads of sweat to form on her brow. Thin strands of lank hair had escaped from behind her ears and were on her face, sticking stubbornly to her forehead, threatening to impair her vision. Her features were distorted with anger. The more she felt her impotence, the more enraged she became.

Maureen became alarmed as the wheelchair crashed into the side frames of the kitchen doorway. She vaulted out of her chair and moved backward into the service porch. Eileen got up quickly and moved toward the doorway, her fists raised.

Maureen stood speechless as she saw her mother recoil in fear.

"Back off." Eileen said, "or I'll lock you in your room and you'll never get out."

Maureen watched wide-eyed as her mother backed away from the door, her thin arms grappling with the battered wheelchair through the shabby carpet to her room. "Why don't you tell her the truth? Why don't you tell that high-caste throwaway what really happened," she shouted as the bedroom door slammed behind her.

Maureen was shocked at her grandmother's raised fists, so reminiscent of the way she had been treated by her mother. A different picture was emerging, one which was easier for Maureen to deny than admit. *Was her mother also abused when she was growing up?*

She stepped back into the kitchen, sitting down again at the table, and looked intently at her grandmother. "What did she mean by that, 'high caste throw-away?'"

Eileen took her time pouring the cognac into the two shot glasses. "I don't know where to begin. How much time you got, and I'll explain everything."

"Well, I've got 'til tomorrow morning," Maureen looked at her watch.

"That'll do it! In the meantime, let's drink." They downed the Cognac. Several minutes went by.

Eileen broke the silence. "When your mother returned after not showing up for two days, your grandfather called her a whore and told her she was grounded for life." Eileen leaned her elbows on the table and pinched her nose. "I figured that was the end of it until a few months later when I realized she was pregnant. I tried to talk to her but it was useless. Eventually she had no choice but to let me take her to our family doctor." Eileen got up and leaned her thin frame back against the kitchen counter. The faucet had a slow drip and Eileen automatically reached back to tighten it as she'd done for the past several months. "I got to thinking about something your mother's girlfriend said."

"What was that?"

"That the sax player looked white but that this was an all black band. So I tracked them down; *SIX TO FIVE* is what they called themselves. They were playing another gig about fifty miles down the road. 'Oh, yeah,' the band leader said. 'Harry Lax, the man with the sax. We ain't seen him since that gig . . .up and left us high and dry.' He was pissed."

"Did they say he was black?"

"What they said was, 'Harry Lax was the whitest black man they'd ever seen'. I told them my daughter was pregnant and I figured he wasn't playing the sax when he got her that way. I told them that if they did see that son-of-a-bitch to tell him he was going to be a father."

Maureen didn't know how to ask the next question. "Are you saying I'm . . . black?" She was unable to assimilate what she had just heard.

Eileen didn't answer directly. She just went on with her story and Maureen wordlessly held her glass out for another shot of cognac.

"You know," her grandmother said, "it was totally unacceptable then, a black man and white woman, not to mention your mother was not quite seventeen. So it didn't surprise me that we didn't hear from him, or that he would disappear from the face of the earth."

"Are you sure *now* that he was black?"

"No, I'm not. Does it matter?"

"Jesus!" Maureen said, angry. "Damn right it matters. You don't think it would matter to you? One day you're white and the next you're black? I'm trying to get my life together here. This is so over the top; I don't know what to think!"

"It certainly wouldn't have made any difference to me," Eileen said. "But I sure was surprised when you turned out white as a snow queen with blue eyes. 'Course there's no way tellin what the future holds, I mean, when you have babies and stuff. I hear sometimes it don't show up til later."

"No wonder she hated me so much," Maureen said. "Why the hell did she have me?"

"Sweetie, this was the forties. You couldn't get abortions back then. It's just this year it's become legal. And anyway, she had some twisted notion that she was going to pay him back by abusing his child."

"Well, she paid him back alright. No doubt about that." Maureen paused. "What did my grandfather have to say about all this?"

"He was very quiet; never said a word. He just pulled away from her as though she wasn't living here no more."

"Did you tell him who the father was?"

Eileen busied herself getting silverware and napkins from the drawer. "Well, yes, but to tell you the truth I didn't tell him everything because I was afraid he'd get a gun and shoot the whole damn band.

"When you were about five your mother and I had a knock-down drag-out argument about her drinking and staying out all hours. I told her we'd take custody and she could go her merry way. But for some perverse reason, probably just spite, she said she was sick and tired of us interfering with her life and she was moving and taking you with her.

"Of course, I didn't believe her. But the next day, both of you were gone."

Ilsa had opened her bedroom door. She heard Eileen's last comment and yelled across the room. "Bullshit! You know damn well why I took her." She maneuvered her chair toward them again. "It didn't have nothin' to do with spite."

"I ain't going to tell you again. Shut your damn mouth. No one's interested in your theories."

"They ain't theories and you know it!"

"Jesus!" Maureen said. "Didn't you look for us?"

"Of course I did. I called everyone — social services, the police. But no one could help me. I was just your grandmother, after all. I found out much later that your mother had moved in with a boyfriend. That's why I couldn't find her. Eventually I stopped trying, figuring she wasn't even in Cleveland any more.

"I've thought and thought about it, always wondering if there was something more I could have done." Eileen dabbed at her eyes. "Then, one day I volunteered at a clinic on the other side of town and spotted you and your mother in the waiting room. She didn't see me and I followed her.

"When I saw you walk out the door I had everything I could do to keep from talking to you. So many years had gone by. I was so afraid you'd hate me. I didn't know if it was right to suddenly reappear in your life. You seemed to have made it without me." Neither of them spoke for several minutes.

Maureen played with her napkin, folding and refolding it and tearing off little pieces.

Her grandmother spoke again. "I was at your graduation, you know. I was so proud of you, your speech and everything."

"You were at my graduation? My God, if you only knew how happy that would have made me."

"I looked for you afterward but no one knew where you were. Where'd you disappear to?" Eileen asked.

"New York. I didn't tell anyone." Maureen brought them back to the present. "Since my mother's accident, all these years, you've been taking care of her?"

"I didn't have a choice, did I? After all, she is my daughter."

"Even so, you could have just shoved her off on the county."

"No. I owed her. It's my penance," Eileen said, her eyes downcast.

"Penance for what?" Her grandmother didn't answer.

"It's a heavy price," Maureen said.

Eileen took her granddaughter's hands in hers across the table. Maureen looked into her grandmother's eyes, the same eyes she saw when she herself looked in the mirror. She recognized the sadness, the regret, the pain. Maureen started to cry.

Ilsa had managed to move closer to the kitchen. "Ain't this a pretty scene? Everyone so lovey-dovey, just like a movie picture. All is forgiven, the truth thrown out with the garbage for a happy ending."

Eileen got up and stood in the kitchen doorway. "There's only one truth. You're a deranged old woman."

"Not so deranged that I don't remember how you stood by when good ole daddy . . ." Ilsa shrieked.

"Shut up. You don't know what you're talking about." Eileen's mouth twisted. Her left eye twitched. She looked at Maureen. "Listen, just ignore her. What's done is done and neither you nor I can change it. You can't keep blaming yourself. Just blame yourself once and then move on."

Ilsa circled the living room. Around and around she went like a trapped animal not knowing where else to go, finally stopping again just outside the kitchen.

Maureen got up abruptly. "I really have to go," she said.

Eileen caught her arm. "Can't you stay a little longer? We have so much catching up to do."

Maureen sat back down at the edge of the chair. "Maybe everything's been said that needs to be said."

Ilsa kept her wheelchair within hearing range but did not interrupt again for fear of being exiled to her room. She listened to the cadence and tone of her daughter's voice as she related the events of the past ten years: college, her abusive relationship with Paul, the fight at

Ramrod, her companions, Lui, Ramon and Alberto. Ilsa thought, *I'll never see my daughter again after tonight. So many mistakes. No more chances!*

Maureen still felt uneasy about the comments her mother had made, but she wasn't ready to pursue it. Maybe she never would be. She looked over at her mother occasionally. There was a connection she'd never felt before, but the feeling was so unfamiliar it slipped away as quickly as it surfaced. She didn't want to risk asking her grandmother the questions that piled up on the floor like dirty laundry.

Ilsa dozed on and off. Exhausted, she finally struggled back to her bedroom without a backward glance. Both Maureen and her grandmother watched. Neither of them said anything, but Maureen's eyes followed her mother until the bedroom door closed behind her.

Once in the bedroom, Ilsa grappled with the bed covers and managed to thrust herself fully clothed from the wheelchair to the bed. She buried her face in the pillow and closed her eyes tightly to stop the tears. *I'm sorry, Maureen. I swear, I'm sorry.*

Back in the kitchen, Eileen broke the silence. "So what do you plan to do when you get to Los Angeles?"

"Get a cheap apartment, a part-time job to keep me in rice and beans. And then I'm going to enroll in law school."

"You want to be an attorney?" Eileen smiled.

"That's my goal. I hope it's not too late."

Eileen looked at her granddaughter. "Hell, no! It's never too late to do nothin'."

Maureen stood up. "I gotta go," she said. Her grandmother walked her to the door and pressed her in a tight hug. "Keep in touch. Please don't disappear again." She pulled a crumpled tissue from her sweater pocket and watched as Maureen walked to Lui's car.

A light drizzle had started and the air smelled fresh and clean.

CHAPTER SEVENTEEN

LUI WAITED IMPATIENTLY FOR Maureen's return. He peered out the window every time he heard a car drive into the parking lot. Finally the Impala drove up. He breathed a sigh of relief, closed his eyes and fell asleep.

Alberto paced, nervous as a caged tiger. He and Ramon had both showered and watched TV.

"So wha'd ya think's goin' on with Maureen," asked Ramon. "She gonna be all right?"

"Yeah. She has family business here."

"What? An old boyfriend or somethin'?" Ramon didn't wait for an answer. He stretched his long frame on the bed. "God, this feels good," he said. "Finally, a pillow I can sink my head into. And clean sheets. I had clean sheets once; I think it was when I was born, but I remember how they felt and smelled. You know how they put newborns in those little baskets? Whatcha call them? Incubators? Yeah, that was the last time." He paused, his thoughts veering off in another direction. "She sure is a good-looker."

"Yeah, but, bro . . . let's keep this . . ."

"I ain't touched her," Ramon said, throwing his hands up.

"Let's keep it that way. I don't want no trouble between us and Lui and Maureen. Once we get to L. A. everyone can do what they want. But for now . . ."

"I hear ya." Ramon looked at the clock: eleven p.m. He closed his eyes, but Alberto waited for Maureen's return. He heard her enter the room next door and waited a few minutes for her to get settled. Then he slipped his jeans on and quietly left the room. He knocked softly on her door.

"You decent?" he whispered.

She recognized his voice.

"Is everything okay?" Alberto asked. "You didn't kill anyone, did you?"

"No. I didn't have to," Maureen smiled, opening the door wider to let him in.

"It ain't none of my business," Alberto said. "You don't have to tell me nothin if you don't want to."

"Alberto, I'm wound up tighter than a virgin on her wedding night. If I don't pour some conversation on the cognac I had tonight, I'm going to combust, so come on in," Maureen said. "There's a coffee machine on the bathroom counter. You want some?"

"Sure, why not?"

Maureen waited for the coffee to perk. "First of all, I didn't need to kill my mother. God has a way of taking care of things."

Alberto breathed an audible sigh of relief. "Amen," he said.

"A couple of years after I left, my mother was in an accident. Some kid was practicing left hand turns for his driving test. She was in the way. That's it! Boom! Next thing you know, some doctor was telling her she'll never walk again."

"No kiddin'?" Alberto said.

"First off, it took everything I had to walk up those three porch steps. Then, to make matters worse, the woman who answered the door wasn't my mother and I thought, *oh shit, I'm at the wrong house.* We kept looking at each other. Then she said, 'Maureen' and I knew right away it was my grandmother."

Alberto sipped his coffee and listened wide-eyed as Maureen recounted the evening. She didn't know why, but she withheld the information about her father; that he might be black.

"You know, Alberto, there were some things my mother said . . . well, not exactly said, but implied . . . that were really disturbing."

"Like what?"

"Sometimes it sounded like my grandfather might have abused her, or at least tried to, and that my grandmother stood by and let it happen. For awhile there I was so disgusted with both of them, I just wanted to leave."

"No way! What did your grandmother say about that?"

"Only that my mother was demented."

"What do you think? You think it's true?"

"I don't know. I can't go back there, you know what I mean? I can't ever forgive my mother, but it's comforting in a perverse way that there might have been a reason."

Maureen looked so forlorn he just wanted to put his arms around her, hold her tight, but he knew he could never stop there. She wore a T-shirt that came down to mid-thigh. The thought that she might have nothing on underneath caused a pain in his groin, but he remembered telling Ramon: *hands off.*

Maureen continued with her story until they agreed to call it a night. Alberto slipped back to his own room.

◇◇◇

They met at seven a.m. for a quick continental breakfast offered by the motel.

"Ramon, any chance you called mama?" Alberto asked. "See if she's okay and find out how Rosie's brother, Joey, is doing?"

"Nah. I was going to do it last night but I was dead to the world the minute I hit the sack. How come you didn't call? You must've stayed up pretty late. I opened one eye around midnight but you weren't there."

Lui's ears perked up, suspicious. *If Alberto wasn't in his room, where was he?*

"I was there . . . probably taking a piss," Alberto answered quickly. "You guys finish up here. I'm going to use that pay phone near the restroom." He looked at his watch. *Ten o'clock eastern time. Mama should be home - probably having her first cup of coffee.* The phone rang three, four times and a man answered.

"Oh, sorry. I must have the wrong number," Alberto murmured. But then, a moment before hanging up, he thought the voice sounded familiar.

"Mr. Cardillo?" he asked, surprised.

"Well, um, yes," Cardillo answered, flustered. "Alberto? Where are you? Why you no come to work?"

"Is mama there, or are *you* renting the apartment now? Or maybe you're just delivering your goods to her," Alberto said, mocking.

Embarrassed, Cardillo said nothing more but handed the phone to Hortencia.

"It's Alberto," he heard Cardillo say.

"*Ah-h, mi hijo. Como estás?*"

"*Bien, mama. Que pasa?*

"*Nada.*"

"It don't sound like '*nada*' mama. Has Mr. Cardillo moved in?"

"No, no. Not yet," Hortencia said, unabashed. "He is just taking care of me. You and Ramon are gone. I have no one," she looked for sympathy, but her voice belied any real sadness.

"Mamacita. I have only one question?"

"What's the question?" she worried that Alberto was about to ask how come Senor Cardillo answered the phone. Alberto hesitated on purpose, stretching the moment, enjoying her discomfort. "Are you still as beautiful as ever?"

"Oh, you devil!" she shrieked and they both laughed.

"Before you hang up - how is Rosie? And Joey?"

"Joey is home from the hospital. Rosie is with him day and night. He can't walk without someone to help him — and his memory. Ay, it is not good. I help her. I shop for her, or I take care of Joey if she needs to leave the house. She is so good, Alberto, so-o-o good. But, about Joey," she continued. "I don't think he has very long. You know what I mean, eh, Alberto?"

"Geez, I'm really sorry to hear all this." He was afraid to ask the next question. "Do you know what happened to Paul?"

"Paul? He is the man who hurt Joey?"

"Yes," Alberto replied.

"The police take him. He killed someone . . . in a bar. You know about that?"

"Yes. We read it in the newspaper."

"Alberto, I am worried about you, and Ramon. He is alright?"

"Oh, yeah, mama. You know Ramon. He's always alright!"

"Where are you?"

"Well, mama, would you believe, we are just leaving Cleveland."

"Cleveland! Where is Cleveland?"

"Ohio, mama. Cleveland is in Ohio. But to tell the truth, I wasn't so sure either where Cleveland was until we got here yesterday,"

Alberto laughed. "By the way," Alberto added as an afterthought. "Mr. Cardillo doesn't snore, does he?"

"No, mi hijo. I keep him too busy." She giggled like a school girl.

Lui came around the corner and motioned with his head that they were ready to leave.

"I gotta go, mama. You take care of yourself. Tell Senor Cardillo I'm going to be a baker in Los Angeles."

"Los Angeles!"

"I'll call you, mama, when we get there." Alberto hung up and joined Lui, Ramon and Maureen.

"So, how's everything?" Ramon asked as they walked toward the car.

"Everything sounds okay. Mama seems happy."

"Yeah, well she's probably glad to be rid of us."

"Oh, I don't know. I think she misses us, but it sounds like she's got a better deal now."

"Whatd'ya mean?"

Alberto filled Ramon in on his conversation.

"Boy, it didn't take her long, did it? I hope the same thing doesn't happen to him as happened to papa."

"I don't think so." Alberto had a big grin on his face. "She said Mr. Cardillo doesn't snore!" Ramon looked at him and snickered.

Lui drove. Ramon kept him company while Maureen and Alberto got comfortable in the back seat. Ramon opened the map. "How long you figure it'll take us to get to L. A.? We got a lot of ground to cover: Indiana, Iowa, Nebraska. His voice trailed off.

"Yeah. We been coasting up to now, but I'd like to get some road behind us. I figure two, maybe three days. Hopefully we'll get there before our money runs out." He turned to Ramon. "I spoke with Charlie Mello. He's anxious to have a new man on board at the auto shop."

"Good!" said Ramon. "I'll be ready soon as we get there!"

"So, Maureen. You get your business taken care of?" Lui asked, pretending indifference. "You bet," she said. "I'm finished with Cleveland."

"You got plans for when we get to L.A.? You know anyone there?"

"Nope, but I'm hoping I can hole up in a YWCA until I find an apartment or room somewhere. I don't need anything fancy."

"We can share a place," piped up Ramon looking back at Maureen.

She rolled her eyes. "Horny young pup, aren't ya?"

Lui laughed and looked at Ramon. "Hey, I live with my brother. He and his wife said they could put you guys up for a day or two, til you get settled."

"Hell, I can lay my head down anywhere," Ramon said with a lecherous grin.

"Don't I know it, bro. Don't I know it!" Alberto agreed.

CHAPTER EIGHTEEN

THE BONANZA FOLDER NOT only contained the Trust documents, but a fairly concise record of Joey's business transactions for the past thirty years. The amount was astonishing, beyond her belief or expectations. She suddenly became aware that her life was about to change dramatically. The Certificate of Deposit was the culmination of assets he had acquired from various sources: private loans on second mortgages, silent partnerships, and several commercial real estate deals, not to mention the stock market.

She dialed their old, long-time attorney, Jack Schneider. The phone rang several times and she began to wonder if he was still alive. Finally his familiar voice answered.

"Rosie, I don't believe it!" Jack said, obviously pleased. "It's been so long. I can't believe you still have my number."

"Jack, I'll always have your number, even when you're gone," Rosie joked.

"Well, I'm not gone. Not by a long shot." His voice sounded strong and alert. "It's good to hear from you but I know you must be calling for a reason other than to just say 'hello'. Is Joey okay?"

"He's very ill and I don't think there's much time." Rosie's voice caught.

"I'm really sorry to hear that. Just tell me what you need."

"Jack, you're an angel."

"Well, not yet Rosie. Not yet!" Rosie knew he was smiling.

They met for several hours the following day. "I don't know anyone who kept such meticulous records," Jack commented. "This man was obsessive. Everything appears to be in near-perfect order."

"I know," said Rosie. "I couldn't believe it either. I can't figure out how he managed to keep this from me all these years."

"Rosie, I think I can safely say you are about to become a very wealthy woman."

She laughed nervously as the word 'wealthy' washed over her. "What good is it if you can't share it with anyone?"

"There are lots of ways to share wealth, Rosie. I'm confident you'll find the right one."

"Besides the Trust, there's one more thing, Jack. Joey wants me to sell the house. Can you handle the negotiations with the county?"

"It shouldn't be a problem. I still have some contacts there. They've wanted to build a small park between those tenements for quite awhile now. If they aren't interested you can always donate it and take a tax write-off. I'll make some calls and let you know." Jack walked Rosie to the door and embraced her. "So what's your next step? I mean after you sell the house?"

"I'm thinking of California. There's another world out there and I think I'm ready to see it." She put the Bonanza file into a canvas briefcase and hugged it close under her arm. She decided to splurge and take a cab home. After all, she was about to become a rich woman.

◇◇◇

The four companions were well on their way from Cleveland to Denver. Maureen had purchased a best seller mystery book and spent a good part of the time reading. They alternated driving, stopping every few hours for a jolt of caffeine, a can of beer, a cigarette and a bathroom. Maureen was sure she would die of asphyxiation before they reached Los Angeles. The car reeked of cigarettes, coffee and beer, not to mention body odor.

"Listen," Maureen said. "How about stopping overnight in Denver and then shooting for Los Angeles the following morning? I'm hallucinating about a hot shower and a queen-size bed."

"I'm game," said Ramon.

"Yeah, that's what I mean. I think all of us are 'game'. If we don't get a shower soon, somebody might shoot us."

"You saying we stink?" Lui asked, surprised.

"You saying we don't?" Maureen retorted. "Better get your nose fixed. If someone had to guess, they'd say they were downhill of either a cattle ranch or a zoo."

Lui was outnumbered and they agreed to find a cheap motel for the night and leave early the following morning for their final push to Los Angeles.

◇◇◇

Rosie arrived home from her visit with the attorney, Jack Schneider. Joey was resting peacefully watching some late afternoon panel discussion. He waved his hand weakly as Rosie entered the room. She thought she was used to the smell of illness, but the smell assaulted her every time she entered his room.

"Did everything go all right?" Joey asked, his voice hardly more than a whisper.

"Yes. It was really great to see Jack again. 'Very impressive,' Jack kept saying. He couldn't get over how organized everything was. And, of course, he was flabbergasted at your cunning, at the investments . . ."

"Just luck. That's all it was," Joey said modestly. "Did you talk about selling the house?"

"Yes. He said he still had plenty of contacts and he would get the ball rolling."

"Good girl, Rosie. For a change you did what I asked."

"It wasn't easy, but now that you're making me a kept woman I can't take any chances you'll change your mind."

"Change my mind about what? Dying, or leaving the money to you?"

"Well, if you want to change your mind about the dying part, I have no objection. But if you changed your mind about the Will, I'd have to kill you myself."

Joey smiled. "You know, Rosie, you're the best thing that ever happened to me . . ." he paused. "Except getting laid when I was . . ."

"Oh-h, you are a disgusting old man, but at least you've still got a good memory! It's a hell of a lot better than mine. I can't remember the last . . . oh, never mind!"

CHAPTER NINETEEN

JOEY LINGERED SIX WEEKS and then died peacefully in his sleep.

He and Rosie spent as much time together as possible, talking for hours about their parents and grandparents, their siblings, aunts and uncles long gone, friends, parties, blind dates, favorite restaurants. They tripped over each other to get the last word in, both trying to pack a lifetime of memories into this remaining time. Joey would lie back totally exhausted and Rosie would say, "Enough!" but as she was leaving the room, he would rally, 'do you remember when' and then they'd start all over again.

Rosie laughed uproariously, as Joey gasped and sputtered, almost with his last breath. They laughed with joy, and cried with sadness, tears streaming from their eyes, their noses running, pounding the pillow, slapping at their thighs. They went through a case of tissues, filling a waste basket every evening.

Rosie wished she could save the tissues in a scrapbook: *these are the tissues from Grandpa in the grocery; these tissues from my first date with Ruben; these tissues represent my college graduation. These tissues are for the morning when I tried to wake Joey, and couldn't. A lifetime of memories*, Rosie thought, *nothing but crumpled up tissues.*

◇◇◇

Rosie called Clara in Los Angeles.

"So, how did it go?" Clara asked.

"As well as funerals go, I guess. You know as well as me, having lost Frank so recently. We buried him next to Mom and Pop and our grandparents. The whole *mishpucha* is buried there. He's got lots of company."

Clara understood that Rosie's Yiddish word meant 'family'. "Who was at the cemetery?"

"Well, the Rabbi, of course . . . and me, our attorney Jack Schneider, and my neighbor Hortencia Esparza. Most of Joey's pals are gone. I'm the last of the *Mohicans* – or the Goldbergs, or the Sanchez's for that matter. Sad, isn't it?"

"Well, it sure gives you a wake-up call. You know you have to do *something* when you're the last one to do it! Did you sit Shiva?"

"Not really. I was home every evening, if that's what you mean. Where would I go?" Rosie unwound the long telephone cord as she moved out to the front porch. "My neighbors came by one by one to express their condolences. They brought soup, enchiladas, chile relleno, flowers and other items; nothing Kosher, that's for sure. Someone even gave me a cross, and a rosary," Rosie laughed. "What the hell. As Joey would say, 'it can't hurt.' I didn't think I was that well-known in the neighborhood."

"Rosie, how long have you been living there?"

"All my life!"

"And you don't think you're well-known in the neighborhood? For heaven's sake, *everybody* knew you and Joey."

"I guess so," Rosie said softly. "I just never gave it a thought. I don't know what I would have done without Hortencia."

"Is she the mother of those twins?"

"Yes, Ramon and Alberto. By the way, they're in Los Angeles now."

"Really? What are they doing here?"

"I'm not sure. Ramon does something with cars. And Alberto has a job in a bakery. Before they left Ramon borrowed three hundred dollars from me. I never expected to see it, believe me. But last week I got a check in the mail for five hundred fifty dollars, with a note from him: *Rosie, thanks again. Three hundred fifty for you, and please give Mamacita two hundred.* I gave the money to Hortencia and I thought she was going to faint. She wanted to know if I thought the money was 'legit'. I told her if the check doesn't bounce we'll consider it legit. She said Ramon never gave her that much money in all the time he lived with her: '*Ramon nunca me dio mucho dinero cuando vivio conmigo.*'

"What did our esteemed principal say when you told him you were retiring?" Clara asked.

"I think he was in shock. He said I was too young to retire. I reminded him that if you're a high school teacher in the Bronx you age quickly."

"Did that get a laugh?"

"Are you kidding? Not even a twitter!"

"How's it going with your baby-sitting for your grandkids?" Rosie asked.

"Some days good, some bad."

"What do you mean, 'some good, some bad?'"

"Well, Hannah usually comes directly home from school unless she's in a soccer game or something. But Martin is a different story. He always has a reason for not coming home. It sounds valid, but I have my doubts. I'm settling for lies because I'm afraid I'll alienate him if I confront him with the truth."

"And what do you think the truth is?" Rosie asked.

"That he's hanging out with the wrong kids; that he's going to get into trouble. He's surly, barely answers when spoken to, doesn't spend any more time with the family than he has to; you've seen the signs."

"Well, he sounds like a typical teen-ager. This is a big responsibility your kids laid on you! Can't you get out of this none-binding contract, get your own apartment and start living your own life?"

"It's easier said than done. I really can't afford my own place on my school retirement money."

"We're not talking about fancy living. Maybe you should get a little part-time job substitute teaching, or in a department store — anything.

"Look who's talking. What're you going to do when you get here?"

"I'm not sure. Nothing drastic, but I know I'm not ready to retire. Maybe I'll travel a bit, buy a business . . . you never know."

"Buy a business? What're you nuts? At your age?"

"Well, look what you're doing at your age. You're a baby-sitter for God's sake! Listen, there's a woman I know, Patty More - owns More Used Books a few blocks from here. She said she followed her dream when she retired and opened this used book store, and . . ."

"A *used* book store? What do you know about used books?"

"Well, no, I wouldn't open a used book store. I'd find something else." Rosie hesitated. "Maybe a grocery store . . ."

Clara laughed. "Now I know you're nuts. You can't compete with those super markets."

"Okay, laugh, you idiot," Rosie joked. "I wouldn't expect to compete. Tell me you don't miss those little corner groceries where they add up your total on a brown paper bag. Then you either pay the man, or you charge it. And if you charge it, you clear up your bill when you get your paycheck. It's a business built on trust."

"Rosie, you're dreaming. Those days are gone forever. People had integrity back in your grandfather's day. If they owed money, they paid it back. Nowadays you're lucky if they don't spit in your eye."

"When did you become so cynical?"

"Let's see. Maybe when God took Frank shortly after we got to Los Angeles, or maybe the first time my grandson looked me in the eye and lied," Clara took a moment. "Okay, let's not dwell on cynicism lest I get seriously depressed. Just tell me when you're coming so I have something to look forward to?"

"A couple of weeks, at most. The County bought the property. They're knocking down the house and building a small park between the tenements. Joey is probably wiggling his arthritic toes right now knowing that children will be playing in his back yard."

"I'm glad you've decided to stay with me for a few days. You know you can stay as long as you like."

"We'll see. For all I know I'll hate California and want to return to New York."

"Everybody loves California, Rosie. There's no way you'll go back to the Bronx."

◇◇◇

Rosie left almost everything behind. She had imaginary conversations with Joey where she spoke out loud and his words echoed back to her.

"Should I take this?"

No, you won't need it.

"I found five broken umbrellas in your closet." She lashed out at him.

I was saving them for a rainy day!
"But they were broken, for God's sake."
It didn't matter. I never went out in the rain anyway.
"You're impossible!" Her anger was unreasonable, but often a sob escaped, unsolicited. She reached into her housecoat for a tissue and loudly blew her nose. "What? It's not enough that you died? You still have to argue with me?"
Oh, stop blubbering.
"Easy for you," she said to his picture. "You're off having a good time in heaven while I'm here trying to squeeze a hundred years of memories into two boxes."
What makes you think I'm in heaven? Maybe I'm a bull in Montana.
"You're full of bull all right."
You don't have to get nasty.
"Stop talking to me; I can't concentrate."
She rummaged through her closet, moving hangers back and forth, looking at each item. *Ugh, this blouse must be a hundred years old! I think my grandmother gave it to me and she's been dead forty years!*
Along with photo albums, and a few favorite items of clothing, Rosie shipped her grandmother's silverware, her mother's dishes and several mementos in Joey's room to Clara's address in L.A. She had watched painfully as ten decades of household furniture, scratched and worn, refinished, stripped and painted and lovingly polished with *Pledge* – were carted away by the neighbors or Goodwill.
Now that Rosie was leaving, the blanket of privacy which the neighbors had respected throughout the years was lifted. They responded to her loss with their own special kindness, helping her pack boxes, and inviting her for meals. During the last two months she and her neighbors found a kinship that had always been present, but had previously been silent. It was helpful that, much like her own Jewish religion and tradition, Rosie knew their language, and identified with their culture. She understood the humor, the optimism, the bitterness, and the hope of these people.
On her last morning Rosie couldn't stop crying. As she walked through the empty house she felt as though she were watching an old movie, a kaleidoscope of her grandparents, parents and siblings —

laughing, crying, arguing, a life taken and one given in return, the smell of Friday night chicken soup with matzo balls, Sunday morning lox and bagels, salami on rye, her mother's prayers over the candles, the wine, her father's toast l'chaim. All the while, Joey's skinny spirit hovered over her like a kid's beanie hat with a propeller. *You can do this Rosie. I'm proud of you*, he repeated over and over.

"I can't, I can't. I'm scared. I don't remember ever being so scared. Everything here is so familiar. I'm too old to make changes."

I know you're scared, but you can do this!

Senor Cardillo and Hortencia drove her to the airport. She wore slim black jeans which sat at her waist, a short sleeve white cotton sweater and a two inch wide black leather belt looped through the jeans with a silver buckle,. Her long dark hair was held back with an ivory clip.

"This isn't me," Rosie had complained to her neighbor's daughter, Gabrielle, as she fussed with the belt buckle.

"Rosie," Gabrielle had said, hands on hips. "This is *you* from now on. You're no longer a school teacher. You have to act like a woman of the world . . . sophisticated, smart, sexy."

"Don't get carried away," Rosie said, smiling.

Her new Nike sneakers were stylish and comfortable. A plain silver chain hung between her breasts; silver loop earrings enhanced the contours of her face and neck. Rosie never had a weight problem, but since Joey's death she'd lost ten pounds and, although pushing sixty, she looked at least ten years younger. The shadows of sadness under her large brown eyes made her even more appealing. This new look was due to Hortencia's prodding, although, according to Hortencia, Rosie was 'wasting away.'

"You are too skinny; *muy flaca.* I have to bring you more enchiladas," she joked.

Hortencia had worried about Rosie's depression after Joey's death. She'd visited her every day, bringing food and neighborhood gossip. In her grief, Rosie hardly acknowledged her presence. She walked through the house, stopping often in Joey's room, fingering the spread, looking at photos, drawing the shade, opening the closet, running her fingers along the back of his chair.

Rosie's depression lifted through an odd sequence of events, a conspiracy of sorts between a neighbor, her twenty-five year old daughter, Gabrielle, and Hortencia. Gabrielle had suggested that what Rosie needed was a new wardrobe.

"What are you talking about, a new wardrobe? The poor woman is grieving for her brother and you think new clothes would cheer her up?"

"Yes, I do. She needs new clothes anyway, especially if she's going to Los Angeles, Hollywood, Malibu," Gabrielle said, imagining herself there. "I wish I was going with her. Rosie's starting a new life. She shouldn't go looking like a dowdy school teacher."

"Well, that's what she is. You want she should look like you? Like a . . ." Gabrielle gave her mother a warning look.

"Okay," her mother said, wiping her hands on her apron. "Maybe you're right. I'll ask Hortencia what she thinks."

The next day Mrs. Santos spoke to Hortencia. Hortencia, whose life consisted of eating and shopping, and could never pass a store without entering it, was in total agreement. "YES!" she cried. "That is the answer. We need to get Rosie out of the house. Do you think Gabrielle would go with her?"

"I am certain she would," answered Mrs. Santos.

And that's how it happened that Rosie's appearance the morning she left for Los Angeles was very different than her customary conservative look. Gabrielle had assured her that jeans were appropriate for traveling, that the silver-buckled belt was *de rigueur*; the long hooped earrings essential; the large hobo bag slung over her shoulder imperative to affect a certain savoir faire.

"You don't want to look like the Bronx," Gabrielle had said. "You want to look like Manhattan. Walk tall, swing your hips a little, - like this." Gabrielle strutted, slightly gyrating her narrow hips and long legs, leaving her upper body intact. Her pelvis angled forward ever so slightly, drawing more than one second look. "New Yorker's must convey a certain inner confidence. You want them to look at you in Los Angeles and say, 'That beautiful woman must be from New York.'"

Rosie relented. As she tried on various outfits, her mood lifted. She turned this way and that in the mirror and found that she liked her new slimmer figure. And she loved the youthful clothes Gabrielle selected for her.

"You look gorgeous," Gabrielle said. "Sleek and chic!"

"You don't think my ass is too big? Look how tight these jeans are in the crotch. You can see my *you know what*."

"Exactly," Gabrielle shrieked.

Now, as Rosie closed the door behind her for the last time and moved to the front porch swing that she and Joey had shared so many times, she felt a sense of adventure, a revival of hope and a premonition of a new beginning. *If only Joey was here to see my new look.* She nervously searched her hobo bag again for the airline tickets and her latest book and smiled as Hortencia opened the gate and walked toward her. "I am so excited for you," Hortencia said. "You look beautiful - like a young girl."

"Well, look at you; you're beautiful too," Rosie smiled.

Hortencia, now down to a mere two hundred ten pounds, turned this way and that, primping. "You like my new outfit?" She wore tight black pants, her thighs and buttocks straining against the latex fabric. Her extra extra large colorful print blouse fell to mid hips. "Henry bought for me," she said. "A gift because I am so good to him." She raised her eyebrows, her dark brown eyes twinkling. "You know what I mean, eh Rosie?"

"How would I know what you mean, Hortencia? I haven't been *good* to anyone in a long time."

"Well, there is always hope. Maybe things will change when you get to Los Angeles, eh?"

Just then Mr. Cardillo drove up with his truck. He got out and walked up the path. "Two beautiful women. I am a lucky man this morning." He put Rosie's suitcase in the back of the truck among the powdered sugar pastries being delivered that day.

Rosie grabbed the carry-on and followed him. She remembered how difficult it was to get Hortencia into the cab when they took Joey to the hospital a couple of months ago. But this time Henry had foreseen the problem and he had a step-stool handy. With Henry's assistance Hortencia climbed up. At the last step Henry put his hands on her buttocks and said, "Ready?" He gave her one last shove, catapulting her into the front seat. She struggled to move her body to the center, keeping her legs to the side to avoid the gear shift. Rosie squeezed in. The ride to the airport took about an hour. Hortencia was unusually quiet. Rosie and Henry also harbored their own thoughts.

"You know, Rosie, I am thinking maybe you will see Ramon and Alberto when you are in Los Angeles."

"Los Angeles is a big place, Hortencia. Do you know where they're living?"

"No, not yet. They call me sometimes - when they remember they still have a mama. They say they are staying with a friend and they don't have their own apartment yet. Where will you be staying Rosie?"

"Well, my friend Clara is picking me up and I'll stay with her a few days. I don't want to stay there too long though."

"*Porque?*"

"I need to be alone for awhile; make some decisions about whether I even want to stay in Los Angeles."

"What will you do with yourself? You have to find something. You think maybe you will teach again?"

"Well, maybe substitute . . . but definitely not nine to five. I would love to open a little business of my own."

"A business?" Hortencia said, surprised. "What kind of business?"

They were approaching the airport and Rosie did not have time to answer.

"You're sure you don' want us to go in with you," Henry asked, putting her luggage on the curb.

"No, it's not necessary. This is easier." She gave Henry one last hug and held Hortencia tight, trying to hold back tears. "I'll call you when I get there," she shouted and waved, pulling a tissue from her pocket and wiping her eyes.

Henry pulled away. Rosie checked her bag and walked into the terminal toward her departure gate trying to remember how long it had been since she'd flown anywhere. *At least five years.* There was still plenty of time before boarding. She stopped for a large black coffee and continued to her gate. Gabrielle's advice came to mind: *You're a New Yorker. Act like one. Hold your head high. Move your hips from the waist down.* Rosie smiled to herself. *Now I know how New Yorker's walk. I wonder how Los Angelinos walk.*

The plane boarded. Rosie looked around unable to figure out how she could be feeling both sadness and anticipation at the same time. *Goodbye New York! Goodbye Joey! I'll see you in my dreams.* She hummed the melody . . . *'See you in my dreams, hold you in my dreams, someone took you out of my arms . . .'*

Joey, Joey. I miss you so much!

PART TWO
LOS ANGELES, FALL, 1973

CHAPTER TWENTY

MAUREEN MOVED HER HAND over several papers scattered on the desk and felt for the shape of the yellow highlighter. "There you are," she said aloud removing the top and marking a passage in her law book. The broken-down black vinyl desk chair squeaked as it swiveled around to the interior darkness of the room. She rubbed her eyes and leaned back. A small alarm clock on the nightstand read two a.m.

Tired to the bone from her four to ten shift at Davey's Deli on Alvarado, she had hopped a bus after work, exited a couple of miles down the road at Highland Avenue and walked two blocks toward her apartment. She slid her key into the iron cage leading into the hallway and walked up one flight of stairs to her room. *First things first — a cup of strong coffee and then hit the books.*

A few hours later, she said *enough.* She closed the book, got out of her clothes and flopped on the bed with a great sigh of relief. Before sleep overtook her she recaptured for the briefest few minutes her quick overnight stay in Colorado two months ago with Alberto, Ramon and Lui. She had been disappointed they couldn't stay longer. No heat and humidity there — just the strains of John Denver's *Colorado Rocky Mountain High* drifting in and out of her head aimlessly like an unfinished thought.

They had been sniping at each other. Too much togetherness. Maureen, especially anxious about staying at Lui's brother's house, picked at her cuticles and became withdrawn. Tired and bedraggled, their spirits were low despite having finally reached their destination.

Lui had called his brother Sam as they neared Santa Monica. "Sam . . . Lui here. Yeah, I know it's late. We're about half hour away. Ya think you can put my friends up?" Lui listened. "Three," he told his brother. "Well, it's Maureen I'm thinkin about. Ramon and Alberto can flop in my room." Lui looked at Maureen. He nodded at her and gave her a thumbs up. "Okay, that's great. See ya in a bit."

"If there's a hotel in the area Lui, you can drop me off . . ."

"No, no problem. Sam's wife, Nancy, said it was okay. They have a small office in their garage. Sam flops there sometimes. You can look around tomorrow. We're all too tired tonight."

"You're sure?"

"Yeah," Lui said.

Lui had honked his horn upon their arrival. Sam Chu and his wife greeted them at the door. Lui introduced everyone. Nancy was gracious, but her voice and eyes were cool. Either Hawaiian or Philippine, with smooth unblemished cocoa butter skin, she looked in her early thirties. Her long dark hair hung past her shoulders. A sleeveless Hawaiian print dress clung to her petite frame. The low scoop neckline revealed high breasts and ample cleavage. Ramon was speechless. If he had to speak he would have been tongue-tied. Nancy could see his appreciative glance and she played up to it, looking directly into his eyes, disarming him completely.

"You must all be exhausted," Nancy said as they filed past her into the entry hall.

Lui's brother Sam was quiet. He seemed less than pleased at the prospect of three guests in his small house. He shook hands all the way around, his gaze lingering on Maureen. He held her hand a moment longer than necessary. She immediately had an uncomfortable feeling, a scintilla of danger. A year of dealing with Paul's capricious temper had heightened her predatory senses. Nancy Chu had noticed Sam's attention to Maureen. She glanced at him and he caught her eye. A signal passed between them. A hint of a smile played on her lips.

Sam Chu was squat; muscular, like a Sumi wrestler without the girth. He owned a very successful body shop – not the kind that did auto repairs, but the kind that taught muscle building and self-defense. He held children's classes during the day and adult classes as night. His military-style short hair was shaved all around, a buzz on the very top. He and his brother were the same height but Lui was slim and agile whereas Sam appeared slow and lumbering. Maureen was on edge. She wasn't sure if she was paranoid because she was tired or because Sam frightened her.

Lui directed Ramon and Alberto to his room and followed right behind. They carried whatever gear they had. The small room had twin beds pushed together with barely any room on either side. Neatly made, each had a simple plaid cotton cover. Alberto eyed the bed, put his backpack down and flopped on it. He was out!

"Ramon, c'mere," Lui showed him a thin quilt and pillow on the top shelf. "There's your bed, kid," Lui said, pointing to the floor.

Ramon shrugged. He didn't care where he slept. Ramon had noticed a small bathroom in the hallway. "I'll be back in a sec. Just have to take a piss."

"Take your time," Lui said. "I'm down for the count."

Nancy Chu took Maureen in tow. "We have a small office attached to the garage. Sometimes Sam works out there but mostly we just use it for storage or an occasional guest." She smiled at Maureen. "I hope it's not a horrible mess. I don't get out there too often. There's a bed and small bathroom where you can wash up. Sorry, no shower, but the sheets are clean. I saw to that myself when Lui called."

"Oh, gee, don't worry 'bout that. I'm too tired to care about anything right now."

"No one will bother you out there." She turned on the outside patio lights and then walked to the garage door with Maureen. "Will you need anything else, sweetie?"

"No," Maureen said. "I really appreciate . . ."

"Don't mention it. No problem, really. Sleep tight." Nancy waited as Maureen switched on the inner ceiling light. She waved at Nancy as she closed the door behind her.

The office was jammed with file cabinets. A twin bed lay against the far wall. A bare window looked out the side of the house where a redwood fence separated this garage from the neighbor's. The paint on the window sill was peeling, the panes thick with grime. A heavy mahogany desk sat against the wall beneath the window where files were piled a foot high. The fractured concrete floor was rough and cold.

Maureen wove her way to the bathroom, set her small suitcase down on the toilet seat and rummaged for her toothbrush and toothpaste. She pulled her T-shirt over her head and removed her bra. *God, what a relief.* She slipped her sneakers off, unbuttoned her jeans and pushed them down over her hips along with her panties, kicking both the jeans and panties aside.

As Maureen walked to the light switch to turn it off, she saw her naked body reflected in the window. *Christ, I hope no one's looking over the fence.* She carefully made her way to the bed and slid in. The sheets were cool and crisp. She was asleep in seconds.

Sam Chu's body threw a distorted shadow across the tiled patio as he stole across the patio toward the garage. But he quickly withdrew when he noticed a tall dark shape, already at the office door. *Fuck!* he cursed under his breath and slid back inside retreating to his and Nancy's bedroom. He saw the look of disappointment on her face before she turned her back to him. She had been looking forward to his re-enactment of his encounter with Maureen.

The office door opened and closed noiselessly. A figure stood unmoving, his back against the door, his eyes adjusting to the darkness. After a few minutes he cautiously wove his way toward the bed, the lightness of his tread belying his weight. He put his hands out in the dark to avoid the erratic placement of file cabinets. His breathing was shallow, tense. He reached the bed where Maureen lay naked. She had kicked the covers half off. The intruder stared at the curve of her hips and the fullness of her breasts. She faced him, the flat of her belly, the length of her long leg exposed as it caressed the sheet.

He sat down softly at the edge of the bed. Maureen stirred. "Wha' the . . ."

"*Shh!* Don't be scared. It's only me," he said. "Move over." He pushed her gently toward the wall.

She recognized the voice. "Jesus!"

"I can't sleep. If those guys snored any louder the building would collapse. Just move over so we can both get some shut-eye."

Too exhausted to argue she turned toward the wall and pulled the sheet over her. "Why can't you just go away?" she said. "If your brother finds out there's going to be holy hell . . ." her voice drifted off as she fell into a deep sleep again.

"I'll leave before morning," he said, but she didn't hear him.

He lay down behind her, waited for the evenness of her breathing, the soft exhale of a whisper on her pillow and then slipped his clothes off. Slowly then, he reached an arm over her and then, lighter than a current of air, moved the palm of his hand gently across her breasts feeling the immediate hardening of her nipples. She moaned but did not resist. He could not tell, dared not ask, whether she was asleep or awake. He moved his body closer, bending her knees to his. His virility, strong, pulsing — throbbed between her buttocks. He slowly moved his hand down the curve of her spine to her waist and down her leg. *Fabric moving sensuously between his fingers, soft, silky.*

She was awake. He sensed it. They both waited for the same thing: a word, a clue! He wasn't sure she wanted him to continue. She wasn't sure she wanted him to stop. They both held their breath, fearful that any sound either of them made would betray their feelings. They would keep it a secret, not breathing a word now and not breathing a word later.

The flat of his hand moved across her buttocks feeling the tightness of muscle against the firmness of flesh. He pulled her closer even as she held back, hesitant, wavering. He caressed her stomach and moved his hand toward her groin. She shuddered. He bent his head to her breast, the palm of his hand pressing and releasing as his tongue circled her nipples. He could feel her body, taut, resisting him outwardly while succumbing inwardly to her own sensuality. He was charged; an electrical current gone awry.

Maureen was barely breathing, emitting small sounds. *I can't fight this.* She knew there would be consequences and that their relationship would change now from the way it had been — friends. Just friends. Maureen was fighting a war she couldn't win. *Oh God! Oh God! I'm drowning.*

"*Shh,*" he whispered.

His hand rested on the silken hair between her legs. He slid his finger into the moisture, finding her core. His head moved downward wanting to smell and taste her. As his tongue worked its magic her pelvis rose, pushing against him. She gasped, either in acceptance or protest, he wasn't sure which. It didn't matter.

He pressed her body to his, aware her resistance had finally been shattered. She entwined her legs with his, pulling him ever more tightly to her. He moved back and forth between her legs. She was ready, moaning; she wanted him desperately.

"Is it okay?" he asked softly; *not that it matters, baby.*

She did not answer. *Yes. Yes.*

"I don't want to do this unless it's okay?" As though he could have stopped! A long lock of dark hair fell over his forehead, dripping with sweat.

Ass hole, you want me to take responsibility for this? You're asking for my approval? Fuck you, I'm not giving you absolution, she cried inwardly, agonized.

"Say it," he said. "Say it's okay." Her body was exploding.

She didn't say it. It wouldn't have mattered; they were totally out of control. He was in such a heightened state of arousal he wasn't sure how long he could continue without coming. Nevertheless he carefully, slowly, penetrated her, taking his time, drawing out the moment. He was gasping, moving in and out, the friction unbearable. He held on as long as he could until they climaxed — a volcano spitting white lava —both crying out from exhaustion and relief. After a few moments she turned away from him, fumbling for the sheet and drawing it around her again. She started to cry, angry that her body and mind had betrayed her, that she had been too weak to resist him. *Why didn't I stop him? What have I done?*

"Hey, everything okay?" He asked the question idly as though they were leaving a theater after having seen a sad movie. Too wrapped up in his own ego and too immature to recognize the damage he might have done, he took her silence for approval, her tears for joy. He lay flat on his back beside her and put his hands behind his head, hardly believing that what he had dreamed of and imagined throughout their journey across country had come to fruition. He projected himself into her future; the two of them making a life together.

"Maureen. I'm crazy about ya. We gotta talk, make some plans."

"Listen," she said, facing him, leaning on her elbow. "You think you can forget about what just happened?"

He turned his head toward her. "Whatd'ya mean, forget about it? I jus told you. I'm crazy about you, baby."

"No, listen. What just happened was nothing . . ."

"Nothing!" he shouted angrily. "You wanted it. You know you wanted it."

"Look, we were both tired, not thinking right. It shouldn't have happened . . ."

He didn't let her finish but got up quickly and walked to the bathroom. Returning a moment later, he put his pants on and walked out without a word, slamming the door behind him.

"You think you can sleep now," she yelled after him. *Son-of-a-bitch.*

Maureen's anger lay there, simmering like stew, mushrooming like a cloud. She dozed fitfully and wondered how she could ward off a confrontation between herself and the twins. She dressed early and walked into the kitchen intending to leave a note.

Nancy Chu, already up and dressed, seemed a little distant. She had had an argument with her husband this morning. "What happened last night?" she had asked him.

"I was on my way but one of the twins was already there," he said, apologetically.

"You're such a pathetic wimp," she said.

"What could I do? Tell me, what did you expect me to do?"

Nancy ignored him and walked out of their bedroom toward the kitchen. She was surprised to see Maureen. "You're up bright and early. I thought you'd be sleeping in. You look like you need a cup of coffee."

Maureen nodded and sat down at the small kitchen table. Nancy poured for both of them and also sat down. She looked at Maureen and paused, holding her spoon but not moving it. "Was everything alright last night?" Nancy arched her eyebrows. The moment lingered. Neither of them said anything. Maureen sensed that Nancy knew about her late-night visitor.

"Of course," Maureen hesitated. "Why do you ask?"

Nancy laughed. "Well apparently one of the twins didn't have such a good night because he's sleeping on the couch."

"Really?" Maureen tried to smile as she stirred her black coffee. "Which one?"

"Ya got me. I can hardly tell one from the other. This one's got his head buried in the pillow, snoring away . . . sounds like an outboard motor about to give out."

"Listen," Maureen said, changing the subject. "I gotta get going. Is there a car rental agency nearby?"

"Sure is. I'll be happy to drop you off. But don't you want to wait for Ramon and Alberto to wake up?"

"No, I already had my wake-up call. Just tell them I'll be in touch."

CHAPTER TWENTY-ONE

ROSIE ARRIVED IN LOS Angeles in October, two months after Maureen and the twins. Clara picked her up at LAX, all excited and full of hugs and kisses. She jabbered away, pointing out various landmarks and making all kinds of plans for the two of them. Rosie just smiled and said, "We'll see."

Clara's one-room apartment over the garage was well laid out, easily accommodating a temporary guest. Martin Ramirez had designed a comfortable retreat for his mother-in-law. A jacaranda tree shaded the window above the kitchen sink, its purple blooms carpeting the yard below. Pale yellow spreads covered ell shaped twin beds against the wall. One slid under a large table which held a fake silk plant. The walls were pale blue with white trim molding. A fifteen inch television sat in a corner. A small comfortable chair and floor lamp allowed for easy reading.

The contrast between Clara's Manhattan apartment, which was dark and cluttered, and this one, was striking and elicited a small *oh my goodness* from Rosie. She was impressed.

"See," Clara said with pride, moving her arm in an arc to encompass the room. "Do you like it?"

"I love it! Martin did a great job. I wouldn't mind something like this."

"You know you can stay as long as you like."

But despite Clara's wheedling Rosie stayed only a few days until she found a small room in a private home several blocks away. Senora Saenz, the owner, had recently been widowed and needed to supplement her income. Although the Senora had lived in L. A. many years, she had not mastered more than a few words in English. Rosie conversed with her in Spanish. Within weeks the two women established a warm relationship, though they were careful to respect each other's privacy.

Each day melted into the next as Rosie slowly slid out of the grief of losing Joey. Alone, or with Clara, she visited museums, went to the beach, read a lot and walked the neighborhood. She tried to engage some of the neighborhood women, but they seemed aloof, disinterested in conversation, perhaps intimidated by a gringo suddenly in their midst. Each day the same women walked the same route, absorbed in pushing a stroller with several toddlers hanging on. Their shoulders sagged; the strain of poverty and repetition showed on their faces.

How can I help them? Rosie wondered. After observing their malaise for several weeks, she began to formulate a plan. Excited, a renewed energy surged through her. The idea of a grocery store became ever more important.

At a Ford dealership Rosie fell in love with a cream-colored 1971 Ford Mustang. "This is the car I want," she said to Martin, who had accompanied her to various auto dealers.

"We can probably find something with lower mileage," he said.

"This car has less mileage than I do." She motioned to the salesman who stood hovering nearby. "We'll take it."

The salesman looked to Martin for confirmation. He nodded, smiling. "You heard the lady."

"Now all I have to do is learn to drive," Rosie joked.

◇◇◇

As Rosie pursued her search for a neighborhood store, the Ramirez family continued to voice their objections. "You've already lost your mind and now you're looking to lose your shirt. This is not the farm community you grew up in," they argued.

"I grew up in the east Bronx. You call that a farm community?"

"You know what I mean," Clara countered.

Despite Clara's warnings, Rosie consulted several business brokers who were familiar with the area.

"This neighborhood is changing; used to be a lot safer. All of a sudden I'm noticing gang bangers on some corners. I can recommend another location."

"Well, maybe that's true," Rosie interrupted the broker, "but this reminds me of where I lived in the Bronx. It's almost like being home."

"But a grocery store! Ya know the people here are not that accepting of gringos. D'ja notice how they look at you suspicious-like? Even if they patronize your store, which they won't, you'll lose your shirt. It's not exactly like . . ."

"I know. I know. I'm going to give it a lot of thought."

A few days later, on a side street, she spotted a large store-front window. JEROME L. GREENE, ABOGADO, showed in bold black letters. Rosie pulled her car to the curb and got out.

A young woman, watering roses in a raised brick planter box, looked with approval at Rosie's Mustang. "Nice car," she said.

"Nice roses." They both smiled.

"You should have seen them a month ago when I first got here." Maureen wiped her hand on her jeans. "I'm Maureen," she held out her hand.

"Rosie Sanchez."

"You're new in the neighborhood?"

"Yes. You work here?"

"I think it's work, but my boss sometimes disputes that. He calls me the plant lady and says he'll give me respect when I can try a case as well as I grow roses. But I refer to him as my savior."

"Why is that?"

"Because he saved me from smelling like a pastrami sandwich with a side of sour pickles. Now he's trying to make a law clerk out of me. You know the old line, 'make a silk purse out of a sow's ear.'"

"Are you talking about a deli? A real deli? Where I come from there's one on every corner. You're making my mouth water. I didn't think they had pastrami in this neighborhood, let alone sour pickles."

"I'll take you there sometime. I get special prices because of my short stint as an employee."

"Can I make an appointment to see Mr. Greene?" Rosie pointed toward the office.

"Sure. Come on in. Maybe he can make time for you now."

"You think it's all right? I feel sort of grungy – these old jeans and sneakers . . ."

"Well, look at me, plant food down my shirt and dirt in my fingernails. I don't think you need to worry about how you look. Mr. Greene only notices what he writes down on his yellow pad. First he looks at that and *then* he looks at you."

Rosie followed Maureen into the store-front. They entered a small waiting area, comfortable but sparsely furnished.

"I'll just be a minute," Maureen said. A few minutes later she returned and escorted Rosie into a larger office.

Mr. Greene rose from a brown leather chair. A big man, probably a football player twenty years ago, he looked to be in his forties. His dark hair was cropped close to his head, his dark eyes intelligent and probing. Rosie felt less inappropriately dressed when she noticed he was wearing jeans and a baseball tee shirt. He held Rosie's hand in a strong handshake and apologized for his informal attire. "I wasn't expecting anyone today. How can I help you?" he waved her to a chair.

"I'm not sure. I'm new to the neighborhood. I'll spare you a long story and give you the scenario in a few words. I'm retired from the New York City school system; thought I was ready to call it a day, but now I find I have a lot left in me. I'm probably too old to start all over again. But that's what I want to do."

"You want to start all over again? And do what?"

"Open a small grocery store." She held her breath for his response.

If Greene was surprised, he didn't show it except by leaning forward. "Hmmm." He rested his elbows on the desk and held his long fingers together in a tower. "And where did you want to open this store?"

"Right here!" Rosie blurted.

"Why?"

"Why do I want to open a grocery store or why do I want to open it in this neighborhood?"

"Both," Greene leaned back in his chair.

"I'm not sure. The grocery store is a hand-me-down from the past, from my grandfather. It's almost compelling. I can't explain it. I've been a teacher all my life and now I still want to teach, but in a different way."

"In what way? You can always get a job as a substitute teacher. You know that."

"Yes, but that's not what I want. To answer your question about why in this neighborhood, all I can say is that I think I can help."

"Help?" Greene was perplexed. "How do you think you can help these people?"

"By example," Rosie said stubbornly. "Especially the women! If I could make them realize they can take more control of their lives. Maybe if they see a woman alone, trying to be independent . . ." She was frustrated, unable to fully express her thoughts.

"What makes you think these women want help? Maybe they like their lives?" He sounded angry. "You want to play God and be a martyr; open a grocery store in an area where you probably won't be accepted? Where the hours are long and tedious? Where delinquent kids will . . ."

"Look, I'm not here to seek your approval, only to ask a few questions." Rosie stood up, confused at his outburst.

"Okay, I'm sorry." He threw his hands up. "I'm just concerned that what you're suggesting is risky, but please, sit down. Ask away."

"Well, for starters, have you had any problems maintaining your store-front office?"

"Not really, other than kids dropping cigarette butts in the planter outside. But, as you know, Maureen takes care of that now."

"Do you know of any business on the street that has had unusual problems, like break-ins, rape, murder, vandalism? I mean, anything that doesn't happen in other areas?"

"Vandalism is always present but it depends what kind of business you have. I mean, what can you steal in a laundry besides someone else's underwear, but in a grocery store there's a lot that can be stolen. You're entire profit, for example."

"I want to provide a place where the locals feel welcome, where they're not looked down upon, where someone speaks their language."

"And do you speak their language?"

"Yes, I do."

"But they don't really speak your language, do they?"

"Not yet. But I'll teach them."

"So, you haven't really told me what I can do for you." Greene became more business-like and pulled out a lined yellow pad.

Rosie slid forward in her chair facing him directly. "I found a store. It's small, but good enough for starters. It's on a little side street, just around the corner from the furniture store. I need you to contact the landlord and negotiate for me. I wrote down his name and number." Rosie rummaged through her purse and pulled out a crumpled piece of paper.

Greene reached for his glasses. They sat below his nose and he looked over them at Rosie. "I know him. George Polenski. He owns the whole block. That side-street store has been vacant forever. I think he'll be happy to deal." Greene took Rosie's number.

"If this works out, I'll also need an architect. Do you know anyone?"

"You bet. Lorenzo Jacobs. He designed the layout of this office and, believe me, it was a challenge. He's kinda retired now - like you," Greene smiled. "One day he's retired and the next day he's looking for something to do. I haven't seen him in awhile. His wife died about a year ago and he's been hibernating. This might be just the thing to get him motivated again. He will *love* this. It's right up his alley."

"Lorenzo Jacobs. Sounds like he couldn't figure out whether he's Italian or Jewish."

"I think he's both. He designs in Italian and hires in Jewish. Lorenzo is a genius." Greene escorted Rosie to the door. "I know I'm not the first to tell you, this is the most ridiculous . . ." He looked at Rosie's determined face. "Okay, I'm not going to say it. What are you going to name this place?"

"ROSIE'S GRINGO PALACE," she said and then laughed out loud. "If that doesn't get 'em, I don't know what will."

CHAPTER TWENTY-TWO

AT LEAST FOUR MONTHS had passed since Maureen's overnight stay at Lui Chu's house. Although she promised herself she would sever all ties with Cleveland, still part of her could not let go completely. She gave her grandmother a quick call.

"This is the first spare minute I've had since arriving here. It's hard to juggle work and law school. How's everything going?"

"Same as always. I'm still using the kitchen as my safety net. Your mother's just as rotten as ever — surly and mean spirited. She's living on her own bile."

"Does she ever ask about me?" Maureen asked.

"No, but she's always got her antenna up when you call." Eileen continued. "So, how's your job going at the deli?"

"That's what I called to tell you. I'm not working there anymore. I put my feelers out and it worked."

"Who'd you put your feelers out to, the bus boys?" Eileen laughed.

"No. A lot of professionals came in, especially attorneys. They'd pour over briefs with one hand, eat a pastrami sandwich with the other, and then go back to the office and work all night to prepare for court in the morning. Attorneys are notorious for letting things go 'til the last minute."

"So who finally believed you had a brain and could type?"

"An attorney named Jerome Greene. He runs a one-man office; had a secretary for twelve years who moved out of state. Put him in a real bind. He was singing the blues one night and I jumped right in; told him I used to work in a law office and I'd be glad to give it a try. He asked me when I could start. He thought I was kidding when I said, 'when do you need me?'"

'Tonight!' he said. 'You think you'll be able to type a brief for me?'

"'How brief?' I asked him."

'An all-nighter.'

"'You bet! What time and where?' Turned out to be the best thing that ever happened to me."

"So-o-o," Eileen asked coyly, changing the subject. "You dating anyone?"

"Get real. Who has time for dating? Sometimes I see the twins on weekends if I have time."

"Yeah, I've been meaning to ask you about them. How are they?"

"Well, Alberto works in a bakery on Fairfax Avenue. It's a Jewish area so now he's learning to make Danish and cheesecake instead of tortillas and churros. He loves it and they love him. He's dating an adorable little Jewish girl. She's eighteen but passes for fourteen. She just enrolled in City College. She may even convince Alberto to go back to school."

"So what does this nice little Jewish girl's family think about their daughter dating a nice little Mexican boy?"

"You know, Grandma, Alberto is so good-natured, he can win anybody over."

"Maybe you should send him to Cleveland. Your mother can use some winning over. What about his brother, what's his name?"

"Ramon," Maureen paused for a moment. "That's a different story. He's working for a guy named Mello who owns an automobile body shop."

"So what's wrong with that? Sounds good to me."

"I don't know. There's something not right about Mello. He's slippery. I have a feeling he's running an illegal operation. So far, Ramon seems to be working on cars that regular customers bring in to the shop, but Mello has hinted that he has other plans for him. Mello is very cagey about those 'other plans'."

"What do you mean?"

"I have no proof, but from what Alberto tells me, I think Mello may be running a chop shop."

"What's a chop shop?"

"It's slang for a business where people disassemble stolen automobiles and sell them as separate parts."

"So, what're you saying?" Eileen asked. "Mello steals cars and then sells the parts separately?"

"Something like that. I'm waiting for Mello to solicit Ramon to steal automobiles. Ramon is so damn cocky, he thinks he's never going to get caught no matter what he does."

"Have you mentioned this to Alberto?"

"Oh yeah! Alberto says, 'ya know what, Ramon has got to take responsibility for himself. I'm tired of gettin his nuts out of the fire.' But I know Alberto is worried. He made Ramon promise that he would tell him if Mello asked him to do anything illegal."

"Does Ramon even know what 'illegal' is?"

"I'm not sure Grandma. I gotta go . . . got some studying to do."

"Me too. Got to look after the wicked witch of Cleveland."

◇◇◇

Rosie got a call from attorney Jerome Greene the next day. He had arranged for a meeting at the premises with George Polenski two days hence. This time Greene was dressed in a charcoal grey suit, white shirt and burgundy print tie. *Very professional* Rosie thought.

Polenski, five feet five in height and girth, was put together like a cardboard box. It was hard to tell which end was up. Sparse strands of grey hair covered an otherwise bald pate. A thick black and white mustache matched his eyebrows in density and color. A heavy gold cross lay on his wiry chest hair; frayed baggy Dockers hung over scuffed sneakers brushing the floor with each step. The buttons pulled on his plaid shirt revealing a white undershirt. He drove an old Dodge which he parked in the alley behind the premises.

He greeted Rosie with a mixture of anxiety and awe, but Rosie put a smile on his face when she showed him her financial statement. Still, in all good conscience, he made an effort to advise her against it.

"I don't see a woman running a grocery store," he said. "But what do I know? It's a different world these days."

They discussed the items that needed to be taken care of prior to the opening. Greene listened carefully and took notes so that he could draw up an appropriate lease.

"You show me the plans and I'll sign. As long as it's okay with the City, it's okay with me," Amiable and smiling Polenski brushed against Rosie every chance he got. She tried to stay out of his way but he artfully maneuvered his corpulent body so that she was forced to back up, duck sideways, or otherwise shimmy past him. Greene noticed, winked at Rosie and whispered, "I think he likes you."

"Yeah," she rolled her eyes.

"When do you think you'll have the store ready to open," Polenski asked.

"I'm meeting with the architect this afternoon. It'll probably be a couple of months, maybe by Christmas if everything goes okay."

"What're you going to call your place?" George Polenski asked.

"Rosie's Gringo Palace!"

The three of them looked at each other and burst out laughing. "Good name, good name," George's belly shook with laughter. "I like it," he waved as he waddled toward his car.

"C'mon," Greene said to Rosie. "I'll take you to lunch at Davey's Deli . . . you know, the one Maureen is always touting."

"Just lead me to a pastrami sandwich; I'll be your slave."

They got into his car and drove to Alvarado Street, discussing lease points along the way and cementing the beginning of a trusting relationship. That afternoon they were meeting at Greene's office with the architect, Lorenzo Jacobs.

At two o'clock Greene and Rosie returned to his office. Maureen had just gotten there. Jerry could never quite remember her schedule although she reminded him frequently and had it posted conspicuously in various places – under his glass desk top, on the wall, and on their mutual calendar. She greeted Rosie like an old friend.

"Guess where we ate today?" Rosie asked, smiling.

"Davey's!" Maureen shrieked. "Did you at least bring me a piece of Halvah?"

"No," Rosie said. "I brought you the half of pastrami sandwich I couldn't eat."

"You darling woman!" Maureen said blowing kisses and diving into the doggie bag. "Oh, my God, I'm starving. Thank you, thank you."

"Don't mention it."

Lorenzo Jacobs poked his head in the doorway and hearing the voices and laughter said, "I think I got here at the right time. Sounds like a party . . ."

"Renzo," Greene said, holding out his hand. "It's great to see you."

"Yeah, yeah. It's been too long my friend. Too long."

Greene turned toward Maureen and Rosie to make the introductions. "Maureen's my new law partner," he joked. Jacobs looked shocked. "Well she's not exactly there yet but give it another couple of years" Greene laughed. Turning to Rosie he said, ". . . and this is the woman who needs your design expertise."

Rosie looked at Lorenzo Jacobs and lowered her eyes as she shook his hand because, otherwise, she was afraid she would just keep staring at him. 'Renzo', as Greene called him, stooped slightly, his graceful height bowing over his six foot frame. His shirt was tucked into belted blue jeans and rolled up at the wrists. He wore cowboy boots. *Randolph Scott reincarnated* Rosie thought. Probably in his mid-sixties. Long, blond-white hair was brushed back behind his ears and curled at the neckline. Slender, yet sturdy, delicate yet strong, his fingers were calloused between thumb, forefinger and middle finger, probably from holding a drafting pencil all these years, Rosie thought. It was amazing how much she noticed about him from the handshake hello to the handshake goodbye. His voice was especially interesting, mellow and deep like a bass guitar, quiet but resonant.

As Renzo followed Rosie into Jerry's office, she managed to bring herself back to the task at hand: the Gringo Palace. But she had trouble concentrating. Renzo pulled a large sketch pad out of his briefcase. She felt mesmerized by Renzo's hands as he sketched various renderings.

"Have you ever designed a grocery store?" she asked, rolling her chair closer to his and bending over to see the sketches.

"No, but after I talked to Jerry I went back to the books and also called some friends who specialize in that field. Would you prefer someone with more specific experience?"

"Oh, no, not at all." Suddenly she couldn't bear the thought of not seeing him again. She wondered what kind of fragrance he wore and moved even closer just to inhale his scent. "I'm confident you can do it." She forced herself to focus on the drawings. "I'm looking forward to working with you . . . *really*."

They talked about the placement of counters, refrigeration, lighting, flooring, shelving. Rosie recalled the layout of Grandpa's store; the memory of Joey came back to her; Joey behind the counter, laughing and joking with customers. Her heart ached for Joey.

Greene watched them for awhile. "You know what?" he smiled. "You guys don't need me for this. I'll set you up in the conference room and you can take all the time you want." They gathered their things and followed Jerry. "I'll talk to you tomorrow. Let Maureen know when you leave. She'll lock up."

CHAPTER TWENTY-THREE

DURING THE NEXT TWO months Lorenzo and Rosie spent a great deal of time together. They poured over design drawings, and Renzo took her to half a dozen 'Mom and Pop' businesses from San Diego to Ventura County.

More than once Rosie found him looking at her as she drank coffee or bit into a sandwich or used her finger to trace a change in design. He never seemed embarrassed to be caught that way, but his craggy face would light up with a smile and he'd say, "Caught me, didn't ya?"

"Well, if we put this here . . ."

"Yes, good idea, or we can combine . . ."

"One of the things I'm most worried about is how you're going to be able to sustain the pace of running that store. It's unrealistic to think you can do everything on your own. This isn't a business for a woman alone."

"Well, you're right. You're absolutely right!" They had stopped at a hotel in Newport Beach for a mid-afternoon espresso on their way from San Diego to Los Angeles. Rosie leaned back in the patio chair and crossed her legs. She contemplated the blue ocean, the white waves gently hitting the shore. She changed the subject. "Do you know how many kids in our neighborhood never saw the ocean?" she said sadly.

Lorenzo looked at her. "Yeah. There's lots of things they'll never see. And lots of things they see that they shouldn't be seeing."

"You volunteer over at the Boys and Girls Club, don't you?" Rosie asked.

"Yes."

"Is it hard? I mean, emotionally is it hard?"

"Yeah. I let them come to me. Sometimes they do but most times they hide their fears, their loneliness. At night they'll stay as late as they can, hanging back until the last light is out, the last door locked. They'd stay there all night if they could."

"What do you think is the most important thing you give them, Renzo?"

"I don't know. Hope. Encouragement. A place to shoot baskets so they can forget the beating they got the night before from their drunken father. They give me more than I give them."

"What do you mean?"

"Well, they gave me a reason to get up every morning after my wife Yetta died, but that's not the only thing."

"Yes. Jerry told me about that. I'm sorry. It's a big loss. I lost my brother Joey a few months ago. People need a reason to go on, whether you're a kid or an adult. You had a prestigious career, probably made enough money to move on, right? I'm surprised you and your wife continued to live in the area."

"I like it here. Yetta was a blue-eyed Jewish *maideleh*." He used the Yiddish term for young girl. Her parents were Polish immigrants. They came to this country like a lot of others to escape the pogroms. What about your family?"

"My father was a Russian Jew. He died when I was just an infant. My grandparents took my mother and her five children in to live with them. They owned a grocery store."

"Ahh, so that's why. . ."

"Yes, I know a lot about the business. I feel like I'm fulfilling a legacy. I cut my first teeth on a crust of rye bread."

Lorenzo laughed. "It's a great neighborhood, but they're very suspicious of newcomers so don't expect to make millions your first year in the Gringo Palace."

Rosie looked at him. He had trouble picking up the small cup with his long fingers. "You ever had espresso before?"

"Sure. You?"

"Never!" They burst out laughing.

"I don't want to leave this place," she said. "It's so beautiful here. The ocean, the beach. I just want to dig my toes in the warm sand."

"We don't have to leave right now, you know." He took her hand across the table.

She blushed, reading the look in his eyes. "It's been quite awhile."

"For me too," he said, getting up. "Finish your drink I'll be back in a few minutes."

She didn't say anything but as he was leaving she gulped down the remainder of her drink and shouted after him: "I think I'll need another."

"Me too!"

They walked hand in hand up to the room. He had ordered a bottle of champagne which he now poured into slender crystal glasses. They clinked glasses and walked to the balcony. He slipped his arm around her waist and, circling lower, he pressed her to him. Their first kiss had been slow, just a touch of softness; then, a little deeper, mouths opening slightly, a taste of sparkle lingering on the flicker of a tongue. His hands moved haltingly as he waited for her response. She slid her hands under his shirt, caressing his back and moving to his chest. He pulled his shirt off and she brought his nipples to her lips, first one side, then the other. She didn't remember taking off her shirt, her bra, falling over each other as they unbuttoned their pants and tried to remove them. They staggered to the bed, their hands sliding in and out and around each other as their passion surfaced. Wheezing, gasping for breath, they reached the finale, screaming with laughter and relief, Rosie moaning about a cramp in her leg, Renzo trying to disengage the sheet which was sandwiched between his thigh and hers.

Afterward, Rosie stood on the balcony and looked out at the wide expanse of horizon. A few sailboats slid by. Gulls pecked away at unseen objects in the sand. Renzo thought, *how could I be so lucky to find another love like this?*

◇◇◇

On the way home, they continued their conversation of three hours ago.

"So, Rosie . . . you never answered my question. How are you going to run the Palace on your own?"

"Here's what I've been thinking: I don't need this to be the normal kind of grocery store. I've decided I'm going to keep banker's hours."

"What do you mean, 'banker's hours?'"

"Look, who's to say I have to be open a certain number of hours? Just because other groceries are open seven days a week doesn't mean I have to do the same, does it? It's not like I'm trying to compete with anyone. This is *Rosie's Gringo Palace*. I want it to be more than a grocery store."

"What do you want it to be?"

"Remember what you said about the kids at the Boys and Girls Club giving you more than you gave them? You know how you feel when you think you've given a kid a reason to come back? How sometimes you see an awakening in a kid's eyes . . . like he's thinking 'maybe I can do better?' Well that's what I want to do. I want to make people aware that they can do better. I looked for that when I was teaching and every so often, there it was — the kid that finally *got it!*"

"Rosie, get real. Look around. There's graffiti everywhere, kids are dropping out of school, drug deals are made on every corner, the Catholic Church preaches abstinence in direct proportion to the rise in pregnancies of teenage girls, and the unemployment rate is sky high. You want me to go on? The stores that do the most business, the ones that are making mucho profits, are the two liquor stores across from each other and around the corner from the Gringo Palace. And you think you can change this?"

"Maybe. I think this is different."

"Why?"

"Because here I may be able to directly influence the parents. That's where it begins."

Lorenzo glanced sidewise at her. "Who do you think your customer base is going to be, the kids or the parents?

"Hopefully the parents, and especially the women. They're the ones I'm counting on. They don't seem to have any direction. I mean, they walk the streets daily, their kids hanging on to them, just trying to kill time, engrossed in the moment and unable to project beyond it. The only way they can think to be more productive is to have more kids. They've been here forever but they don't speak English. . ."

"Sounds like you're being judgmental," Lorenzo interrupted.

"No — I don't mean it to sound that way at all. I know what they're up against. I come from that kind of neighborhood. They're wonderful people. They just need a new perspective. They need to think 'outside the box.'"

"That's a corporate expression. I don't think they'll understand that concept." He moved easily in and out of traffic.

"Well, now who's sounding judgmental?" Rosie retorted.

"Okay, touché!" They were silent for awhile. "Do you have any idea how the hell you're going to do this?" he asked.

"Not in the least," she laughed.

"Okay." He took her hand and squeezed it. "Whatever you do, I'm in!"

CHAPTER TWENTY-FOUR

ANARPOL AYALA'S FRIENDS CALLED him Chicory. From the time he was a toddler, his color of preference was black. His clothes were black; his early childhood drawings were black; his mood was usually black. The nickname *Chicory* came from a long-forgotten source - a mother whose amniotic fluid was so laden with alcohol that her son was born drunk. She left him on the doorstep of an unsuspecting distant relative with a promise to return *as soon as I get my life straightened out, baby.* He had to hang on to something so he conjured up a memory of someone holding him close, saying *my sweet baby, forgive me for not being able to take care of you; my son with the coffee eyes and black curly hair; Mommy will come back to get her little Chicory!* So that's how it was.

Shuffled from relative to relative, none of whom had the wherewithal or desire to care for him, Social Services took over and, without malice aforethought, sent him to one foster home after another where he paid for the sins of his mother and learned about the sins of humanity. Still, each time they moved him he'd ask: "Will my Momma know where I am when she comes for me?"

At eight years old, thin and wiry, undernourished and hyper, he now lived with his Aunt Rita Davidson in a low rental garden project. She was the third relative he had been 'banished' to; Social Services had dug really deep to find her. Surprised as hell when they tracked her down, Rita looked hard at Anarpol to find a familiar family trait.

"You sure this puny kid belongs to my family? Why, he ain't even the same color as me. He too light to be . . . He what? . . . His mama did it with a what? I don' remember nobody in our family named Ayala. Stand up, boy," Rita said. "What kinda name is Anarpol?" She confronted Chicory and then questioned the social services rep.

"That's what was found on him; a birth certificate with the name Anarpol Ayala, mother's name Georgia James, father John Doe." The social worker had dark circles under her eyes and a pile of folders on her desk that would take a month to go through. *Twelve years to retirement. I don't think I'll make it,* she thought.

"Well, now you talkin. James. James," Rita repeated, tapping her forehead. "That's different. Maybe I 'member someone's kid named Georgia James from way back in the fambly. Lemme see them papers. You say his mama's gone? Well, what about his daddy? Never been one you could find, huh? This boy say his name Chicory, not Anarpol. What kinda name is Chicory? Not as I blame him. Chicory be much better than Anarpol . . . And how much you say you payin' for him every month?"

Aunt Rita was in her thirties, medium dark skin with big boobs and a big ass and a lot of hair. She was forty pounds overweight and loved every inch of herself. She'd been married twice. Her boyfriend Reggie Wallace, a gambler, drinker and womanizer had moved in with her six months ago. Reggie had two things going for him: a big dick and a steady job. Rita worked part time at a discount women's clothing store. Chicory was left alone a lot.

Occasionally she took him shopping with her. By the time they got home he'd have his pockets full of candy or some other fanciful items that an eight-year-old is attracted to. Aunt Rita observed this and said nothing. In fact, she took pride in his ability to *steal from da man.* But then she worried: *Lordy, jes a little more experience and I be visitin him in juv'nile detention or jail, and dere go my extra income.* So one afternoon she unexpectedly grabbed him by his scrawny arm and threw him down hard on a kitchen chair.

"Empty your pockets," she screamed. She watched as his thin little arms pulled candy, gum and a whistle out of his pockets and laid them on the table. "Look at this crap! Only eight and already you be a criminal heading straight to prison or hell." She put her angry face against his. "But what're you stealin"? She slapped him hard. "Shit stuff, that's what. It ain't like you stealin' something worthwhile, somethin' you can be proud of."

He was whimpering and his cheek stung; he didn't understand why she was so angry. She'd seen him steal before and never said anything. Now, Rita showed repentance for the slap.

"Stop your bawlin and come on over here and give your aunt Rita a kiss." She sat facing him. She slid to the front of the chair, opened her legs and let him stand between them.

"Here, baby, Aunt Rita's not mad at you anymore. We can forget all that and you can make me happy. C'mere. Yeah, like that. Stand in front of me and give me a big hug."

She held him close and took his small hand and put it between her legs. He felt the warmth and softness and tried to pull away. "No, no honey. It just hurts a little and your hand is gonna make it all better. That's right honey, just move your hand around a little." She pulled her panties aside and maneuvered his hand back and forth. "There you go, that's the way. Oh, yeah, Aunt Rita likes that a lot." She brought his ear close to her mouth. "It's okay, sweetie. Yes-s-s, that's the way, that's real nice. When I breathe hard like this it means I like what you're doing. Yeah, this is real nice," she moved forward. "You like it don't ya?" She answered for him. "Yeah, I knew you would. We can do this a lot, you and me."

Chicory's small body trembled with fear and revulsion. His stomach tightened and he was on the verge of vomiting; he felt that first drop of uncontrolled urine in his pants. He worried that if he put his hand there it would get suctioned in and never come out. And he was fearful he'd give Aunt Rita a baby.

That night at dinner he wanted to ask Reggie whether putting your hand down there could give a woman a baby. But he didn't ask because he was afraid of the answer. And also Aunt Rita had said this was special, *just between you and me, baby.* He'd heard the older boys talk about pussy at school. He wondered if this was what they meant. They'd know. They were nine and ten year olds.

◇◇◇

At fifteen, Chicory and Aunt Rita had an arrangement. He gave her what she needed and she kept a roof over his head. As long as he fucked her she wouldn't put him out. She was his *ho*. In fact, all women were *ho's*, only good for fucking and taking care of their man.

As the years passed his anger smoldered, revealing itself more frequently in short bursts of groundless violence. After a particular outburst he'd ask himself *why*, but he couldn't answer the question. He had a good life didn't he? Better than some. At least no drunken bastard beat him up every night like some of his friends.

After school Chicory and his gang gathered around the music store for their daily bout of bullshit. The build-out of ROSIE'S GRINGO PALACE was the foremost topic of conversation. It took precedence over previous discussions which included gang activity in other communities, so-and-so's mother's late night visitors, which high school girl was putting out, music rappers, the current drug of choice, and who was dealing. Smoking and dice were their entertainment. Their own personal exploits took up a good amount of time.

"Yeah, I remember when . . ."

". . . she gave it up to me right then and there."

". . . my mama just dropped me off — never came back."

They were family; still, some things were too painful or shameful to reveal. However, through emotional means or actual physical evidence, each kid was aware of another kid's problem, like whose father beat whose mother, which of them never had a father, whose father had a pregnant girlfriend, whose mother was dying of breast cancer, whose father lost his job. They never talked about how lonely they were, how scared, their lack of confidence, or their personal abuse and degradation.

"Ya ever get down in the dumps?" one of them asked. "Ya know, sad?"

"What the hell kinda question is that? What I got to be sad about?"

"Jus askin, jus askin. I don't worry 'bout that neither," one of them answered.

Hector, one of Chicory's boys, paced back and forth in front of his friends. He had just applied for a warehouse job but couldn't fill out the application because he couldn't read it. He scratched his crotch and hitched his pants up, like a cowboy getting ready for a gun fight. "What the fuck? They think I can't do some fuckin job lifting boxes and loading trucks? Bunch o' shitheads. Just 'cause I can't read good don mean I can't do the job. It don't pay nothin anyway," he muttered, spitting on the sidewalk. "You offer me a good job and I'll take it any time, but ain't no good jobs waitin for me. They don' know how good I am . . . what they're missin." He threw his hands up and lit another cigarette. "You just can't win. Makes no sense to me, you gotta read to load boxes," he mumbled, angry and frustrated.

No way would Chicory tell his boys what he had to do to keep a roof over his head. One of the boys was beat up regularly by his father; one of the boys had a ten year old sister with Down's Syndrome whose family was embarrassed because she was still in diapers. They never took her out. The women felt powerless; they cowered under the oppression of cultural mores. What could they do? There was no money. They couldn't read, couldn't even speak English. "So, what can we do?" they asked each other.

Chicory and four other boys slouched against the brick façade of the building. Marty Ramirez, Jr. was one of them. Marty was raised in a normal environment — working parents and grandparents that all lived together; a nice kid that didn't really fit in as a gang member. His family had confidence he would come to that conclusion on his own

"Hey, Marty, you know this Rosie who's puttin up that store?"

"Yeah, what of it?" Marty moved away from the building. Feeling trapped by the question because of the relationship between his grandmother, Clara, and Rosie, he didn't answer immediately but took a lighter from his T-shirt pocket, flipped it open and lit a cigarette. "She taught high school with my grandmother in New York."

"So maybe you can tell me, what the fuck is the Gringo Palace? We don need no gringos coming into our turf."

Marty had to be careful how he answered. "It's just a grocery. No one's gonna do business with her anyway. She'll probably have to close the store a month after she opens it. Chicory, why are you so nervous, man?

Chicory gave him a hard look. The other boys kept their eyes averted. "Marty, when I'm nervous, you'll be the first to know." Chicory pointed his finger and poked it at Marty stopping just short of touching him. "You stickin up for her?"

"No, man. I'm just saying, let it go for now. See how it plays out."

The boys looked uncomfortable but no one said anything. When Chicory got like this it was best not to contradict him. But he managed to get the last words in: "Yeah, well, ya know what? If she don close the store on her own, maybe we can help her a little, huh?" he smiled.

PART THREE
LOS ANGELES, FALL, 1974

CHAPTER TWENTY-FIVE

UNDER LORENZO'S SUPERVISION THE Palace began to establish its image in the community. His relationship with Rosie deepened and he suggested they live together.

"I have to open the Palace first," she said.

They got into face-to- face combat squabbling over safety versus décor and practicality. Sometimes she would give in, sometimes he would.

And in all of this bickering they learned more about each other.

"You're late," he said, looking at his watch.

"You said twelve-thirty."

"I know, but it's twelve-thirty-five."

"What time did you get here?" she asked, raising her eyebrows.

"Twelve fifteen."

"So, if I understand you correctly, I'm late because I didn't get here early."

"Exactly," he said. "You see, if we lived together we wouldn't be having this discussion."

She laughed, he scowled, but they both stood as close to each other as they could while poring through the plans yet one more time. They began to take personal liberties with each other, little criticisms that went hand in hand with their intimacy.

"You need a haircut," she said.

"Why?"

"You look like a sixty-five year old flower child. All you need is an earring and a guitar."

"I already have a guitar," he grinned. "Want to come up and listen tonight?"

"Are you cooking?" she glanced at him sidewise.

"My specialty is bacon and eggs."

". . . but that's breakfast!" She swiped at him with a newspaper.

"I know," he smirked.

And so it went. Amidst the noisy disharmony of hammer and nails and ringing telephones they continued their teasing and petty arguments. Rosie's friend Clara came by every day. Maureen stopped in from time to time before reporting for work. Slowly the Gringo Palace took shape. Chicory strutted by nonchalantly with his small gang in tow. He waited.

◇◇◇

The twins shared a one-bedroom apartment on a side street in a less hospitable area of Hollywood. Alberto worked at a Jewish bakery on Fairfax Avenue. They hesitated to hire him because his previous experience had been in a Mexican bakery, but his personality prevailed.

Ramon's boss, Charlie Mello helped both of them find used automobiles. Neither twin questioned Mello's source. Their mother, Hortencia, was solicited for the down payments.

"You're calling me for money? I am choking on my tortilla," she sputtered. "First you send me money, now you ask for money. *Donde esta el dinero que me promististe?*

". . .well, we've only been here . . ."

"Every day I look in the mail for the money. Then, when the money is not in the mail I listen for the doorbell and I am thinking, maybe this is the man on television who gives a million dollar check to the lady in the apron. She is so surprised, she is screaming and crying; they are showing her the check and she is smiling in front of the camera. *Te diga mijo*, when the doorbell rings, I run to put on my apron and I pinch my cheeks for color, just in case."

"Mama you don't need to pinch your cheeks. You will always be beautiful — unless you got ugly since we left," he teased.

"Oh, Alberto, don give me your bullshit. I am still beautiful, don worry," she patted her hair and sat down heavily on a dining room chair.

"Anyway, Mama, if you want a million dollars from Reader's Digest or some other magazine, you have to enter their contest."

"*Hay un concurso?* A contest?" she asked, surprised.

"*Si* Mama, ask Henry to explain the contest to you if you are still seeing him."

"What do you mean, 'if I am still seeing him'?" You think he would leave me? I am the best thing that ever happen to him."

"Mama, you are the best thing that ever happened to us, too."

She sent them the money.

CHAPTER TWENTY-SIX

MAUREEN WELCOMED SUNDAY MORNING and was excited about meeting Rosie at Davey's Deli. Although Davey's had a reputation as the best Jewish delicatessen far and wide, the Sunday morning crowd was primarily Latino. Despite this mostly Catholic contingency, lox and bagels were still the main choice for breakfast.

Because of Ramon's sexual advances at Lui Chu's house when they had first arrived in Los Angeles, Maureen was careful to include Alberto whenever they got together. She didn't want to give Ramon any reason or opportunity to speak of that incident or to pursue his feelings for her. Yet, despite her resolve, her heartbeat quickened when she saw him. Ramon, afraid to risk never seeing her again, also hid his innermost feelings. He had never mentioned anything to Alberto about that evening.

On the way to the restaurant Maureen told them about her new job with attorney Jerome Greene. She spoke of her studies and how demanding her schedule was between work and school. She turned to Ramon.

"How's your job with Charlie Mello?"

"Ya know, he's hardly ever there. He has something else going for him but I haven't figured it out yet. Like, he thinks nothin about calling me two in the morning to tell me a customer's car gotta be ready by nine. I don't ask no questions. I just get my ass down there."

"You mean you go to work at two in the morning?"

"Hell, yeah! For the kinda dough he pays me, I'd go back to the Bronx."

"So what're you saying? The customer can't wait to have his car fixed during normal hours?" Maureen looked at him across the table. "Doesn't that sound weird to you?"

"I guess. But, hey, it ain't none of my business. I don't ask and I don't care . . . long's I get paid, I'm good."

"I keep tellin him," Alberto said. "There's something fishy . . ."

Conversation lapsed as they approached Davey's and looked for a parking space. Ramon lit a cigarette. It reminded her of when they were traveling across country.

The place was jammed, but the waitress knew Maureen so they were seated almost immediately. Coffee was ordered all around. Maureen smiled at Alberto as she unwrapped three pink sugar packets. "So how come you didn't bring your *yiddisha maideleh*," she asked.

"She wanted to come but she's studying for an exam."

"Boy, do I empathize with that! I'll be doing the same thing this afternoon. What's her name?"

"Annie. Annie Robbins. Used to be Rabinsky."

"I don't hear wedding bells, do I?" Maureen teased.

"C'mon, I'm still a baby."

"Some baby!" Maureen laughed. "So how about you, Ramon? Got any girlfriends?"

"A few," he said quietly, looking directly at Maureen. "But I'm saving myself for my one true love."

Maureen blushed and then spotted Rosie at the front entrance and waved. "Oh, there's my friend, Rosie."

The twins looked up. "Rosie!" They shouted her name at the same time.

Rosie walked toward them. They flew out of their chairs, Ramon's chair sliding backwards banging into the table behind him and Alberto's chair almost tipping over. "Jesus! Rosie!" they shouted.

Maureen's eyes widened. "What the hell . . ."

"Ramon! Alberto!" Rosie shrieked. "Oh, my God! I can't believe this." They hugged and kissed her and lifted her off her feet, happy to see someone they knew from the Bronx. They hadn't realized how lonely they were for the old neighborhood, for their mother, Hortencia, for *Ramrod* and their friends.

"You guys know each other?" Maureen was confused.

When they settled down, laughing and shaking their heads at what a small world it was, they brought Maureen into the sequence of events.

"Do you remember when Lui told us we'd need three hundred dollars to get across country?"

"Of course. It was an insane ride from *Ramrod* to the Bronx. Alberto was in a daze from his fight with Paul. The police were practically on our tail."

"Well who do you think gave us the money?" Ramon said, smiling. "Rosie?"

Rosie nodded. "I'm still not sure why I trusted these bozos. But they paid me back, with plenty extra. Just goes to show, sometimes you have to trust your instinct."

"What a night!" Maureen said.

"So, Rosie, whatcha been up to," Alberto asked.

She told the twins about the Gringo Palace.

"You gotta be out of your mind. How you gonna do this?"

"I don't know. We'll see."

"You ain't gonna make no money, that's for sure," Ramon commented.

"If I make enough to pay the rent, that'll work for me. Hey, you want to see the place? They're working today. I'm sure my friend Lorenzo is running everybody ragged. I'll introduce you."

"You bet. I'm dyin to see it," Alberto said.

Rosie took a moment to look at them, all talking at once, reminiscing about the Bronx, laughing and patting each other on the back. *This is family* she thought . . . *warm, loving.* She sensed Joey's arms around her. *This is good, Rosie. This is real good,* she heard him say.

As they parked their cars at the Gringo Palace, Ramon noticed Chicory and a few of his honchos standing nearby. They were passing around a joint. "Who are those kids?" Ramon asked.

"They're usually at the music store around the corner, but now they may have a new hangout." Maureen sounded worried.

One of the boys was Clara's grandson, Marty. "Hi, Marty," Rosie waved. He nodded and Rosie proceeded into the store. Chicory gave Marty an angry look and was about to make a nasty comment but suddenly Ramon stood right in front of him, his eyes narrowing as he and Chicory looked each other over. If Chicory was unsure of himself he didn't show it. His eyes said *you don't scare me* but his head said *who is this mother fucker?*

Ramon's six-foot-four frame towered over Chicory. "I know you, don't I?"

"I don't think I had the pleasure," Chicory said sarcastically, drawing slowly on his joint, pinching the end with his thumb and forefinger and putting the roach in his T-shirt pocket. His boys snickered. Marty turned away.

"Oh, yeah. I know you alright. I met up with assholes like you in New York a few times."

"I ain't never . . ." Chicory started to say.

Just then Alberto called to Ramon. "Hey, what're ya doin'? You gotta see this. This is really somethin."

"Find another place to hang out," Ramon said quietly as he walked toward the Palace. He turned back momentarily and looked again at Chicory.

"I don't want us to ever meet again. You get it?"

Chicory could hardly wait to take up the challenge. Under his breath, "Maybe you're the one that's gonna get it! Not now mother fucker, but later."

CHAPTER TWENTY-SEVEN

WHEN THE TWINS RETURNED home there was a message from Lui Chu.

"Ramon, I gotta see you right away. Give me a call when you get in. It's really important."

The twins had picked up a Sunday paper and were looking forward to watching football and reading the sports page. "Jeez, last thing I want to do is talk to Lui right now."

"So don't call him."

"Yeah. Good idea." He removed his Levi jacket, threw it over a chair and clicked the TV to a sports station. *New York Giants vs. Washington Redskins.* Great! He pulled a beer from the refrigerator and settled into an easy chair, his long legs stretched out in front of him.

The small apartment came furnished. It sat in a courtyard of bungalows reminiscent of old Hollywood where would-be stars were often photographed going to and from MGM studios. Although the courtyard was not well maintained, it still suggested the nostalgia and history of a more glamorous era. It was certainly different than anything the twins had ever imagined when they lived in the Bronx. It was the closest they'd ever come to owning their own private home; it even had a back yard. No more harassment from Mama; no more rules. They were feeling their first euphoria of adulthood.

"I can't believe we caught up with Rosie. Were you as surprised as I was that she and Maureen knew each other?"

"Like they say, 'small world.'" Alberto removed his shoes and socks, sighing with relief as his bare feet hit the floor. "Rosie looks terrific."

"Yeah. But once she starts working the Gringo Palace she's going to get tired real fast."

"Maybe she can find someone in the neighborhood to help her."

"U-m-m, maybe."

"Did you see that group of kids hanging around?" Ramon asked.

"Kinda. But I didn't pay much attention."

"Well, there's one kid, Chicory. I had a little conversation with him when all of you were going into the store."

"So?"

"So, he's a real smart-ass. I think he's planning to give Rosie trouble. Also, you know Rosie's friend, Clara?"

"Yeah, what about her?"

"Her grandson Marty was there, hanging with these kids. They were passing a joint around."

"That ain't good." Alberto said. ". . .guess we'll have to keep an eye on things."

"I hope I'm wrong, Alberto." Ramon lay back and closed his eyes. He dozed on and off, watching the game in-between, cursing when he disagreed with the referee's call.

The phone jolted him awake an hour later. It was Lui.

"Hey, man, why didn't you call me back?" he snapped.

"Take it easy Lui. Don't have a heart attack. We just walked in. I was about to call you. What's up?"

"I'm in deep shit, that's what's up! We need to talk, man."

"So talk," Ramon said.

"Not over the phone. We gotta meet."

"Okay, how about I meet you tomorrow after work?"

"Jesus, Ramon. Ain't you hearin me man? We gotta meet — right now!"

"Now?" Ramon asked. "Cryin out loud. It's Sunday," Ramon said, pissed off.

"Don't ya think I know it's Sunday. I'm tellin you, Ramon. We gotta meet right now," Lui's voice escalated. "It's a matter of life and death." He sounded desperate. "You owe me!"

"Hey, asshole, I don't owe you nothin."

"Okay, okay. I'm just asking you. I'm putting a please on the end of it."

Ramon looked over at Alberto who had been listening to the conversation and was now shaking his head, *NO!* Ramon shrugged, rolled his eyes, and mouthed the words *have to.* "Okay," Ramon said. "Where? Good . . . Okay, half an hour."

"What could I do?" Ramon held his hands out. "The guy sounded desperate," he said before Alberto could come down on him. "Maybe he's right. Maybe I owe him something."

"You don't owe him shit. This whole business with Lui and Charlie Mello. It just don't sound right."

"Are you seein something I don't see?"

"Not yet. But I don't trust Lui. He's a sleazebag. I don't want him pulling you into something you can't handle."

"Hey, bro. Don't underestimate me." Ramon got defensive. "I can take care of myself good as you can."

"Yeah, yeah. I know. Just be careful, okay. I'll see you in a couple of hours." He walked Ramon to the door.

"Aren't you seeing your little Jew girl tonight?"

"Ramon . . ." Alberto warned.

"Okay, don't get your ass twitching. Whaddya say I pick up a couple of rib eye steaks and we'll watch 60 Minutes together like an old married couple," he laughed. "I'll have this little conference with Lui and be home in no time."

◇◇◇

When Ramon didn't show by six o'clock, Alberto started to worry. By eight o'clock he was frantic. He called Lui Chu's house.

"Yeah we met, but I left him a couple of hours ago. No, I have no idea where he is," Lui said.

"You're lying, you son-of-a-bitch. Anything happens to Ramon, you're finished."

"Hey, calm down, *amigo*. He probably met someone . . ."

"What was the big rush you had to see him today?" Alberto raised his voice.

"Yeah, well my brother Sam and me — we had a little disagreement and he was tellin me to get out. You know how it is sometimes between brothers, right?"

"So how come you're still at your brother's house, huh?" Alberto paced back and forth on the kitchen floor, feeling its stickiness and thinking, jeez we gotta mop this floor. "You're lyin. I know you're lyin."

"Hey, man. You don't believe me, call the police and file a missing person report," Lui said sarcastically.

"What's Charlie Mello's number?"

"Why you wanna bother Mello? It's Sunday night. Don't worry so much about Ramon. He can take care of himself."

"Give me Mello's number, you cock-sucking bag of sh . . ." The phone went dead before he could finish his sentence.

◇◇◇

Rosie was still on a high after having spent time with Ramon and Alberto at the Deli. She brought the leftovers home for dinner with Senora Saenz.

Rosie grabbed a couple of plates from the cupboard and spread the paper wrapped corned beef, rye bread and potato pancakes on the small table. "So, did you have a chance to talk to your kids?"

"Si. I called them." Calista got a couple of forks and napkins. "What is this?" she asked.

"Oh, I brought us a few potato pancakes."

"Potato pancakes? *Que es* potato pancakes?"

"Believe me, they're addictive. Just add a dab of sour cream and applesauce, like this." Rosie put some on her potatoes. "Well . . . what did they say?"

"What did who say?" Calista concentrated on the pancakes "Ay! These are good!"

"Your kids? What did they say about me renting the house from you?"

"Oh, that." Calista got up and put some water in the kettle for tea. "They are worried."

"What about?"

"There is one little thing I didn't tell you," Calista said as she searched the cupboard for the teabags. "Actually there are two little things." She pulled out a kitchen chair.

Rosie looked up as she was taking a bite of her sandwich. "Uh oh. Spit it out."

"First of all — I didn't want to tell you before," Calista hesitated. "I have diabetes and . . ."

"Oh, no, Calista. That's not such a little thing," Rosie said.

"I know. But that is not the real reason my children want me to sell the house. The real reason is that my son wants to buy a few acres of land to expand his vineyard — and they need the money from the house."

"But this is your nest egg!" Rosie bent over to pick her napkin up from the floor.

"Nest egg? What is 'nest egg?'"

"A nest egg is an asset that you have that sees you through hard times, or old age, or emergencies."

Calista mulled over Rosie's explanation. "No, Rosie, I don't think you understand. My son is, how you say, my 'nest egg'. *Mi hijo es mi familia, mi vida.*" Calista dabbed at her eyes with her napkin, looking for a corner that did not have mustard and ketchup on it. "My son, not this house, will see me through hard times and old age and emergencies."

Rosie looked into Calista's eyes and took her hand. "Calista, you're absolutely right. You're a very lucky woman to have such a loving family."

"You have no children, no family?"

"No. My husband died too soon. I had my brother Joey. He died a few months ago and I decided I had to make a change in my life. So, here I am, for better or worse."

"Oh, Rosie, I think it is for better. Here you have friends. Sometimes friends are as good as family and maybe even better."

"Yes. Look at you and me." They smiled at each other. Rosie told her about meeting Ramon and Alberto and about the Gringo Palace. The sadness of the previous conversation passed and the two women laughed as they cleared the table and discussed the possibility that Rosie might buy the house.

CHAPTER TWENTY-EIGHT

ALBERTO DIDN'T KNOW WHAT to do. He couldn't call the police and he wouldn't leave the house for fear he'd miss Ramon. He knew in his gut that Lui and Charlie Mello had something to do with this. Finally he called Maureen.

"Hey, perfect timing. I was about to take a break."

"Maureen," Alberto interrupted. "I think something terrible . . ." he broke off, choking up.

"What is it?" Her hand tightened on the receiver.

"Ramon . . ."

Maureen gasped. "What?" she screamed. "He's not dead is he?" She held her breath. She felt Alberto's fear, pictured him doubled over, filled with pain.

"He left."

"What do you mean, 'he left'?"

"Lui had some sort of emergency. Ramon went to meet him. He said he'd be home in a couple of hours. It's nine o'clock and he's still not home."

"Did you call . . . ?"

"Yeah, I called Lui at home soon as it got dark. He gave me some stupid reason he had to see Ramon . . . said he had a fight with his brother. I didn't know what the hell he was talkin' about. But he said he left Ramon a couple hours ago."

"Well, you think maybe Ramon ran into someone? It's still early, you know."

"He would've called. I know Ramon. He said he was going to pick up some steaks for dinner. He knew I was waiting for him. He would've called."

"Listen, it's only been a few hours. I don't think there's anything to worry about. But, I'm coming over." She closed her book and reached into the closet for a clean T-shirt.

"Okay, Maureen. Thanks, thanks." Alberto's voice broke.

"I'll be there in fifteen," she said.

◇◇◇

Ramon lit a cigarette and ordered a cup of coffee as he waited for Lui. The coffee shop was only a few blocks from the body shop and Ramon knew it well. Usually packed with breakfast and lunch customers, on this Sunday afternoon the place was almost empty. *Everybody's watching the ball game, except me! Damn Lui.* He picked at his cuticles and bit the edge of a nail. Finally, through the window, Ramon watched as Lui parked his red Impala.

Lui's eyes were red and puffy like he'd been up all night. He wore a faded blue cotton pull-over, over his designer jeans. His shoulder twitched as he slid into the booth.

"This better be good," Ramon said.

"You seen today's paper?"

"Yeah. What about it?" Ramon asked. The waitress came over. Lui ordered coffee, black.

"You seen the front page?"

"Yeah. They had a whole article on quarterback Sonny . . ."

"What're you talkin' about? I mean the *front page* asshole, not the sports page."

"Nah. I never read anything 'cept the sports section. Why? What was on the front page?"

Lui looked down. His hands cupped the coffee mug. When he looked up again, Ramon thought he saw fear in his eyes.

"Listen. I'm gonna tell you something. You'd find out sooner or later, but I guess it has to be now." Lui looked around. No one was within hearing distance. "Mello runs a little business on the side." He rolled and unrolled his napkin, his hands in continuous movement scratching his nose, folding his arms, cracking his knuckles. Ramon was all ears now.

"So, on today's front page," Lui continued, "there was a little section that said 'Underworld Kingpin's Car Stolen. See pg.8.'

Ramon had a blank look on his face. "So? What's that have to do with anything? I think it's kind of funny. Here's this guy always stealin from everyone, now he gets a little payback."

"Were you born yesterday or somethin?" Lui interrupted. "A well-known criminal had his car stolen." Lui put his hand alongside his mouth and whispered. "You think that's something to laugh about? Fuck. Who do you think stole that car?"

"How the hell would I know?" Ramon paused. "Not you, I hope." Ramon's elbows were on the table now, his face leaning forward to meet Lui's. He was beginning to get the picture. "Okay, let's go back a few minutes. Ya wanna tell me what Mello's little side business is?"

Lui hung back. Finally, he muttered under his breath. "He runs a chop shop." He wiped his sweaty hands on his jeans.

Ramon looked at him. "Shit! I been working for this guy several months and now you decide to tell me my ass could wind up in jail?"

"No, no. I swear! The work you do for him is legit. Honest. He's had that body shop eighteen years. Everybody knows him. Nobody knows about the other thing."

"So, I still don't know where you're going with this or why I'm here." Ramon made a move to leave.

"Okay, listen. For starters, I didn't steal that car. But I'm like a scout for Mello." Lui talked fast. "For every car that comes into Mello's shop, I get a commission. Mello gives me the order, I find the car and I find the guys to do the job. But last night my usual man stands me up at the last minute . . . calls me and says he ain't available. Suddenly I'm in a bind, right? I figure maybe to call you, but I don't think you're ready, and besides, I'm a friend, right?"

"Yeah, right!"

"So I'm thinkin, who can I call? And I finally think of this scumbag who's done a couple jobs for me. He says yeah, he can use the money. So I give him the lowdown on the car, a 1970 white Mercedes-Benz S 600, beautiful job with a gorgeous tan interior. I tell the guy where to find it."

"Get to the point Lui. Who'd you steal the car from?"

"The guy's name is Willie . . . it don't matter what his last name is. It's in the paper. Just read the damn article. The police call him

Maestro because he orchestrates most of the drug runs. They got a list on him as long as a porno star's cock. He's not a nice guy."

"Where was the car?"

"Well, here's the beauty of it," Luis's eyes glinted with excitement. "I have this girlfriend, see, lives on Beethoven Street in Venice. I'm there a couple times a week and all of a sudden, last few weeks I'm noticing this Mercedes a few doors down. So, I'm interested, right? Come to find out whoever owns that Mercedes also has a little cherry he's giving his banana to." For a few minutes Lui became so engrossed in the successful theft of the car, he forgot to be scared shitless. He couldn't restrain his pride in having pulled this off.

"Ya know, Lui, I wanna hear the rest of your story, but I'm outta here." Ramon slid toward the outside of the booth.

"Hold on. I'm getting to it."

"Getting to what? Whaddya need me for?"

"Well, here's the thing. This guy I told you about who stole the car?"

"Yeah?"

"He delivers the car to Mello's little side business, like we planned. Mello pays him and the guy is gone before he even finishes counting his money. Mello has plenty of time after the guy leaves to take a good look at this gorgeous automobile. And he's drooling because he's got ten buyers he could call right now that would pay a premium to have this gem."

"So, happy ending," Ramon said. "Everybody makes a buck. You get your commission. Your guy gets his money. Mello makes a handsome profit. What's the catch?"

"Well, when Mello inspects the car he realizes this wasn't stolen from some rich shnook who lives in Beverly Hills. This is a car that's well-known because of its owner. See, every time Willie Hooker gets his name in the paper, his automobile is mentioned along with him. The car has as much notoriety as Willie. Suddenly Mello says, 'Call your guy, and have him return the car from where it was stolen.'"

Ramon was shaking his head. "This is unbelievable. He's already got the car. Why not keep the fucking thing?"

"Charlie thinks there may be drugs in the car. He's paranoid that one way or another Hooker will find out where the car is and blow his head off. 'Get this fucking car out of here,' he says. 'You got 'til tomorrow morning.' So, naturally, I call my guy again because now I want him to return the car." Lui hesitated. "Okay." Lui took a deep breath. "You want to know why you're here?"

"I can't wait," Ramon said.

"I can't get hold of my guy. For all I know he's in the Himalayas. I been calling and calling . . . no answer. Bottom line is, I need you to return the car to Beethoven Street. That's it!" Lui let out a sigh of relief. He wiped his forehead with his napkin. "That's it!" he repeated.

Ramon leaned back and felt the coolness of the vinyl booth through his T-shirt. "I gotta think about this."

Lui waited for his answer, tapping his foot, signaling the waitress for more coffee.

"Why the hell don't *you* take the car back?"

"Listen, Ramon, there's no way I could do it. I'm a fuck-up, big time. I get too nervous. You can see — look at me. I'm a mess just talkin about this."

"I don't know." Ramon closed his eyes again. "This is big, Lui, real big." Finally, he said, "What's in it for me?"

"Enough for a down payment on a small house."

Ramon opened his eyes. "In cash, the money up front, right?"

"You got it," Lui smiled, putting his cigarette out in the coffee cup.

◇◇◇

What the hell am I getting into, Ramon thought. *There's only one way to handle this without getting my head shot off. It's risky, but what've I got to lose except my life? First I'll call Willie Hooker and just talk to him, mano a mano, tell him a mistake was made and let bygones be bygones. And if that don't work, I'll worry about what to do next.* He dialed the number Lui gave him.

The phone rang three times. Someone answered. Suddenly Ramon was practically wetting his pants.

"Yeah?"

"Is this Hooker?"

"Who wants to know?"

"I need to talk to Hooker. I know who has his Mercedes," Ramon blurted out. Silence, and then, "hold on." Another voice came on the phone.

"This is Hooker."

Ramon cleared his throat. "Listen, to begin with, Hooker, I'm not the one who stole your automobile, okay?"

"Who the hell are you?"

Ramon ignored the question. "But I know where it is and I can get it back for you."

"Sounds interesting. So what's stopping you, punk?"

"I'm too young to die." Ramon's response took Hooker aback with its frankness and actually brought a small smile to his face, something his bodyguards rarely saw.

"How old are you kid?"

"I'm going on twenty-two. I'd like to celebrate my next birthday."

"So how come you're such a good guy?"

"Listen, Hooker, I'm not such a good guy," Ramon said. "I'm so scared, I'm about to piss my pants. The car was taken by mistake."

"You find anything interesting in it?"

"No, man. I'm tellin you. The car ain't been touched. The whole thing was a mistake. I just wanna get it back to you. I'm doing somebody a favor."

"And who would that be?"

"See, this is what I was afraid of — that you'd be asking me a lot of questions instead of just telling me you want the car back and all's well that ends well."

"So how come you haven't called the police?" Hooker's voice was smooth, educated, like a public speaker or actor.

"I'm not a 'call the police person.' Besides, I didn't think they'd believe me. And I thought they'd ask me the same questions you're asking, like who stole the car in the first place."

"Well, if the police wouldn't believe you, what makes you think I would?"

"I don't know. Do you?" Now Ramon really had to pee. He was at a gas station. The men's room was ten feet away but what was he going to say to Hooker, 'hey, give me a minute, I need to piss?' He opened the booth door slightly, unzipped his fly and sent a steady stream out the door. He wasn't about to piss on his own shoes. "Listen, Hooker. All I want to do is leave the car in a dark alley where you can find it." There was silence. "You still there, Hooker?"

"Yes. I'm thinking, kid. I just don't like the idea that someone could get away with this without being punished. You know what I mean? Someone steals my car, it doesn't seem right not to get some justice."

"Here's the justice," Ramon said. "You get your car back and I get to go home alive. Whatd'ya say?"

Hooker nodded to his man. "Okay. Where's the car?"

"I'll call you in half an hour and tell you where it is. You pick it up and we're all square, right?" There was no answer. "Hey, that's the deal," Ramon said. "You pick your car up and that's the end of this. Do I have your word?"

"What makes you think my word is any good?" Hooker asked.

"I don't know," Ramon said. ". . . Guess I'm just a believer. I still think there's a Santa Claus."

Now Hooker laughed out loud. "Okay, kid. We have a deal!" As Hooker was about to hang up, Ramon said, "Hey, Hooker, I really appreciate this. You ever need your car worked on, gimme a call. I'm the best mechanic there is."

"Yeah? That's good to know. I always need a good mechanic."

"I'm talkin' about *auto mechanic*. Is that what you're talkin' about?"

Hooker laughed. "I like you kid. Tell you what. Leave your phone number in the car and I'll give you a call.

"You're not planning to kill me or anything, are you?"

"No, kid. Good mechanics are hard to find. Just leave the car where you said."

Ramon parked the car in an alley a few blocks away, called Hooker and then watched from a safe distance as Hooker's man picked it up a short time later.

CHAPTER TWENTY-NINE

AT FOUR A.M. RAMON headed home. At the same time, Alberto was leaving for work at the bakery. They just missed passing each other on Olympic Boulevard.

Ramon had thought about calling, but he knew Alberto would order him to come home immediately. And he also worried that Alberto would want him to quit his job once he found out about Charlie Mello's little side business. He liked being caught up in this little intrigue. He thought of it like a movie with Humphrey Bogart. He felt that he and Hooker had established some sort of relationship. The guy had respect, money, women! He was a wheeler-dealer. Ramon wanted some of that. Also, he knew Lui would owe him, big time.

Maureen and Alberto had been awake all night waiting for Ramon, or his call. Before Alberto left for work, he asked Maureen to wait 'in case Ramon calls.' Unable to keep her eyes open, Maureen had curled up on Alberto's bed and fallen fast asleep.

Ramon, hyper from the night's activities, was whistling as he entered the apartment. He had forgotten that Alberto might have already left for work. When he walked into the bedroom and saw Maureen there, he was so shocked he lost his balance and fell back against the dresser, knocking the alarm clock to the floor. The sudden noise woke Maureen who bolted up and screamed, thinking it was an intruder.

When he saw Maureen in Alberto's bed, Ramon's jealousy rose like an uncorked bottle of champagne, spilling over irrationally and uncontrollably. After Alberto left this morning she had taken off her bra and thrown it on the nearby chair. She had loosened the button on her jeans and pulled the zipper half-way down. Ramon took in all of this. Maureen watched as Ramon's face twisted in pain and anger. He strode to the bed and roughly pulled her out.

"What is this? Some sort of game? First me, and then my brother?"

"What the hell are you talking about? You don't understand," she screamed. "We were waiting to hear . . ." She tried to pull away but he tightened his grip.

Ramon was beyond listening. Maureen was crying now, trying to gather up her things, hopping on one foot to get her shoe on. Her nose was running and she instinctively looked around for a tissue but Ramon was pushing her toward the door. She stumbled and as he lifted her off her feet both of them lost their balance, winding up against the wall. The more she fought against him, the greater his surge of adrenalin.

As they fell against each other, Ramon could feel the hardness of her breasts through her thin cotton T-shirt. He lifted her shirt and ran his hands over her. His hips pressed her harder against the wall and his passion mounted. He found her mouth and kissed her, holding her immobile as he pulled her jeans and panties to her ankles, awkwardly unbuckling his belt and dropping his pants as well. A small sound escaped Maureen's throat. All the memories of that night several months ago came back to her when, despite her resolve, he had aroused as much passion in her as he had in himself.

But this was different. Now he was angry and filled with an outrage that only punishment and revenge could satisfy. She kicked and screamed, pulled his hair and scratched his face, but he quickly pinned her down. Had he not been so angry, she might have been more willing. She had been applying herself so rigidly to her studies these last few months she did not recognize the signs of neglected libido: anxiety, headaches, shortness of temper and a dull ache in her groin.

He mounted her to the wall. Gasping for breath, incapable of fighting him, she felt her fury rise to match his until both of them were beyond reason. He pulled her head back and forced her mouth open in a kiss that was both angry and passionate. She bit at his lip but that inflamed him all the more. Finally, with a wild animal groan, her mouth opened wider and moved with his. They established a rhythm, an erotic beat played note by note like a symphony soaring to an urgent crescendo.

Afterward there was nothing. A void, as though all the air had been sucked out of the room; the only sound was that of Maureen crying softly. Ramon stepped back, awkwardly pulling his jeans up.

His anger abated, he sat down on the bed and watched silently as she gathered her belongings. Her dark hair hung loosely around her face. She looked at him, her face drawn and tired. In that moment, in that brief second when their eyes met, he realized that he had committed an irreversible offense.

"Call your brother," she whispered and walked out the door, leaving it open behind her. Ramon turned to the empty room. He had a brief premonition of the loneliness he would be feeling for a long time.

◇◇◇

Ramon didn't call his brother. He sat down heavily on his bed and searched for a cigarette in the drawer of the night stand. He couldn't find one so he pulled the entire drawer out and dumped the contents on the floor, tossing it aside so that it splintered against the wall.

The events of the evening crowded in: his meeting with Lui, his conversation with Hooker, his delivery of the Mercedes and his violation of Maureen. He moved back and forth between guilt and righteousness. *Oh, God, what have I done? She betrayed me. NO! She didn't do nothin' asshole, she was tryin' to tell you something.* He berated himself. *You weren't thinking! You never think except with your dick.* He dismissed Alberto's involvement. *Alberto don't care about her. He's got his own little girlfriend that he's crazy about.* Ramon's head was pounding. *I should have given her a chance. Maureen, Maureen,* he groaned. A terrible sound emanated from deep within him that he did not identify as his own. Exhausted, he fell back on the pillow, his thoughts tripping over one another. Finally, weakened with fatigue, he fell into a deep sleep. He didn't hear the phone ring.

◇◇◇

Alberto tried to concentrate on his work but his co-workers only had to look at him to know something was wrong. Usually upbeat, this morning he was anxious and morose as he absent-mindedly put together the ingredients for the day's orders. He waited for the call from either Maureen or Ramon. The longer he waited, the more convinced he was that something terrible had happened. Normally his shift ended at one p.m., but today he left at noon without an explanation to anyone.

As soon as he entered the apartment Alberto knew that Ramon was home. He smelled the lingering odor of cigarettes. He walked into the bedroom and saw the broken drawer against the wall, the contents on the floor, Ramon in a deep sleep. Alberto sat on the other bed, anger and relief vying for first place. He figured Maureen had gone to her classes. But why didn't one of them call him? He was so tired, he couldn't think straight. He lay back and closed his eyes, waiting for Ramon to wake up. They would have a long talk. Maybe it was time to consider each going their own way. It wouldn't be easy. He remembered Hortencia's comments about their birth:

"You think you came out like normal babies? No! You think one of you gave me a rest between pushes? No! I tell you, even when you were taking your first breath, one of you hung on to the other."

"Which one was holding on to which one, Mama?" Alberto had joked.

"What? I had nothing else to do while I was screaming? You think I stop to ask who is holding who?"

Alberto really missed his mother.

◇◇◇

The twins slept several hours, both opening their eyes within seconds of each other. Alberto sat up, threw his legs over the bed, pinched his eyes together and picked a speck of sand out of one corner. He looked at Ramon and then waved his arm to encompass the broken drawer and the items strewn on the floor.

"What happened?" he asked. "Were we robbed or somethin'?"

Ramon didn't answer.

"Goddamn it, Ramon. Answer me. What time did ya get in? I asked Maureen to call me the minute you walked in. How come I didn't get a call from either of you?"

Ramon put his hands behind his head and looked up at the ceiling, still not answering.

"Okay. You don't want to talk to me. I'll talk to you." Alberto reached for a cigarette. He held it in his hand and put it to his lips without lighting it. "When you didn't come home last night I got crazy. I didn't know what to do." He ran his hands through his hair, tamped the cigarette, put it back in the pack, got up and walked barefoot to the bathroom. Ramon heard the toilet seat go up, the splash of water in the sink and the squeak of the towel bar. "I called that asshole, Lui," he shouted from the bathroom. "He told me he left you several hours ago; he didn't know where you were."

Alberto came back into the room and paced in front of Ramon's bed. "I was worried sick, so I called Maureen. She was the only one I could think of. She got hysterical when I told her you went to meet Lui and weren't home yet."

"Lui!" she screamed. "That sleazebag isn't going to be happy til he gets Ramon in trouble. I'm coming right over," she said.

"It was past ten o'clock. I really felt bad calling her so late, but I gotta tell you, bro', I don't know what I would've done if she wasn't here. We drank coffee all night, just waiting for you, waiting for your fuckin' call. Finally, I had to go to work. Maureen said she'd stay until we heard from you." Alberto sat back down on his bed. He took the cigarette back out of the pack again. "So now, you want to tell me what happened?"

"Yeah." Ramon said. He got up and walked into the kitchen avoiding the splintered drawer, still wearing his jeans and shirt from last night. Alberto heard him put up the coffee. He knew Ramon would take his time, delay the discussion. He waited patiently until Ramon came back with two cups of coffee and sat down on his bed facing Alberto.

Ramon lit a cigarette. "Remember when we first got to Lui Chu's house several months ago?" And then he told Alberto the whole story of how he had gone to Maureen's room and made love to her; how he couldn't get Maureen off his mind; that he was in love with her.

"Jesus, Ramon."

"Yeah, ain't that a bitch . . . being in love with someone and knowing you don't have a chance?" Ramon said.

Alberto looked at him. "Well, nothing is impossible."

"You ain't heard the worst of it Berto," Ramon continued. "After I met Lui this afternoon . . ." Ramon told his brother about Charlie Mello, about the Mercedes, and Hooker.

"Shit, this is bad Ramon. You could be in a lot of trouble."

"I know. But that still ain't the worst of it."

"Christ! There's more?"

"Yeah. There's Maureen. She was in your bed when I got home and all I could think of . . ."

"You thought that I . . .?" Alberto jumped up. "Jesus, Joseph & Mary! What the hell's the matter with you?"

"Listen . . ." Ramon was pleading with him now. "Her bra was on the chair, her jeans zipped down; I was crazy jealous. You gotta understand. I mean, what would you think, right? What would you think? I fucked up. I really fucked up." His voice faltered. He put his head in his hands. "She'll never want to see me again."

Alberto put his arm around his brother's shoulder. "You know, Maureen was pretty upset when I told her you went to meet Lui." He paused. "I don't think she would've come over if she didn't care about you."

Ramon looked at his brother. "If I thought there was a chance with Maureen, I'd do anything."

"I don't know what to tell you, bro. Maybe we should talk to Rosie."

CHAPTER THIRTY

DANIEL BRACCO WATCHED THE build-out of the Gringo Palace. He was of medium height and stocky. His arms, shoulders and chest were muscular, but his stomach already showed signs of too many tortillas. He and his high school sweetheart had moved to the neighborhood when they married eleven years ago. Their five children ranged in age from two to ten, the first being born four months before their first wedding anniversary. She had insisted they both graduate high school despite her pregnancy.

Until three months ago he worked for a large market chain, but when the market merged with another entity, he found himself out of a job. His unemployment checks were running out. Desperate for work, he took odd jobs in the neighborhood, painting, plumbing, carpentry and simple electrical problems. Not only was he versatile, but he established a reputation for honesty and reliability.

From the first day of construction Daniel had made it a point to arrive every morning about the same time as Lorenzo and the other workmen. He stood by, watching quietly, waiting for an opportunity to talk to Lorenzo. Eventually, Lorenzo noticed him and they began to talk.

"You live around here?" Lorenzo asked.

"Yes, just a few block away."

"You've been coming by every day. Are you looking for work?"

"Yes." Daniel held out his hand. "Whatever you got. My name's Daniel Bracco."

Lorenzo shook his hand. "Lorenzo Jacobs," he said. "Do you know anything about construction? Cabinet making? Electrical?"

"I know a little bit about everything. I'll take anything you got." Daniel met Lorenzo's eyes. "I never worked construction, but I learn quick. You show me once and I get it."

"Where'd you work before?"

"I had a great job with Ranchero Market for three years but, you know, they sold out to some new owners who brought in their own people.

"You worked in a market for three years?" Lorenzo's eyes lit up. "So, you know a lot about grocery products, stocking shelves, pricing, and that kind of stuff?"

"Anything that has anything to do with markets - just ask me!"

"Do you know what we're building here?" Lorenzo asked.

"Well, I ain't sure," Bracco said hesitating. "Another liquor store maybe?"

Lorenzo didn't answer. He looked at his watch. "Come back around ten. I may have a job for you."

◊◊◊

As usual Rosie arrived at nine-thirty bringing coffee and donuts for the workmen. Lorenzo immediately cornered her.

"Listen. You know how worried we've all been about you being here on your own?"

"Lorenzo, damn it!"

"Listen, Rosie, this is great!" He put his arms against the wall and blocked her escape. "I met someone this morning . . . someone from the neighborhood. His name's Danny Bracco. He's been hanging around, looking for work. This morning we got to talking. This guy's in the business."

"What business?"

"The grocery business."

"So what?"

"Rosie, do me a favor, okay? Just do me one little favor. Meet with this kid. He's going to be here in a couple of minutes. Just meet with him, okay?"

"Okay, okay." She slid under his arm. "You're so damn pushy. I suppose if I didn't say yes you'd keep me here all day."

"And all night too!" he grinned.

Following his conversation with Lorenzo, Daniel Bracco ran home to tell his wife that he might have a job. He threw his arms around her and spun her around.

"Jenny, you'll never guess what happened," he said laughing.

"A Brink's truck lost a bag of money and you picked it up," she teased. She had not seen him so excited in months.

"Better than that. I think I have a job."

"You *think*? And you are so excited just from *thinking*?"

He told her about his conversation with Lorenzo.

"Well, I am very worried," she frowned, trying not to smile at his exuberance. She pointed him to a kitchen chair and sat on his lap wiggling her small body until she felt comfortable. He automatically put his arms around her, holding her tight. She ran her hand through his hair and felt his head. "Oh-h, I think you have a fever. Yes, I am certain. It is from *thinking*."

Within a few seconds she could feel the beginning of his erection. "You know what I am thinking now?" he asked as he slowly unbuttoned her blouse.

"You are thinking, where are the children?"

"Not exactly," he said as he carried her to the bedroom.

◇◇◇

Rosie and Daniel Bracco were as compatible as nuts in a pecan pie. They sat on boxes in the back room away from the construction crew. Two cups of coffee and an unfinished donut sat between them. Rosie shook her head. "I can only hire you temporarily, Daniel. Right now I need someone to set up everything, but I can't make a commitment for when the store opens because I'm not sure I'll be able to afford you."

"Senora Rosie," Daniel said quietly. "Why don't we worry about that after the store opens? If there is not enough money, you can always pay me in trade."

"What do you mean?"

"Work for food, or food for work." He smiled. "I am a good worker. You said you only want to keep the store open in the mornings. Why not keep it open longer? You can open in the morning and I will close in the afternoon."

"Well, that's a thought." Rosie stood up and looked around at the boxes of products that had to be priced and put on the shelves. "I'll tell you what. Suppose I hire you temporarily for minimum wages. Last I heard it was a dollar sixty an hour, and let's see how we work together."

"Done!" Daniel said quickly. "When can I start?"

"Right now, I guess. Just write your hours down every day and give them to me the end of the week."

"Thank you. Thank you very much. You won't be sorry Senora."

"Call me Rosie, please," she smiled. "I feel too old when you call me 'Senora'."

As the Gringo Palace neared completion Rosie's friends distributed flyers around the neighborhood and posted them on light poles. Lorenzo insisted on a New Year's Day opening because he thought it would bring her luck.

ROSIE'S GRINGO PALACE
GRAND OPENING
8:00 AM TO 6:00 PM
TUESDAY, JANUARY 1, 1974
Free Donuts and Coffee

Everyone pitched in. Clara came every day. Maureen poked her nose in from time to time, but she seemed distracted. Rosie noticed a change in Maureen but couldn't put her finger on it. She attributed it to Maureen's obsession to get her law degree.

Ramon and Alberto showed up whenever they could, but usually only one or the other was there. Sometimes Alberto brought his girlfriend, Annie. The twins weren't spending as much time together as they used to. Alberto said they both agreed to pursue different interests.

Even Clara's grandson, Marty, showed up after school to help. Chicory wasn't happy about it. He intercepted Marty outside the high school one afternoon.

"Hey, man, we ain't seen you around much lately. Our little group ain't the same with one of us missin', right boys?"

Marty kept walking. Chicory matched his stride. Four others maintained positions, two in front and two in back. Chicory wore his signature black. "I hear you been helping out the gringo." Chicory said. He waited for an answer. Marty took his time.

"Yeah, well, ya know Chicory, I got better things to do than just hang around."

"What? You don't like us no more? If you're bored, we got lotsa things to keep you busy, don't we boys?" He looked at his entourage. They snickered. Chicory grabbed Marty's arm and spun him around. "In fact, we was just goin over . . ."

Marty gave Chicory a threatening look and pulled his arm free. "Hey, keep your fuckin' hands off — and don't tell me what I can and can't do." It irked him that Chicory was taking more and more latitude with bossing him around.

"Yeah, well you either with us, or . . ." Chicory was in his face.

"Hey, let me tell ya somethin. I've been doing some serious thinking lately. And I don't like where my head is."

"Hey, don't be blaming me for this fucked-up world. I know where your head is. It's up your ass." Chicory said.

"I'm not blaming you. I'm just saying, I don't like me so much anymore. I feel like I'm on the edge, like I'm going to a place I might not be able to return from. Yeah, I've been helping out at the Gringo Palace and I like it. This guy, Lorenzo, he's the architect, he's been showing me the drawings."

"Save your message for someone who gives a shit, Marty. I'm guessin' we can't count on you no more."

"I'm guessing you're right." He looked squarely at Chicory and held out his hand. "No hard feelings then? Are we good?" Chicory ignored his hand and motioned to his gang. "We'll be seein you."

Marty watched as they walked away. He felt good. Better than he had in a long time.

◇◇◇

The last thing Rosie wanted to do was move. And next to the last thing was buying a house. She asked Calista Saenz to hold off putting it on the market. She spoke to Lorenzo over dinner one evening.

"So what's the problem?" he asked. "You can move in with me. I'll move my two pair of jeans over and you can have the rest of the closet." He raised his eyebrows and looked at her sideways, waiting for her response.

"I'm not ready to escalate our relationship."

"You don't have to escalate anything. I'll do all the escalating." He put his head down so she couldn't see him grinning.

Despite herself she started to laugh. "I appreciate the offer but I'd kind of like to stay in the neighborhood so I can be close to the Palace. That way, if Danny needs me I can be there in a few minutes."

"Why don't *you* buy the house?"

"I'm taking on such a big commitment with the grocery, I can't even think about another obligation."

"You still have some time. Something will come up," he said.

"Well, as a matter of fact, something has come up. I had dinner with the twins a few nights ago and they told me a very interesting story. Kind of a sad story, really."

Lorenzo leaned forward. "What's going on?"

"They wanted my advice about an incident involving Ramon. He almost got himself in a lot of trouble the other night. Something to do with his boss and a stolen car."

"A stolen car?"

"Yes. But more important, there was an incident between him and Maureen." Rosie told Lorenzo the whole story, about the car stolen from Willie Hooker, about Charlie Mello's chop shop, about Ramon's misinterpretation of Maureen's presence in his apartment and about his violation of Maureen.

"Jesus! Someone's got to take that boy under his wing! I wondered why Maureen has been so distant lately."

"Yes, I wondered about it too until I heard the story."

"Have you talked to Maureen?" Lorenzo asked.

"No, haven't had a chance. But, listen to this. Ramon got a couple thousand dollars for getting Mello's cajones out of the fire, and he's wondering if he should buy Calista's house. If he does, I can still have my room there and it would help him pay the mortgage."

"What about Alberto? What does he think?"

"The twins think they should live apart for awhile; see how it goes. Alberto is seeing Annie more regularly and if Ramon buys the house, she may move in with Alberto."

"Wow! When did you find all this out?"

"The other night when I had dinner with them."

"And you waited all this time to tell me?"

"I have to keep *some* secrets from you don't I?" Rosie sat back, crossed her legs and signaled the waitress for more coffee. She watched as Lorenzo cut minute pieces of fat off his prime rib.

"So, the big question is, is Ramon going to keep working for Mello?"

"That's sort of up in the air. He makes real good money."

"He's a great mechanic. He can make good money anywhere," Lorenzo said.

"Yes, but here's the biggest question Ramon asked me. Did I think there was anything he could do to win back Maureen?"

"How can you win something back that you never had?"

"You know, 'Renzo, I think Maureen really likes Ramon. Maybe even more than *likes*. I think if he played his cards right he could do it."

"What does that mean, 'played his cards right?' What do you think he'd have to do?"

"He'd have to prove himself and improve himself. Maybe open his own mechanic's shop and make a million dollars. I don't know exactly. He's thinking maybe he could buy the house and fix cars in the back yard and then, as business picks up, he'd get a regular shop. It's a little unrealistic. He's only twenty-two and he hasn't quite matured yet."

"And you don't think that's a problem . . . that he's twenty-two and she's how many years older?"

"Why should it matter? You think men are the only ones who like sweet young things?"

Lorenzo shrugged. "What about a good old fashioned apology from Ramon?"

"That wouldn't be enough. He has to catch up to her. She's going to be an attorney and she's going to want someone who can fit in."

"You really think Ramon could reach that level? He's just a street kid from the Bronx."

"And what were you when you were twenty-two?" Rosie asked.

"Point taken." Lorenzo signaled for the bill. He put his arm around her as they exited the restaurant.

"You know, if Ramon buys the house and starts a mechanic's business in the back yard, you're not going to be happy with the noise, the grease."

"I know."

"So what would you do?"

"Well, then . . ." she paused. "I guess I'd have to let you escalate our relationship." She laughed.

"In that case I'll talk to Ramon tomorrow."

CHAPTER THIRTY-ONE

DANNY BRACCO MET ROSIE at the store at seven a.m. to prepare for the eight o'clock opening. Clara and Lorenzo showed up shortly thereafter. It was a beautiful morning — sixty-eight degrees and sunny.

Rosie blessed the day Lorenzo introduced Danny to her. They set up a table outside the store. Boxes of fresh-baked Mexican *empanadas* had been purchased from a nearby *panaderia*. Danny took care of inside grocery sales while Rosie greeted and socialized with potential customers many of whom merely came for the free give-a-ways or because they were curious. Danny had wisely suggested marking down certain grocery items so that customers would come into the store and familiarize themselves with the layout and products.

Everyone was excited about the opening of ROSIE'S GRINGO PALACE. They did not recognize the subtlety of Rosie using the name *Gringo* before they themselves used it. Since the owner herself had given it that name, the negative connotation was not only diminished, it was impotent. In time the store came to be referred to in three different ways, any of which was self-explanatory and none of which were considered derogatory: "Rosie's", or "Gringo's" or "The Palace."

Rosie's command of Spanish and Danny Bracco's familiar face were helpful in garnering small clusters of customers throughout the day. Still, the community was suspicious and distrustful of newcomers. While the grand opening drew a fair crowd, the number of people who actually made purchases was not particularly encouraging.

Bracco was quick to clue Rosie in regarding money habits in most Latino households. "You gotta understand, Rosie. In this neighborhood the men make the money and they decide who spends it, and where. Maybe they give their woman a few bucks to put aside for emergencies. But you can bet the husbands check and if there's money missing the wife better have a good explanation. And it's much better if she tells him about it before he checks."

"So, what are you saying? Women will never shop here without their husbands?"

"Not at first," Bracco said. "When they get to trust you, when they get to know you, the husbands will tell their wives to 'get it at the Gringo's place'. That's when they'll start coming in — when their husbands tell them it's okay."

When the store closed that evening Lorenzo walked Rosie home. She told him what Danny Bracco had said.

"Don't be too discouraged. Once they get to know you . . ."

"Look, 'Renzo. I'm not expecting miracles. This is just a little neighborhood store. People will probably stop in for milk, tortillas, and everyday items. They're not going to buy huge bags of groceries. It'll probably wind up more like a social club."

"What do you mean, 'a social club?'"

"I don't really know. I've been thinking that the women need to do something more stimulating than pushing strollers back and forth with one little, two little, three little *ninos* trailing after them."

Lorenzo looked at her as if she were crazy. "You don't think they have enough to do?" He sounded angry.

"You don't get it 'Renzo. The key word is *stimulating*. They need something more *stimulating*. Just because they have a lot of kids it doesn't mean they can't do something more meaningful with their lives . . ."

"I think you're the one that doesn't get it. Having kids *is* what's meaningful in their lives."

"Well, maybe nobody's shown them any other way." She suddenly realized they were having their first argument. She crossed her arms.

Lorenzo hadn't seen this side of her, adamant, confrontational. He pulled her to him and kissed her hard on the mouth. She tried to push him away but his arms held her steady until she responded to his kiss. He didn't break away but whispered in her ear, "They don't even speak English for God's sake."

"You're right! They don't." She mumbled into his shoulder, "at least not yet!"

The phone rang later that evening and Calista Saenz picked it up. "*Oh, si, hola Ramon. Quiere Rosie? Una momento.*" She called Rosie to the phone.

"Ramon, thank you for helping out today."

"I'll do anything for you, Rosie. You know that. How'd it go?"

"It was okay; really too soon to tell."

"Rosie, here's why I'm calling. A few weeks ago you said your landlady wanted to sell the house and I been thinkin' maybe I should buy it. What do you think?"

"Whoa! Big step, big responsibility. Have you talked to Alberto?"

"Yeah. He thinks it's a great idea. But he don't want in."

"Whatd'ya mean? Why not? Is it the money?"

"No. He's got a few bucks saved. I think he and Annie want to move in together."

"A nice Jewish girl . . .?"

"These are different times Rosie."

"Don't I know it? Suddenly I feel really old, Ramon," Rosie said, pulling the phone cord into the living room and plopping heavily on the couch.

"What about your job?"

"Well, I ain't going to work for Mello much longer — just until I get a little ahead. Mello wants me to get *more involved* and Alberto convinced me Mello's trouble. Not that I needed convincing. After what happened with Willie Hooker, I'm on to it. I'm thinking to go out on my own. Start fixing cars right in the back yard. You know, start small and get my own shop eventually."

"You want to open up an auto mechanic's business right here in the back yard?" Rosie asked, skeptical. "Jesus! I don't know Ramon. I don't think the neighbors will take kindly to it; a lot of noise, a lot of grease, old cars all over the place."

"Rosie, there's more cars in this neighborhood need fixing than in all of Los Angeles. I'll be busy from day one." He listened to her silence. "You don't like the idea, huh?"

"I think it's a great idea for you to buy the house. But I'm not so sure about setting up an auto shop. You don't even have equipment or anything. Maybe you should look for a small shop . . ."

"Okay, okay. I see where you're goin'." His voice softened and he suddenly sounded dejected. "Maybe I'll have to work for Mello longer than I thought."

"You know," Rosie tried to bring him up again. "You could take one car at a time, still work for Mello, but just put it out in the neighborhood that you do this kind of work."

"Yeah. That sounds good." Ramon's spirits rose again.

"So, should I start looking for another room?"

"Hell, no! I'm countin' on you staying there."

"I'm warning you, I'm a neat freak and I don't plan to do anyone's laundry but my own. We can try it for awhile but I don't want any hard feelings if I decide to move out." She laid her head back and slid her shoes off. "I just hate to see you and Alberto split. Both of you are going to be really lonely, not to mention your mother's going to have a fit."

"I know." Ramon already felt the tight grasp of loneliness. "That's why I need you there Rosie. I don't think I can do it alone."

Rosie hesitated. "Have you spoken to Maureen?"

"No. Ain't no point. No matter how I spin it, I gotta admit Maureen's taking a higher road than I can climb."

"Hey, look. The worst that can happen is you can be friends."

"Yeah, maybe . . ."

Rosie hung up. She closed her eyes and listened to the muted sounds of a news commentator on television: *world population exceeded four billion, heiress Patty Hearst was kidnapped by a revolutionary group known world-wide as the SLA; and, oh yes, President Nixon met with Brezhnev in Moscow to discuss arms limitation and nuclear disarmament while, almost simultaneously, India successfully tested an atomic device and became the world's sixth nuclear power.*

In June of '74 the Gringo Palace barely met its expenses. Rosie and Danny Bracco established a routine for opening and closing, overlapping each other at times. Both worked Saturdays. Business improved but the community still held back.

This was due in great part to Chicory and his boys having made this their after school hangout. The music store had gone out of business and a Chinese Restaurant took its place. Rosie called them the *Insignificant Four;* she was glad Marty was no longer part of their group.

Chicory wore his usual black costume every day. Out of respect for him and in deference to his leadership, no other person in the *Insignificant Four* was permitted to wear black. But the others managed to make their own statements with other types of bizarre clothing: T-shirts with scrawling death messages, smoking guns and foul language. They whistled and made lewd gestures at passersby, especially the women. They spoke to each other with signs and posturing, using their wrists, hands and fingers like contortionists.

Almost every afternoon they swooped down on the *Palace*, purchasing some items but blatantly stealing more than they paid for. Rosie dreaded their after-school forays. She forbid them to come into the store, but they defiantly ignored or distracted her. "Hey Rosie, look what I got for ya," they taunted as they laughed and danced down the aisles scratching their balls and making obscene gestures. Danny was not exempt from their mockery.

"I'm not comfortable with you being in the store alone when these bozos come in" Rosie said.

"Hey, don't worry so much. I got this baseball bat I keep behind the counter. I can take care of myself," Danny said.

Then, one day, a near-death incident changed everything.

◇◇◇

It had been five years since Felicia Delgado, a good Catholic girl from the poverty-ridden town of Nogales, Mexico, met and fell in love with Reynaldo Cormier, a twenty-three year old truck driver who was making a run from Los Angeles.

Reynaldo, called Ronnie by his friends and family, was six foot five with broad shoulders, big arms and a thick waist. A good two hundred forty pounds, he cut a memorable figure with his deep-set eyes, dark curly brown hair and mustache. He loved the freedom of trucking and was well-known by his co-workers for his sense of humor and kindness.

Cormier drove a refrigerated trailer from Los Angeles, making a drop in Tucson and then driving empty to Nogales to pick up produce. On his way he stopped first in Ehrenberg, Arizona where he fueled up, hit the men's room and grabbed a slice of pie and coffee. He didn't dally because the thought of putting his hand between Felicia's legs was very motivating and, at the same time, painfully distressing. The last sixty miles on Highway 19 from Tucson south to Nogales was as boring as a nightshift at a graveyard. But the image of Felicia spurred him on.

Felicia's home life was dismal. There were eight children. Her father was an alcoholic. His only pleasures were drinking, smoking and copulating. He tried to extend the copulation beyond his wife to the female members of his family but the two youngest were diminutive and adept at hiding when he came home drunk. They could squeeze under beds or in small places their father could not reach. Senor Delgado wheezed and snorted and coughed and cursed as he tried to reach them, but eventually he would give up and fall dead away, sometimes blocking the very place where the girls hid. Then the older boys would pull him away by his arms and legs not hesitating to bestow well-deserved kicks in the ribs or ass. Many mornings Delgado wondered where his bruises came from, why his ribs or buttocks ached. He had his suspicions but could never prove anything.

"I know you did it, you cockroaches," he yelled in Spanish. "I see your footprint here on my ass." Sometimes he even pulled his pants down to show them the bruises, but they scurried out of the house laughing.

Delgado's daughter Felicia was not so fortunate. She favored her brothers in build and girth and was more like a linebacker: five feet eight, broad shoulders, thick thighs. So the first time her father tried to molest her at age fourteen, she threw him against the wall, much to his astonishment. To convince him further that he better not mess with her, she picked up a knife and held it threateningly against his throat. She was tempted to call him a mother fucking son-of-a-bitch but she was a good Catholic daughter and would not disrespect him by using foul language. Despite her size Felicia was very pretty with long dark hair and big brown eyes that sparkled with fun and good will. Her heart was as big as her body.

Out of necessity Felicia dropped out of school and got a waitress job at the pitiful truck stop in Nogales which, during the harvest season, was an extremely busy border town surrounded by produce packing houses. It took a big girl to handle the truck drivers and therefore Felicia was very well suited to the job. All her wages went to feed the family.

It was by accident one time that Cormier was unable to find a suitable spot to accommodate his truck, so he stopped instead at the small run-down *CAMION CAFÉ* where Felicia worked. Since then he deliberately stopped there every trip so he could continue his courtship of Senorita Delgado. They spent whatever free time she had making love in the sleeper bunk. Fortunately this was a huge space which easily accommodated them. However, when Felicia became pregnant and had trouble lifting herself into the truck, there seemed no option but to marry her and bring her back to Los Angeles.

And, thus, it was because of Felicia Delgado, now Felicia Cormier, that the success of ROSIE'S GRINGO PALACE was secured.

On a warm June morning, now five years since Reynaldo had married her, Felicia kissed him goodbye as he left for another run to Nogales. When the door closed behind him she looked around at the unmade beds, breakfast dishes, and basket of dirty clothes. The heat and humidity were already thrusting invisible fingers through the screen-less windows of the small apartment. Her chest tightened as she felt the beginning ache of depression. In a flash of insight she realized no one was pushing her to clean the house or do anything else. She could make the decision, be in charge. This was the first inkling Felicia had of her own power.

She loosened the oldest boy's tug on her trouser leg, wiped her three-year-old son's nose, stuck a pacifier in her nine-month-old daughter's mouth, prepared the stroller with diapers and a bottle and left the apartment. Just that one act of independence brought a small smile to her face.

The baby was distracted by a string of colorful painted beads on the stroller tray. She cooed and gurgled and found them more to her liking than the pacifier which dropped into her lap. The three-year-old boy sat makeshift in the stroller behind his nine-month-old sister.

Felicia's five-year-old held on to the stroller, running ahead at times and then coming back. She headed for the park inhaling deeply as the stress of the morning dissipated. Maybe she would ask her mother-in-law to baby-sit after dinner while she went to a movie with her sister-in-law. *The Sting* was playing with Paul Newman and Robert

Redford. She hadn't been to a movie in months. A surge of energy lifted her spirits and she resolved to do this more often.

As Felicia passed the Gringo Palace on her way to the park, baby Jessica began to sputter and cough. The oldest boy noticed that the string of beads had torn apart and Jessica's little fist was in her mouth, the colored beads dropping off and falling to the ground. "Mama," he said, but Felicia didn't pay him any attention. "Mama," he repeated, louder, pulling on her pants. *Jessica!* He shouted, pointing. Felicia moved forward to see what he was talking about. *Blood?* The baby's mouth was open, gagging, her eyes squeezed shut in a silent wail; red drool fell on her yellow shirt in a long wet line. Felicia froze. She just stood there, screaming.

Rosie heard the commotion and ran out. In a split second she assessed the situation. She tried to pull the baby from the stroller but Felicia blocked her, not understanding her intention. Rosie shoved her aside, pulled the infant out, and administered a Heimlich maneuver. The other two children were screaming now as they observed their mother trying to pull Jessica from Rosie's arms. While Rosie worked on Jessica she spoke to Felicia in Spanish. *Estoy tratando de ayudarte. No te preocupes. Todo estará bien.* I am trying to help. Felicia loosened her grip. Her eyes wide with fright, she watched as Rosie pressed, *one, two, three.* There it was — the red bead popped out of Jessica's mouth and the baby's familiar cry pierced the air. What they thought was blood turned out to be the red dye from the bead. Rosie carried the child into the store, wet a paper towel and wiped the red dye from the baby's mouth. Felicia and the other two children followed close behind.

Rosie sat Felicia down in the back of the store and put baby Jessica in her lap. She leaned against a shelf to catch her breath and wiped her brow with her apron.

The children stopped crying. Still whimpering, the baby looked wide-eyed at her mother's face and sucked obsessively on her pacifier unaware that the incident could have taken a different turn. The two women made eye contact. The ordeal was over, the relief so intense they started to giggle.

"Oh, my goodness! That was a scare," Rosie said.

Rosie pulled a crate forward and sat down. She reached for a box of crackers and offered them to the children. Felicia shaken, was both laughing and crying, tears rolling down her face. The children had no idea what was going on, but seeing the adults, they also started to giggle. The baby cooed, some of the red dye still on her tongue.

When the two women settled down, Rosie spoke Spanish and asked Felicia, "Do you speak English?"

"*No. No habla mucho Inglese.*"

"How long have you lived here?"

"Five years with my husband Reynaldo."

"Is your husband the truck driver that comes in here sometimes for cigarettes and milk? Do some people call him Ronnie?"

"Yes, he is the same."

"So how come you don't speak English?"

"I would like to learn but I have no time . . ."

"Listen," Rosie said. "If you really want to learn, I can teach you."

"Really?" she hesitated. "You know, I cannot pay you — and the children?"

"For goodness sake, nobody said anything about money. Just bring the children with you. You see these two little tables in the back here?" Rosie pointed to two wobbly wood tables. "Well, if you come back every day for as much time as you can spare, I'll have a lesson ready for you and I'll try to find something to keep the children busy while you study."

Felicia's eyes lit up. "You mean, you will really teach me to speak English?"

"Yes, and to read too!"

Several neighbors had been passing by when the incident occurred. A small circle now gathered outside the Palace as one neighbor told another. Slowly they crowded into the back of the store and joined the two women in laughter, patting each other on the back, jabbering in Spanish.

"You know, the *gringo*, she pull the little one . . ."

"Si. I saw it too . . . if not for Rosie, baby Jessica . . ."

"I think she is one of us now, no?"

"Yes, she is one of us now."

CHAPTER THIRTY-TWO

SEVERAL MONTHS LATER, THE life-saving incident was still a major topic of conversation. News had traveled quickly through the neighborhood. For the first time in almost a year, Rosie's Gringo Palace became profitable. Danny Bracco was hired full time. Although the *Palace* was still closed Sundays, the daily hours were extended from seven to seven daily. Clara's grandson, Marty came in after school enduring the taunts of Chicory and his followers.

"Hey, Marty, baby, you bangin' Rosie? She puttin' it in your face? Gotta be *some* reason you're working here, right?"

Marty tried to ignore them. He expected a fight and he held his fists ready for the first punch.

On their way to the park or to do other errands, women now stopped with their children to chat with each other and Rosie, but if Chicory and his boys were there, they moved on. Often the gang surrounded them and would not let them pass, teasing, tormenting. Thus far none of the women had been hurt, but the taunts from Chicory were intimidating. When Rosie intervened, Chicory just said what he always said, "Hey, bitch, it's a free country."

Felicia, in particular, was taunted when she picked up her English lesson. Sometimes she took the lesson home, but whenever time permitted she and the children sat in the back room with Rosie alternating between tending customers and tutoring. In short time Felicia's English skills improved considerably. As an added benefit, one which Felicia valued most, while the children listened to their mother and Rosie, their language and reading skills also improved.

Because of Chicory there were times Felicia considered discontinuing the lessons. She spoke to her husband about Chicory's jeers and insults. "We are all afraid of him."

"How come Chicory is there all the time? Doesn't he go to school?" Reynaldo asked.

"When he's not in school he just hangs there. If not for Chicory, Rosie would be busier teaching English than she would be selling groceries. Many people have asked whether Rosie would teach them what she is teaching me. We all know it would be easier to get jobs if we can read and speak English."

"Well then," Reynaldo said. "Some of us will have to get together and discuss what to do about this."

"I hope so, because otherwise, someone is going to get hurt."

◇◇◇

Rosie was in her element teaching English to Felicia. Other neighbors had approached her and she began to think seriously about starting classes. She decided to talk to Maureen about it.

"Hey, I haven't seen you in weeks. How about dinner?"

"It would have to be a quick one."

"When's the last time you had a decent meal?"

"Let's see. When was the *Last Supper*," Maureen laughed.

"That's what I thought. Why don't we play catch up at my place? Besides, I need an attorney's advice."

"Well, I'm not an attorney yet, but I'm working on it."

"I know," Rosie laughed.

"I'd rather not do it at your place," Maureen said. "It would be too awkward if I run into Ramon."

"You're not going to run into him. I've hardly seen him myself since he bought this house from Calista," Rosie said. "He's been working his ass off to make the mortgage payments."

"Is he still working for Charlie Mello, still hanging with that loser, Lui Chu?"

"He's not hanging with Lui — not that I know of. He's still working for Mello but he's got something up his sleeve. He's obsessed with opening up his own business. He was even talking about doing it right here in the back yard. I told him I wouldn't be able to stay here with all that noise, the dirt, ugh!" She paused. "What the hell happened between you two anyway? I thought he was crazy about you . . ."

"Yeah, well, things change."

"Things change for you, or things change for him?" Rosie asked.

"Both."

"You don't have to worry about Ramon being here. He's gone before I get up and he's still gone when I get home."

Maureen's thoughts went back to Mello. "He's a real sneaky little bastard, that Mello. He'd screw Ramon faster than a *Makita*."

"Ramon said he's trying to get a friend to sponsor him, then he'll quit Mello."

"Who the hell is going to sponsor Ramon? He doesn't have a dime!" Maureen said. She pulled the phone cord over to the bed and looked around at her studio apartment; the sparse furnishings, the worn rug, the khaki colored walls. *God! This place is awful.*

"I don't know. I'm too tired to listen to him when he gets home. He's all wound up and I'm already half asleep. He said he and a guy named Willie Hooker are trying to work a deal."

"Willie Hooker?" Maureen yelled. "Jesus!"

"What? You know Willie Hooker?" Rosie asked, surprised.

"Everybody that reads the paper knows Willie Hooker."

"Well, that leaves me out. I'm too busy to read."

"Hooker is a well known kingpin," Maureen said. "He's involved in everything – drugs, women, car thefts. If it's illegal it has Hooker's name on it somewhere." She thought for a minute. "How'd Ramon get cozy with Hooker?"

"I'm not sure; something about Hooker's white Mercedes and Ramon having done him a favor. He's very secretive about Hooker. Not that I didn't ask."

"So, what you're saying is he can't wait to quit his job with a low-life like Mello so he can work for a low-life like Hooker? Why doesn't that surprise me? Sounds just like Ramon," Maureen said, disheartened. *Stupid son-of-a-bitch.*

"Well, he doesn't want to work *for* Hooker. He wants to be in business for himself."

"If Hooker lends him the money for this, believe me, he'll be working *for* Hooker.

◇◇◇

A week later, Maureen left work a half hour early and walked to Rosie's, a short five blocks. She smelled dinner as she approached: tomatoes, oregano, cumin. Rosie met her at the door with a glass of Chianti. "We're having *Italian*," she said.

"I'd never have known," Maureen said smiling. "You don't know what a break this is — a whole hour just for dinner. Without a book in front of me!" she added. She sipped her wine and walked around the room settling on a bar stool overlooking the kitchen. "What a neat place."

"Yes. I probably should have bought it myself instead of touting Ramon on it."

"I can't even imagine the twins not living together. How're they surviving without each other?"

"Well, at first they were on the phone a lot. I think Ramon was really hurting. He wasn't eating, he wasn't sleeping; he didn't quite know what to do with himself. I don't know about Alberto, but at least he's got Annie. I'm sure that helped. Suddenly Ramon became obsessed with opening his own business. So things seem to have settled down somewhat. They miss each other, but they're involved in their own separate pursuits."

"What did their mother have to say about it?"

"Hortencia? She said it was about time."

"Is she planning to come out to visit sometime?"

"I think she's waiting for when Alberto gets married."

"I need your advice," Rosie said as they sat around the dining table after dinner drinking espresso.

"I hate when I eat this much," Maureen said. She sat back, giving Rosie her full attention. Her blue eyes looked tired. Makeup didn't hide the dark circles.

"Maureen, you look like . . ." Rosie said.

"I know," she said. "I look like shit. I've been studying my ass off. You've no idea how many times I thought I should chuck it all."

"You know you're not going to do that. I've been meaning to ask you. How's your grandmother?"

"I talk to her a couple of times a month. She's not great, but she doesn't complain. My mother is dying — and that's a good thing. It's harder and harder for my grandmother to take care of her."

"And how do you feel about your mother dying?" Rosie asked.

"As I said, that's a good thing."

"So what advice do you need?" Maureen asked.

"I started teaching English to one of my customers, Felicia, in the back room of the Palace. She brings her three kids with her and they sit and listen. Unbelievable how good those kids are, like they know this is important to their Mama. She's from Nogales; been here five years and hardly speaks a word of English. We've been one-on-one for a couple months and the results are astounding. I've been asked by several others, some men and some women, if I would do the same for them."

"Hmm, that's interesting. Go on," Maureen said.

"Well, I'm thinking I should open a classroom in back of the store. Those guys would have so many more job opportunities if they spoke English and if they could at least learn how to fill out a job application."

"That's for sure," Maureen said. "You already have teaching credentials, so what's your question?"

"I just want to know if I need any special permit, and also what you think of the idea?"

"It's a great idea," Maureen answered. "But you need two things that you don't have."

"What?" Rosie asked.

"Time and energy," she said, smiling. "You're not superwoman, you know."

"I'll just whittle down my hours in front of the store and spend time more time in the back. All I need are some real tables and chairs. I can't keep using the crates."

"You know," Maureen said. "That kid Hector who hangs with Chicory is a helluva carpenter. My boss used him a couple of times to build some shelves and stuff. I bet he could fix up that back room in nothing flat."

"You think Hector would do it? Defy Chicory?" Rosie asked.

"He's desperate for a job. His parents are ready to kick him out of the house."

"How do you know all this scuttlebutt?"

"It's a small neighborhood. Word gets around. He might even decide to attend your classes. Wouldn't that be something?" Maureen said as she got her belongings together to leave. "The whole damn neighborhood is going to be knocking your door down."

"We'll see. I think I'll put a small sign in the window."

Rosie escorted Maureen to the door. Just then Ramon pulled into the driveway. He spotted Maureen.

"Where's your car?" Rosie asked as she hugged Maureen.

"I walked over," Maureen tried to pull away. But Rosie held tight. As Ramon was getting out of his car Rosie yelled to him, "Hey, Ramon, Maureen needs a ride back to her car."

"Don't do this," Maureen whispered to Rosie.

"You and Ramon need to be friends again," Rosie whispered back. Anyway, it's not a good idea you walking back to the office in the dark," she said.

"I really need some air . . ." Maureen was trying to extricate herself from Rosie's embrace.

Ramon couldn't believe his luck. He pressed his advantage. He took Maureen's elbow forcefully, opened the passenger door of his car and pushed her in. She didn't have a choice. He pulled out of the driveway and talked nervously, not letting her get a word in.

"All I could think about on the way home was how I was going to treat myself to a long, hot shower. But there ain't no better treat than seeing you. I'm sorry I don't smell better."

She held her nose. "Tell me about it."

He glanced at her. "Maybe we can go to your place and I can shower there," he laughed softly.

"Well, that would be okay except I don't have a shower. I have a room and at one end of it there's a toilet and a tile floor. The tile floor has a drain in it; someone pasted some plumbing on the wall, attached a small round thing that spouts water, and called it a shower. The landlady advertised the room with shower. I remember jokingly asking her 'what if you want the room without the shower?'. She never cracked a smile but said it would be ten dollars less and she'd convert the shower back to a closet." They both laughed and the tension was broken.

He had wanted to talk to her ever since that misunderstanding at the apartment when he thought she had slept with Alberto. But he didn't have the courage. This was a good opportunity to apologize.

"My car is just a few blocks from here — in back of my office," Maureen said.

"We're not going there. We're going someplace quiet where we can talk."

"There's nothing to say, Ramon."

"Unless you jump out of the car, Maureen, you're gonna have to listen."

"Ramon, I have a lot of studying to do. I swear, I don't have time for this."

"It won't take long, I promise." He drove west out of the barrio. Twenty minutes later he found a parking space in Marina Del Rey, overlooking the ocean. Maureen did not speak the entire trip. Her mind was in overdrive. *Remember Paul. Don't go from one bad relationship to another. Don't get distracted from your goal. Repeat after me — you're going to be a lawyer. That's it! You're going to be a lawyer.*

S-O-S. Mind to body, I know you're horny, but don't let your physical needs contaminate your judgment. Mind to brain — think! Think! This is a goddamn test, Maureen, and you need to pass it. No 'F's allowed.

"Let's walk," Ramon said. The beach looked white in the half-moon light. As they approached the sand, he took off his shoes and socks and nodded to her to do the same. She removed her sandals and followed him toward the water. She shivered, wondering if it was the cold sand beneath her toes or if it was the smell of him. They got to the water's edge and watched the white caps outline the shoreline from Santa Monica to Malibu. He sat down and pulled her beside him. She drew her knees up and looked out at the vast darkness. The partial moon cast a luminescent glow on the ocean's surface. He threaded his long fingers through the sand.

Ramon could have posed for a body-building magazine. His body was angular with well-defined muscles and a slender waist. His energy was electric, exciting, powerful. He put his arms around her, but she pushed away using every ounce of resistance she could muster.

"I'm sorry," he said. "You have to believe me — how sorry I am about what happened. When I got home that morning all I saw was you in Alberto's bed half dressed. I just got crazy. I thought you and Alberto . . . I made a mistake."

"It doesn't matter," Maureen said.

"Yeah, it does. I'm crazy 'bout ya. It won't happen again."

"No, you don't understand Ramon. This can't work between us."

"Yeah, it can baby. I'm gonna open my own business, make lots of money. I'll be able to give you anything you want. I'll be able to take care of you real good."

"No, Ramon. You don't get it. I have to finish school."

"Yeah, but that's just it baby. You don't have to finish school or worry about nothin."

"What the hell are you talking about, 'I don't have to finish school?' What do you think I've been doing for the past two years? You think I'm going to give all that up so you can support me? Jesus, Ramon, grow up!" She made a move to gather her shoes but he grabbed her arm. She pulled away, angry.

He blocked her way. "Okay, listen, you can do what you want. I mean, you don have to quit school, but, I got a deal goin' with a friend . . ."

"What friend for God's sake? Willie Hooker?"

He looked at her wondering how she knew.

"Rosie told me. You think he's your friend? Christ, Ramon! Hooker is nobody's friend."

"I'm tellin' you, you're wrong. Hooker and me are buddy-buddy. I did him a big favor a couple months ago and he's gonna loan me the money to set up my own auto shop . . ."

"And what do you have to do for him?" Maureen stood up and started walking back to the car.

"Nothin." Ramon picked up his shoes and socks and ran after her. "He's got cars all over the city — probably enough to keep me busy for years. He'll pay me to fix them and I'll pay him back on the loan. It's a simple deal. He don't care if I fix other cars, as long as I give him priority. He just needs someone he can trust. Ya know, he don't like strange mechanics working on his cars."

"No kidding!"

"Baby," Ramon threw his arms up. "You gonna be mad at me forever? C'mon," he pleaded.

"I'm not going to be mad at you forever. I'm just going to do my thing and you're going to do yours." They got back to the car and she leaned against it to put her sandals on.

"So can I call you sometime?" he asked, hopping on one foot as he put a sock on.

"Yeah. Call me when you're thirty."

"When I'm *thirty?* But that's eight years from now," he said, angrily.

"Ramon, we're on different tracks." She opened the car door and got in. "All I'm gonna say is just watch your ass with Hooker. Get an attorney or something before you sign any papers."

"Look, I know you're pissed at me but can you do me one favor?"

"Ramon, I don't owe you anything and I especially don't need to do you any favors." *Okay, that's a little harsh,* she thought. She turned to look at him. His shoulders were hunched and his head down. He looked totally dejected.

"What?" she asked.

"I want you to meet Hooker."

"No, I'm too busy. Wait until after I take the Bar."

"When will that be?"

"I'll be studying for it all summer."

"Hooker's giving a party for his daughter . . ."

"I didn't know he had a daughter," Maureen said.

". . . in two weeks. Yeah, hardly nobody knows. She's gonna be sixteen and he's throwing a big bash for her. I want you to go with me. Please."

"I don't have anything to wear."

"No, baby, it's a barbecue — an afternoon thing at his home, two, three hours, that's all. He's hired a band and all. C'mon, just this one little favor and then I promise I won't bother you no more."

She felt bad about hurting him. "I'll think about it."

"C'mon, please, gimme a break. I got no one to go with. When Hooker sees a classy broad like you on my arm he's gonna know I'm not just another bum." She didn't answer until they got to her office.

"Maureen," he said hesitating. "This Sunday, pick you up at two?" He got out of the car and ran around to open the door for her.

"Okay, okay. But only for a couple of hours." She'd study in the morning, take a break and then study again when she got home.

Ramon had a big smile on his face. He picked her up and spun her around. She laughed.

"Ugh!" she said. "I hope you smell better on Sunday than you do right now."

As she got into her car she yelled over. "By the way, what does Alberto have to say about this deal with Hooker?"

"Not much."

"Ramon, you're an idiot." Maureen said as she slammed the door shut.

"Yeah, that's what Alberto says."

CHAPTER THIRTY-THREE

AFTER SPENDING THE EVENING with Maureen, Rosie was certain her calling was to teach again. This time she'd be teaching English instead of Spanish. She hadn't been this excited in months.

Whether they were buying groceries or not, stopping at the Gringo Palace became part of the community's routine, like going to church. Rosie loved shmoozing with the neighbors, giving advice and getting advice. But the thing she loved the most, the thing that really turned her on, was teaching. So it was not surprising that the following sign appeared in her window a few days later:

FREE
ADULT ENGLISH CLASSES
MONDAY THRU FRIDAY 5-7 PM

She solicited Clara's help. They had worked together twenty years at the high school in Manhattan and now Rosie hoped they would work together again.

"What do you think?" she asked Clara.

"I think you're crazy."

"You don't want to do it?" Rosie asked, crestfallen.

"Did I say I didn't want to do it? No! I said I think you're crazy."

"Then you do want to do it?" Rosie screamed.

"Yes, yes, yes. Of course! I'm so fucking bored. Oops, did that come out of my mouth?" Clara laughed. "When do we start?"

"I have to set up the back room so it will accommodate more people. Right now there's only room for four or six."

"You think you'll have a lot of takers?" Clara asked. "They may be a little reticent about revealing their illiteracy. Could be a macho thing, you know."

"Well, we'll see. Lorenzo is designing an efficient layout and I'm going to ask Hector if he can do the carpentry — you know, tables, shelves, that kind of stuff. "

"Hector?" Clara was surprised. "You mean Hector that hangs with Chicory? Can you trust Hector in the back room?"

"Why not? What's back there besides a couple boxes of canned goods? He can't steal more from me than he's stealing now," Rosie laughed.

"I don't know if Hector will leave the gang."

"More to the point, will the gang let Hector leave?" Rosie said.

"Chicory's not going to like this." Clara said.

"No, he's not. But maybe if one breaks away the others will have the courage to do so too."

"It's a stretch, I'll grant you that. We can only hope, right?"

"Right!" Rosie said.

In the end it was Lorenzo who held out the carrot stick to Hector.

He approached the boys as they leaned against the brick building next to the *PALACE*. They were watchful, suspicious. Chicory ignored Lorenzo and deliberately spit right past him onto the sidewalk.

"Anybody here looking for work?" Lorenzo addressed the group. Chicory moved forward.

"Yeah, why? You got a bank job for us?"

"No, I'm looking for a carpenter."

Hector moved away from the building. He threw his cigarette down, stepped on it and moved toward Lorenzo. "I'm listening," he said.

Chicory narrowed his eyes, looked briefly at Hector, then smoothly stepped between him and Lorenzo blocking any further dialogue.

"We ain't got no one here . . . "

"Hey, man," Hector tried to elbow Chicory aside but Chicory gave him a hand sign and Hector backed off.

Lorenzo held his ground. "I'm looking for someone to do some carpentry work next door. We need shelves, things like that. Just a few days' work but maybe it could lead to something more permanent."

"Yeah, we seen the sign in the window. So, what's the gringo gonna do now, turn the store into a school?" He snickered. "Maybe she gonna give out free lunches." He looked at his cohorts to make sure they appreciated the humor. "We don need no old woman comin into our hood fuckin with our people." Chicory was in Lorenzo's face.

"If you weren't so stupid you'd understand . . ." Lorenzo lost his temper. His heart was pounding. *Shit!* He knew he'd said the wrong thing.

"Hey, who you callin stupid!" Chicory grabbed Lorenzo's shirt and pulled him close. Two other boys moved in. Lorenzo clenched his fists. Hector ran over and shoved Chicory back, breaking his grasp and stepping between them. Surprised, the other two boys retreated.

"Look, I'm sorry," Lorenzo said. "I didn't mean to call you stupid." *Fucking asshole is what I really meant.*

Chicory was beyond hearing him. He was scuffling with Hector to get at Lorenzo again. Hector knew he'd pay a price for his interference. He'd never gone against Chicory before but the temptation of a job offer was more than he could ignore. Hector was dead broke, about to be kicked out by his family who were hanging by a thread to make ends meet.

Chicory had been talking lately about buying a gun. "It's all to help you out bro, ya know, we're family, right?" Chicory had been mentioning a gun for some time now and he was looking for an excuse to buy one. Hector didn't intend to be his excuse. He wasn't stupid; he just never had the opportunity to be smart.

Hector had made it quite clear a couple of weeks ago. "Hey, I ain't goin along with you buyin no gun, so don't be sayin you're doing it for me. First thing you know, you'll get in trouble and you'll be blamin me for it. You buy a gun and I'm outta here!"

"Whatd'ya worried about? We ain't even seventeen yet so what can they do to us?"

Hector was thinking now, as he held Chicory back. *It's a good thing this son-of-a-bitch don't have no gun or for sure he'd use it right now and we'd all be doin time.* He gave Lorenzo a nod, *get goin'.* As Lorenzo left he looked directly at Hector. "Think about it and let me know."

"He ain't gonna let you know nothin. You hear me asshole? Nothin!"

Chicory shrugged off Hector's arm and spit at Lorenzo's back. He was livid, losing face in front of his boys like that. He stalked away, slouching, his fists tight.

"This don look good," Snake said. They called him Snake because his tongue was always flitting out wetting his lips, a nervous gesture he had acquired when he was learning to read. He never learned to read properly, but the habit was there to stay.

"You fuckin right about that!"

All eyes were on Chicory as he headed in the direction of home.

His Aunt Rita was there to greet him. "Well, lordy, lordy, look what jes blew in — and jes in time to give your old Aunt Rita a little treat." She pulled him to her but he pushed away. She said, "I had a real bad day, baby, and I kept thinkin all day long about us havin a little slip and slide. I wuz jes waitin on you to get home."

He looked at her with disgust. "I had a bad day too and I'm not in the mood."

"Well, ain't that too bad," she shot back, crossing her arms. "Maybe I won't be in the mood to keep supporting you. Ya know. I do my job and you gotta do yours." She walked toward the bedroom and beckoned him to follow her. She pulled her dress up and sat on the edge of the bed, her fat thighs and stomach spreading out to accommodate her upper body.

He got the message. *It's a job* he reminded himself. *A filthy disgusting job.* He hated the look of her, the taste, the smell. He gagged just thinking about it. *When I'm ready, bitch, you'll get yours. A knife right up your decayed black cunt.* The thought of it made him hard.

"See," Aunt Rita said. "I knew you'd be hard for me. Well, don't just put it in, boy. Gimme a little lovin first. You know, lookit this. Feel how hard this nipple is." She took his hand and put it on her breast.

He hated most women. The guys talked about getting laid. This one was hot, that one was putting out. He never cared. He wasn't interested. His Aunt Rita had been giving it to him since he was eight. What was the big deal? But sometimes he wondered what it would be like to make love to a young girl — maybe someone like Marty's sister. She was about fourteen now. He'd seen her walk by ROSIE'S with her girlfriends. *Cute little ass, high tits. Yeah, that would be nice payback for Marty, show him a thing or two about loyalty.* Chicory hadn't forgiven him for leaving the gang and going to work for Rosie. He was on a slow burn, simmering.

◇◇◇

Sunday came around all too soon. Ramon called Maureen several times to remind her about the party at Willie Hooker's place. "Yeah, yeah, I'll be ready. Stop calling me."

Ramon arrived promptly at two. Maureen was waiting outside. He watched her approach. *The girl sure can move. God, she is gorgeous.* She knew she looked good and it lifted her spirits. Her eyes opened wide as she saw what Ramon was driving, a shiny red Corvette.

"One of the benefits of working with Hooker," he said as she appraised the car.

She wore a sleeveless navy-blue dress which clung to her long legs as she walked cat-like toward the car. The low-cut halter neckline crossed in front and tied behind her neck. No bra. A slight hint of nipple pushed through the silk fabric. On one arm she carried a small white purse; on the other a wide-brimmed navy blue straw hat. Her long dark hair was pulled back and knotted with her own hair at the nape of her neck. *Hooker is going to have a heart attack when he sees her.* Ramon met her at the car door and opened it for her. "Baby, you look gorgeous," he smiled. She welcomed his look of appreciation.

Ramon drove toward Hooker's place just off Benedict Canyon. He was wearing white double pleated trousers, a black short sleeve knit shirt, and white tennis shoes. His black hair was slicked back and he smelled divine. Maureen breathed him in.

"I'm glad you're not wearing the same outfit from the other night. You smell a lot better too."

He laughed. "Yeah, that was called cologne d' grease. It comes with my Chevy image."

"And what is this," she asked.

"This is Armani and it comes with my Corvette image," he laughed.

They made light conversation, mostly about Alberto.

"So how are you guys managing without each other?"

"It was tough at first. Even now I still listen for Alberto to finish in the shower so I can get in there. He's like a shadow. When I look in the mirror I see a double image. Him and me. He's always behind me, in front of me, at my side.

"Well, that's a good thing, isn't it?"

"Yeah," he said. "It's always a good thing to have Alberto with you."

They were approaching Hooker's house, a white two-story job with a circular driveway. Valet parking had been arranged and Ramon left his key in the car as he came around to get Maureen. He noticed the looks Maureen got as he helped her out.

"Wow!" she said. "Nice place."

The backyard was huge. A flagstone path led to a pool and tennis court, visible in the distance. A bandstand had been set up nearby on top of which hung a colorful Happy Birthday banner. Waiters walked around with drinks and hors d'oeuvres, caviar on thin imported crackers, shrimp and lobster in pastry shells, chicken liver wrapped in bacon, pate, grilled baby lamb chops. The variety was endless.

Maureen spotted Lui Chu in animated conversation with several men and started in his direction. Ramon lagged behind shaking hands with this one and that. She had not seen Lui in over a year. Once they had arrived in Los Angeles there was no reason to keep up a friendship. He had put on some weight.

As she approached to greet him the men parted and turned toward her. They seemed to be dumb struck. "Jesus!" one of them muttered. *Where'd this doll come from?* Lui didn't recognize her.

"Hello, Lui." He just stared. She gave him a broad smile and went to hug him. He pulled back a little in surprise. One of the other men said, "Hey, me next, okay?" At that moment Ramon caught up to her. When Lui saw Ramon he peered more closely at Maureen and suddenly realized who she was. "Jesus Christ, Maureen! You're a sight for sore eyes, baby. Where you been? Ramon, you been keeping her locked up or something?"

Ramon laughed. "Hell, no. She's been keeping herself locked up with her law books."

"I guess you really meant what you said about being a lawyer, huh?" Lui asked.

"Yep. Plugging away at it," she said. "How's your brother Sam and everyone?"

"Great! Great! He's still got his little Kung Fu studio. Everyone's okay."

As they gathered around Maureen the circle was suddenly broken by Willie Hooker. "Hey, what's goin' on here? What am I missing?" When he saw Maureen he stopped dead.

"Hey, Mr. Hooker," Ramon said, moving to her side. "I want you to meet my girl."

Maureen held out her hand and Hooker took it, lingering a bit and rubbing his thumb over her wrist. Maureen pulled her hand away. Hooker moved his lips a bit, like a smile that couldn't quite make it.

"You've been holding out on me, Ramon," Hooker said as he stared at Maureen appreciatively.

"No, no I ain't. I been tellin' you about her, so here she is in person." Ramon was exuberant, showing off his prize possession, stumbling over his words. It was obvious he was in awe of Hooker. The contrast between them was so vivid that Maureen was embarrassed for him.

Maureen looked Hooker over. Tall, medium dark skin, well built. His eyes were intelligent, his speech flawless, his voice a deep baritone; enticing, seductive. He knew she was appraising him and he smiled inwardly. *Sassy little broad. Smart. Classy. What the hell is she doing with Ramon?*

"This is a lovely party," she said. "Wouldn't it be nice to be sixteen again? Your daughter will remember it forever. Thank you for inviting us."

"My pleasure," Hooker said as he took her elbow and steered her away. She waved goodbye to Lui and the others. Ramon was on Maureen's left and he followed a couple of steps behind. Hooker ignored him.

"I don't think I'd want to be sixteen again. I'd rather be your age, twenty something," he said, more of a question than a statement.

"Almost thirty," she smiled.

"So, I hear you're going to be an attorney," Hooker said. "I need attorneys in my business."

"Yes, I bet you do," Maureen said. Hooker looked at her sharply. She smiled, raising an eyebrow. "Your reputation precedes you, Mr. Hooker." *Sharp little bitch,* he thought.

"I understand you also need auto mechanics and that you and Ramon are about to make a deal where you put him in business and he services your cars. Maybe I can take a look at the paperwork before you finalize the transaction," she said, looking him straight in the eye.

"Whose side would you be on, mine or Ramon's?"

"Whoever needs me the most," she said.

He looked at her for a long moment, shrugged his shoulders and said, "Well, you're not an attorney yet, are you?"

"No, but I'll be studying for the bar before you know it."

He saw her contemplate the margarita bar near the bandstand. "Studying for the bar or heading for the bar?" he asked with a tight smile.

"Both," she said, laughing, breaking the ice. She motioned to Ramon. "C'mon." She deftly slipped her arm from Hooker and took Ramon's hand. "Let's dance." She pulled Ramon toward the outdoor dance floor. Hooker's eyes followed her until she got lost among other dancers. *Nice piece of ass*, he thought. Hooker loved a challenge and Maureen was a challenge.

The band was in full swing. They had just finished an Eagles number for the kids and now they announced something "more mellow, for the grown-ups." A saxophone player opened the set with a smooth rendition of "All the Things You Are." He was so good you could close your eyes and think it was Stan Getz.

Ramon was awkward; the only thing he knew was that he had his arms around Maureen and *to hell with the dancing*. He was happy just moving back and forth with her, smelling her hair. The music ended and the black bandleader spoke into the microphone. "Ladies and gentlemen, give it up for Harry Lax, the man with the sax." The dancers and other guests applauded. "We'll take a short break and be back in fifteen minutes," he announced.

Maureen heard the bandleader's comment but it took her a moment to absorb what he said: *Harry Lax, the man with the sax*.

"Oh my God!" She extricated herself from Ramon's arms and walked quickly to the bandstand. "I'll be back, Ramon. That may be my father," she said. Puzzled, he thought he'd heard her wrong.

Lax was putting his instrument down. He was a tall, thin man, probably in his sixties. Except for his tightly curled dark hair which showed twists of grey he did not appear to have any black features. He and a couple of others were setting their instruments down or just chatting and smoking. He surveyed Maureen as she walked up the two steps to the bandstand and approached him. The other band players glanced over, curious.

"Do you have a minute?" she asked.

"I always have a minute for a beautiful woman," he smiled.

His face was deeply lined; his hazel eyes showed a lot of hard living and more than a trace of skepticism.

"What can I do for you?"

"Well, I'm wondering how good your memory is," she said.

"Used to be pretty good. If you goin back to yesterday, forget it! But now," he paused. "You go back to my childhood and I remember every piece of pie my grandmother ever put on the windowsill to cool. I remember the smell of cherries or apples, the oven so caked with grease the door cried every time you opened it. The kitchen was always hot; too hot in summer and not hot enough in winter, but none of us ever complained."

"How many of there were you?"

"Oh, least nine or ten," he said, scratching his head, wiping down his instrument. "We never knowed whether they belonged to us or not. They just came and went."

"Where was this? It sounds like you were on a farm or something."

"Oh, no. Nothin like that. Just some small town in Louisiana a city slicker like you prob'ly never heard of," he said.

"Your grandmother raised you?"

"Yep. Left her husband and my mother in France. She just threw me under her arm like a piece of baggage and came on to America to start a new life. My mama followed eventually but Louisiana was never a place she cottoned to. New York was more to her liking."

"You play a mean sax." She complimented him. "How long have you been at it?"

"Oh, a long, long time. It's the only thing I ever got to know intimately . . . the only relative I have." He patted the saxophone affectionately.

"Maybe not," Maureen said, looking directly at him. He raised his head and put his hand over his brow to shade his eyes and look more closely at her.

"Whatd'ya mean?"

"Do you remember a band called *SIX TO FIVE*, thirty years ago, Cleveland, Ohio?"

Lax didn't answer but you could see he was struggling to locate the forgotten piece of information, to find a path in his brain from the past to the present. "*SIX TO FIVE*," he repeated under his breath. "Gimme a minute."

Maureen waited.

"Yeah, it's comin to me. Band leader's name was Ezekiel. They were on to another gig down the road but I got a call my Mama died in New York and I took the train there to see to her for the first time in years . . . and for the last time." He paused. "There a reason you're askin me these questions?"

"Well, I think so," Maureen said. "I believe I'm your daughter."

Harry Lax's mouth fell slightly open and he raised his eyebrows. He slowly reached his hand out and lifted her chin with his long fingers. Hazel eyes, the same as his mother; white skin with just a hint of color the same as his; the tilt of her jaw, the same as his grandmother. And the hair. That was the thing that triggered the memory; her hair, dark and thick like molasses. Ilsa! That was her name. A cute kid who had watched in awe as he played his sax all those years ago. He recalled the two nights he spent with her. She had given him a cock 'n bull story about her age but he never believed it for a minute. He didn't really care. She was a hot little number and he wasn't going to turn down a free lay.

Instead of denying their possible relationship, Harry Lax laughed; a deep thunderous laugh that shook his whole body. "Don't go away," he said as the band members took their places for the next set. They put out their cigarettes, finished up their drinks and conversation.

He picked up his saxophone, lovingly, tenderly, and got ready for the next number. "Except for this," he said, "You may be the best thing that ever happened to me in my whole life."

CHAPTER THIRTY-FOUR

CHICORY'S BOY HECTOR, WALKED into the Gringo Palace a few days after Lorenzo's offer of employment. It was not an easy decision. It wasn't as though he could solicit advice from his family or peers. This was an act of bravery; a casting aside of a familiar and somewhat safe lifestyle, one where Chicory was the chief organizer, the security officer, the family advisor. Most decisions were pre-ordained. Thinking was not required, only passive resignation or acquiescence.

Following the altercation between Chicory and Lorenzo, Hector cleared a space in his mind so that, for the first time, he was able to see Chicory objectively — a sneering, angry, black-clad figure whose only power was to surround himself with hangers-on who had nowhere else to go. It came to Hector in a flash that Lorenzo's offer gave him someplace to go.

Danny was at the front counter. When Hector walked in he nodded toward the back room. "She's back there," he said. Lorenzo had alerted Danny that Hector might be coming in to do some carpentry work.

"Not a good idea," Danny had said.

"Everyone needs a chance," Lorenzo answered, looking directly at him.

"Okay, I got ya."

Rosie looked up as Hector entered. She was surprised and pleased. "No smoking back here," she said. "Too dangerous!" Hector put his cigarette out. He looked around. The room was about twenty by thirty. Boxes of merchandise were strewn everywhere along each side and the far end of the room. Rosie was trying to clear a space in the middle.

"What're you tryin to do?" he asked.

"Well, I'm expecting 'Renzo any minute. He's going to lay out a plan that will give us the most space. Meantime, if you're ready to start working, give me hand with these." She pointed to several heavy boxes. They worked for about twenty minutes until Lorenzo showed up.

"Hey, Hector, I'm glad to see you. C'mere. I want to show you something." Renzo squatted down and opened a set of plans for rehabbing the back room. "Can you read blueprints?" Hector squatted alongside him.

"Yeah. I worked after school in a copy place. The construction guys used to come in with these huge sets of prints. They was showing me how to read them, but then I got laid off. I could see from the drawings the way it should be, but the trouble was I couldn't read the instructions too good."

Lorenzo looked over at him. "Chicory okay with this?"

"I don't know. I didn't ask."

"You think there'll be trouble?"

"I don't know. I need this job. But if you wanna change your mind, I'll understand."

"No," Lorenzo said. "I just want to make sure whose side you're on."

"To be honest with ya, Mr. Lorenzo, I'm on my side and the way I see it, right now my side is to be working. You teach me, I'll learn."

"Deal," Lorenzo said. They shook hands. Hector smiled for the first time in a long time.

"So how much lumber you think we'll need for the shelves if they run along this side?" Lorenzo asked Hector. He could see that Hector was calculating linear feet, depth, and height.

"I think we'll need . . ."

"Yes, but did you figure in . . ." Lorenzo asked. And so it went, back and forth, the architect leading, teaching, encouraging; the student absorbing, showing strength and knowledge he never thought he had, smiling a lot, proud of himself.

Chicory observed everything from a distance, waiting, biding his time. His entourage was shrinking. From five there were now only three, and Snake's family was moving. Marty had left him to work for Rosie and now Hector had abandoned him.

The back room took shape: tables, benches, a small bookcase, a blackboard — surrounded by a jungle of corrugated boxes.

When Marty arrived at work that afternoon, he was surprised to see Hector. "Hey, Hec, what happened between you and Chicory?"

"Nothin," Hector shrugged.

"Somethin must have happened, or you wouldn't be here."

"Yeah. I decided I needed a job more than I needed Chicory."

"What about school?" Marty asked. "We only got another year to go."

"You know I ain't no good in school, Marty. I always had trouble reading. I don't see the letters right. They're all backwards."

Marty looked around. "You did all this? Organized the boxes and everything?"

Hector shuffled his feet, embarrassed.

"This looks great! The room hasn't looked this good since the first day Rosie opened." Hector smiled at the compliment. Marty gave him a thumbs up.

Lorenzo was impressed with Hector's grasp of carpentry and his ability to read blue prints. They worked together for a week building tables and benches that fit comfortably into the configuration of the small back room. For the first time, Hector began to think of himself as someone other than Chicory's running mate. Lorenzo made several calls:

"Yeah, I got this kid, name's Hector, no real experience, but terrific at figuring dimensions . . ."

"Hey, how ya doing 'Renzo? I thought you were retired . . ."

"I am, I am. But I'm doing a small job for a friend and this kid pops in looking for work, so I try him out — and I'm wondering if you need anyone. Just a start-up job but I think you'll like him and wind up thanking me."

"Okay, send him in. Maybe I can use him in the lumber department, see how he does and we'll go from there."

"Thanks, Mike. Let me know how he works out."

Hector got the job.

◇◇◇

Felicia's progress with reading and speaking English was spectacular. Partly it was due to Felicia's innate intelligence, but much of it was attributable to Rosie's teaching ability. It affected a broader spectrum of Felicia's life than she had anticipated. Her comprehension expanded and grew like an amoeba, feeding on itself and multiplying. She began to think of herself differently, slowly losing the weight she had gained after the birth of her three children and taking more pride in her appearance.

Now that she could read and understand pattern instructions she began making her own clothes with an old sewing machine a neighbor had given her. She took her children to the library, reading to them from books Rosie had recommended, stumbling over the words, yet determined to progress.

But she worried. She worried that Reynaldo would not approve.

When they were in bed one evening, after a lengthy truck run, she embraced him and ran her hand smoothly along his arm, feeling his muscles ripple beneath her fingers.

"A-h-h," he said. "*Cuanto te extrano cuando no estoy contigo. I miss you so much when I am gone.*"

She whispered into his shoulder. "No more than I miss you."

"What is it about you that has changed, my Felicia? You look different; you smell different. It is like coming home to a new woman." He turned toward her and pressed her to him running his hand along her spine, her hips, pulling her buttocks closer.

She smiled inwardly, pleased that he had noticed. "You are not angry that there is not so much of me anymore?"

"No." He laughed.

"You think you'll be able to find everything? Or do you need my help?" she teased as she moved his hand between her legs.

"Don't worry, wherever it is, I'll find it."

"*Eres mas deseable que nunca. Estoy orgullosa de ti.*" You are more desirable than ever. I am very proud of you," he said as he pulled her body on top of him barely containing his need to enter her.

◇◇◇

News of Felicia's improved English skills, and Hector's job, filtered through the barrio. Neighbors stopped each other on the street.

"The Gringo Palace is teaching English in the back room. Are you going?"

"I don't know. Are you?"

"Senor Fernandez has already talked to Rosie."

"How do you know?"

"He told me he thinks his chances of working would be better if he could speak and read English. There is no charge to learn. It can only help us."

"That is true. We all know that."

"So? What do you think?" Carmen from the hair salon asked.

"I agree there would be more opportunity. I don't know if my husband will say okay."

"You can both go."

"Yes, that would be better — if we both go!"

Rosie and her friend Clara sat at a small table outside the Gringo Palace and took the names of those who wanted to attend. Only a trickle registered before classes started. First one, then two, then three. Within a week twenty men and women had put their names on the schedule. When asked why they wanted to take this class, the answers varied:

"I want a better job."

"I want to speak English to my children so they don't think I am ignorant."

"I love this country and I want to learn the language."

"If I learn to read, maybe I can get a job and help my husband."

"People think I am stupid because I can't read or write English. But I am not stupid. I want to show people that I am smart."

On Monday, October 7th 1974, a palpable change began to take place in a small pocket area of Los Angeles between Alvarado Street on the East, Western Avenue on the west, and between Pico and Olympic on the south and north. An air of excitement coursed through the small group of people gathered in the back room of the Palace.

"My heart is beating like a guitar."

"You mean a drum . . ."

"Yes, like a drum. I am so scared. I have never been to school. Even in Mexico I was not able to go."

"Me too!"

They seated themselves on the benches. The tables in front of them were those that Hector had erected. They squeezed close. Pencils and lined yellow pads had been given to them as they entered. They didn't think they would ever learn to use them, but within the first five minutes Rosie was writing their names on the blackboard and they were copying their names on their pads.

Rosie had her back to the students when she heard the back door open. Suddenly conversation ceased and a hush descended on the room. Rosie turned. Hector stood at the door, hesitant, uncomfortable. She put the chalk down and walked toward him, a big smile on her face. "Hector, welcome." Senor Fernandez moved over making a place for him.

Rosie introduced Clara as her co-instructor. Most people already knew Clara and felt comfortable with her. She walked around unobtrusively, helping those who appeared to have trouble with the letters.

Rosie was in her element. For so many years she had taught Spanish. Now she was teaching English, an easy transition. Rosie and Clara devised a curriculum that was humorous as well as informative, imaginative as well as realistic, elementary yet complicated. Rosie's Gringo Palace bustled with good will, hope, optimism and expectation.

CHAPTER THIRTY-FIVE

THE GRINGO SCHOOL HAD only been ongoing for six months but already there was a palpable change in the community. The changes were subtle, but taken cumulatively, they were impressive.

For starters, Rosie's acceptance into the community now entitled her to be called Rosie. She was no longer referred to as "the gringo."

Felicia Cormier continued to be a role model for several women who had a natural predisposition toward design. Her husband, Reynaldo, encouraged his wife. "If you're happy, I'm happy," he said.

The women met at Felicia's small apartment and she taught them how to use the sewing machine, how to read a pattern, how to make their own clothes, pillows, tablecloths and other saleable items. As they became proficient in English and more professional in their product, they began to discuss a means of marketing their goods and earning additional income for their families.

Some husbands resisted; some even threatened their wives and forbade them to participate. Eventually, however, the women used their most potent weapon: sex — or the deliberate withholding thereof. The husbands capitulated out of sheer frustration and exhaustion.

As the women gained confidence, an unpremeditated transformation took place among the men. A delicate competition arose between them and their wives. To avoid being outdone, several husbands attended the English classes, even asking Rosie or Clara for additional one-on-one assistance to fill out employment applications or to read *want ads*. As a result, a number of men obtained jobs. Their income, along with potential income from their wives, provided the incentive for others to follow suit.

But it was the children who benefited most. They watched closely, absorbing the new activities of their parents: learning English, reading, sewing, working, redefining themselves as Americans while retaining their Hispanic culture. Along with their parents they felt a sense of inclusion rather than exclusion. Every Sunday their prayers could be heard, thanking God, America, and Rosie.

◇◇◇

Chicory was unable to adjust to the new direction the neighborhood was taking. He watched sullenly from a distance as Marty Ramirez's name was called up to the podium for his high school diploma. Marty was already enrolled for the fall semester at Los Angeles Community College as an accounting major. Rosie had taught him to do her books and he loved it. He wanted to work with his dad, bidding contracts, estimating job costs on new construction, maybe get his contractor's license.

Hector continued his job at the lumber yard, attending Rosie's English classes in the evening whenever possible. Rosie told him about dyslexia and he realized it wasn't due to stupidity that he couldn't read. He met a young girl who worked in the sales department of the company and for the first time in his life he was able to maintain a steady relationship without mucking it up. In addition to helping support his family, Hector was putting aside money so that he and his girlfriend could get married in a year or two.

Chicory's friend Snake was the only one left of the old gang. Annoyed with Chicory's bossy attitude Snake made no effort to continue their relationship after his family moved to a new neighborhood. Within a short time Snake was recruited into another club whose members spent their time in a similar fashion, leaning against brick buildings, spitting on the sidewalk, tugging at their balls, doing small jobs, dealing drugs and generally intimidating the residents.

Alone and scared, Chicory began to think he was dying, or maybe already dead. Headaches, loss of appetite, jitters, and feelings of persecution were only a few of the symptoms he developed. Everyone abandoned him — first his mother, and now Marty, Hector, and Snake. There was nowhere to go, no one to talk to. *It was all Rosie's fault.* Living with Aunt Rita was no longer an option. He was repulsed by her hands clawing at him, her sexual demands, sagging body, and foul breath. He wanted out! *She had money hidden somewhere in the apartment. First the money, then Rosie. She's the one who started it all. Marty and Hector wouldn't have left him if not for Rosie.* He called Snake. "Get me a gun."

"You sure you wanna do this man?" Snake asked. He didn't wait for an answer. "Prob'ly take a day or two."

"Whatever. Just get it!"

Snake delivered it early next evening.

Chicory had never held a gun before. He fondled it as he walked home caressing the smooth metal with his thumb, feeling the grooves, the trigger. He pictured himself twirling it like in the cowboy movies, shooting it out with the sheriff.

Aunt Rita was lying on the couch when Chicory got home. He had hardly stepped in the door when she said, "I got me one of dem sickly headaches, baby. Go get me some of dem pills I got in the cabinet . . . you know the ones I mean."

Chicory interrupted her as he closed the door behind him. "Get 'em yourself, whore." He had never talked back to her that way, but the gun in his pocket made a difference. He felt empowered but petrified at the same time. The sweat under his arms spread into larger circles. His legs felt weak.

"What? Whatd'ya say? Did I hear you right?" She swung her heavy legs off the couch. Her dress was scrunched up to mid thigh and she tugged at it as she stood up. "Who you think you're talkin to, you little bastard." He backed away as she came toward him pointing her finger. "This is the thanks I get for keepin you wit a roof over yo head the last ten years?"

"You didn't do nothin for me. I paid my way. I had all I could do to keep from puking every time I touched you, you sick bitch."

"You scrawny little shit. I shoulda kicked you out long ago," she screamed.

Now she was inches from him and he took the gun out of his pocket and waved it at her.

"Don't come any closer," he warned.

"A gun? I always knew you would never be nothin," she shouted trying to knock it out of his hand. But he held tight.

Her mouth was wide and gaping, dark like a cave, her tongue black against her uneven white teeth. He suddenly flashed on the abuse he had withstood all these years: her tongue snaking down his throat, gagging him, her tongue flicking his penis, his balls, her fingers disgustingly penetrating him, making him do the same to her. How old was he? Eight? Ten? Twelve? He was shaking. "Don't . . ."

He pulled the trigger. She fell back, a look of hatred on her face. For a moment he thought it was a painting that had fallen off the wall and crashed to the floor. A red blotch formed on her blouse just above her left breast. He started to laugh and then suddenly he was screaming hysterically like a madman, choking from fear, his tears and laughter mingling with snot and sweat. He fell to the floor, holding his stomach and writhing in pain and relief.

The room was quiet now and he tried to think beyond the sight of Aunt Rita who lay dead a few feet away. He walked over to the cabinet where she kept the liquor and took a couple of swigs of cheap scotch, not bothering to put the cap back on the bottle.

The money! Where would the money be? He walked to the bedroom and pulled out the drawers searching through them and under them. Under one he found his birth certificate. *Mother: Georgia James Ayala; Father: John Doe; Baby Boy: Anarpol.* Funny, he never thought of himself as actually having a mother and a father. *Anarpol.* He repeated his name over and over as if to convince himself that he had been born of parents and not simply uprooted from dirt.

The Money! He needed to find the money. He searched the closet; he pulled down every shoebox and slid his hand in every pair of shoes and in every jacket pocket. Nothing. He went back to the living room.

At the side of the couch was a pair of slippers. These were the same slippers she put on from the minute she came home until she retired. He walked over and picked them up. Aunt Rita's toe had worked a hole through the front. The inner cotton padding protruded slightly and he instinctively pushed it back in. He walked over to the dead body and fit the slippers on Aunt Rita. "There ya go." He felt kindly toward her now and was tempted to cover her with a blanket but he forced himself to turn away to focus again on searching for the money.

The freezer! Nothing there except a tin of Maxwell House coffee and two boxes of frozen vegetables. Nothing in the refrigerator section either. He stood for a few minutes leaning against the kitchen counter.

His mind went back to the coffee. It seemed to him it had been there a long time. He'd never given it a thought before. He took the container out of the freezer and opened the plastic lid. Coffee grinds spilled out onto the floor. *Shit!* Angry and disappointed, he threw the can to the floor and stomped on it. More coffee spilled out and he started to walk away, disgusted. But he turned back because he thought he heard a clinking sound, like coins. He turned the can upside down and poured out the grinds. Three one hundred dollar bills and an assortment of change came out with it. *YES!* He looked at the clock. Almost 7:00 p.m. Rosie would be finishing her class. Everyone would be leaving and she would remain there to close up. *Perfect!*

◇◇◇

Rosie was tired. It had been a long day and an especially long night because Clara was unable to help her. Instead, Clara's granddaughter Hannah pitched in. Hannah had just turned fifteen. A year ago she had dyed her hair blond. The contrast between her olive complexion and blond hair was interesting and provocative. It was parted in the center framing a soft oval face and piercing dark eyes highlighted with dark brown eye shadow and eyeliner. She was long-limbed for her age. Her slender body slouched slightly to compensate for her height. She glided through the classroom picking up odd pieces of paper and pens, pushing the benches under the tables and otherwise clearing the area while Rosie held the back door open as everyone exited, smiling, *adios, buenos noches, see you tomorrow evening.*

Chicory squatted near a dumpster and watched until he was sure everyone had left. He couldn't believe his luck. *Hannah!* She and Rosie were about to walk out the back door. Rosie had already turned off the interior lights but now she said, "Just a minute. I forgot to turn the outside lights on and change the sign in the front window saying we're closed." Hannah held the door and waited.

Chicory pressed his advantage. He stepped from behind the dumpster and quickly moved forward, grabbing Hannah and forcing her inside. She let out a small scream before he covered her mouth and dragged her across the floorboards. Rosie thought she heard a noise.

"What the hell . . ." She turned around before changing the sign in the window from OPEN to CLOSED.

"Hannah?" she called. There was no answer. She heard movement, scuffling, and her heart started beating furiously. She felt her way back holding on to the narrow stainless steel shelving which separated one aisle from another. She stopped just short of the doorway, straining to see into the darkened classroom, calling out again to Hannah.

Chicory had Hannah pinned against the wall, his dark clothing giving him invisibility in the darkened room. Hannah was so frightened she started to collapse, but he held her firm with his body. "First I'll take care of that bitch Rosie and then you," he whispered into her ear. "I bet you can't wait for me to do it to you, right, cunt? You're still a virgin, right?" She could feel his sweat, the smell of him, as he pushed against her.

Hannah was still holding stray pens and pencils in her hand when Chicory accosted her. She moved one hand free of his grasp and jabbed one of the pens hard into his side and he let out a yell, temporarily letting go of her. "Rosie!" she screamed. "Don't come in. Call the . . ." She never finished the sentence. Chicory swung his fist back and gave her a knockout punch to the jaw. She fell to the floor unconscious. Rosie heard the thud. She moved silently toward the phone at the front register. Chicory moved stealthily into the grocery section, his sneakers silent against the hardwood floor. He crouched, moving along one aisle and then sliding over to another. *I got a gun, bitch. You ain't goin nowhere. First Aunt Rita, and now you. And then I'm going to use my joystick to fuck that little cocksucker in the back room.*

◇◇◇

Ramon was driving home from a meeting at Willie Hooker's downtown office. He had just dropped Maureen off. Maureen had taken the Bar exam the previous week and she was totally exhausted. But as a favor to Ramon and at Hooker's insistence she had reluctantly attended the meeting.

"I don't want to do anything your girlfriend doesn't approve of," Hooker had said, his voice eloquent, his delivery smooth. But Ramon knew, as did Maureen, that Hooker was looking for an excuse to see Maureen again.

They were trying to finalize the deal where Hooker would set Ramon up in business with a ten-year payback. Hooker wanted Ramon to work on his cars exclusively. Maureen had said *NO!* She convinced Ramon that if the deal proceeded that way, Hooker would own him. So this was the issue still to be resolved. He was tired and his mind was frazzled with all this business crap. "Let's think on it overnight and talk tomorrow," Ramon had said.

Driving home, he looked at the empty pack of cigarettes on the dashboard. *Damn!* He decided to stop at the Gringo Palace. He thought the store might be closed, but he'd take a chance. *Good. The OPEN sign is still in the window. Funny though, no lights on.* He parked his car at the curb and walked toward the front door. He pulled on it but it was locked. *Something ain't right.* "Rosie," he shouted. "Are you still here?" Rosie didn't answer because she knew Chicory was nearby and she did not want to reveal her location.

Ramon walked around the back to the classroom. The door was unlocked and he entered quietly closing it quickly behind him and staying low. The room was dark. There was an unusual odor. *Blood!* Ramon had smelled enough blood in his life to easily identify it. He listened carefully allowing his eyes to adjust to the dark before moving again.

He spotted the crumpled body of Clara's granddaughter, Hannah, about ten feet away and moved toward it. She was just coming to. "Ramon!" she whimpered. He put a firm hand across her mouth. *Shhh.* Their eyes locked. He took his hand away. "Chicory," she whispered. "I think he's in the front." He helped Hannah up. "You okay?" She nodded.

He raised his hand and signaled her to go out the back door and get help.

Chicory heard the small sound the back door made when Ramon entered. He wasn't sure what to do, whether to continue to stalk Rosie, or go back to the classroom. He removed the gun from his jacket pocket and held it in front of him, his finger on the trigger, his body tense except for his hand which was shaking uncontrollably.

He listened intently. There! On the other side of the shelving unit, a small noise and Rosie's silhouette. He pushed hard from his side. She screamed as the entire unit came crashing down on her, six packs of soda and beer, pretzels, potato chips and cookies.

Ramon sprinted into the room his six foot five body lurching toward Chicory in one final leap. Chicory let off several shots. No one moved. A dead silence surrounded him. In the distance, sirens. He ran out the back door and kept running until he collapsed outside his home. *Aunt Rita will know what to do,* he thought as a police car pulled up to the curb.

Ramon fell, his mind peaceful, not afraid. He closed his eyes slowly. He was sure Alberto was holding his hand. *You're always here when I need you, aren't you, mi hermano?* He pictured his mother's face.

Even when you're crying, you're still beautiful as ever, Mama!
Bullshit. Always with the bullshit!
Ramon smiled.

.

CHAPTER THIRTY-SIX

LORENZO APPEARED TO HAVE aged ten years in the last three days. Unshaven and disheveled, he sat in a hospital chair a few feet from Rosie. He had slipped his shoes off and closed his eyes which were red-rimmed and had dark circles under them. His back was killing him; when he stood up a sharp pain ran down his legs.

Rosie had suffered a severe concussion in addition to cracked ribs and a broken leg. Shattered glass from a case of beer bottles had resulted in two serious cuts, both needing sutures — one on her right arm above the elbow and another on her left thigh. Her whole body was bruised. She looked like she'd been in a boxing match and lost.

Lorenzo stirred, changing his body position. He looked over and saw that Rosie's eyes were open for the first time since the accident.

"Rosie . . ." He grimaced as he stood up and walked to her bedside. He took her hand and sat at the edge of the bed. "Rosie," he said, unable to utter anything else, so overwhelmed was he with emotion, so thankful that she was alive. He bent his head to her pillow sobbing and she stroked his hair until his shaking subsided. After a few minutes he lifted his head and met her eyes.

"Ramon?" she asked.

He shook his head. Her face contorted with grief. A sorrowful low scream escaped her lips, a sound so soulful that Lorenzo was sure it had reached to the heavens where God Himself knelt down to pray.

"Hannah?"

"Shaken up, but okay except for a bruised jaw."

Lorenzo filled Rosie in on the rest. Chicory had been immediately apprehended by the police, the body of his aunt found in the living room. He seemed to be in the throes of a nervous breakdown and could barely remember the sequence of events. The question was whether to try him as an adult or as a seventeen-year-old. Ironically, he wanted Maureen to act as his defense attorney.

Alberto was so inconsolable he had locked himself in his apartment and would not speak to anyone for days, not even his fiancée, Annie. Alberto blamed himself, saying this would not have happened if Ramon and he were still living together, if he had not encouraged Ramon to buy his own house, if he had paid more attention to Ramon's business dealings with Willie Hooker. Alberto could not be convinced that none of this had anything to do with Ramon's death. Hortencia was flying out to see her son for the last time and to be with Alberto. The funeral was to be held the following Tuesday.

"Do you think I'll be well enough to go?" Rosie asked Lorenzo.

He looked at her bandaged body, her raised leg supported by a sling hung from ceiling hooks. "I don't think so. It's going to take at least three more weeks before you're up and about." He looked at her crestfallen face. "But I'll tell you what," he said trying to cheer her up. "The minute you're out of here we'll go to the cemetery to see Ramon. I promise."

"What about the Gringo Palace?" she asked. "Was there much damage?"

"Yes, but nothing that can't be repaired," he said. "It's not like we'll have to start from scratch."

"I wouldn't have the strength to do that," she said.

"We'll see," he said. "No sense worrying about it now."

Rosie closed her eyes. "Don't go away, Renzo."

"No chance of that, Rosie," he said. But she didn't hear him.

◇◇◇

Maureen's boss, Jerome Greene, made the funeral arrangements. Neither Alberto nor Maureen was emotionally capable of doing it. Hortencia was prostrate with grief. She and Henry Cardillo had married a year ago. He had closed his bakery for a week and accompanied her to Los Angeles. She clung to him and Alberto as she viewed her son for the last time. "Mi nino," she murmured. She bent over and kissed his forehead, sobbing as she and Alberto held on to each other for support and comfort.

Maureen had called Lui Chu. She saw him walk in with Charlie Mello. Willie Hooker showed up. He and Charlie gave each other strange looks. Hooker knew it was Charlie who had stolen his white Mercedes a year ago but this was no time to pursue the matter. Charlie disappeared immediately after the service. Hector showed up with his girlfriend. Danny Bracco came with his wife. Clara and her entire family were there, as were Rosie's first student, Felicia Cormier and her husband Reynaldo. The church was crowded with neighbors, friends and family.

Conspicuously missing were Rosie and Lorenzo. When the service was about to begin, and only the mournful sounds of the congregation could be heard, the church doors opened and in walked Lorenzo pushing Rosie in a wheelchair. Nothing Lorenzo could do or say would convince her not to come. She wore a black scarf around her bandaged head. The sight of Rosie provoked a new wave of moaning and sobbing and nose-blowing, as though Ramon's death was not enough, but now they suffered the additional agony and reminder of Rosie's close call with death. Lorenzo wheeled her to the front of the church. Hortencia embraced her. "Rosie, *mi amiga*," she said.

Maureen sat in despair, a wad of tissues tight in one hand. Her face was pale, her blue eyes red-rimmed from lack of sleep and weeping. Next to her sat her father, Harry Lax. He put his arm around her and she leaned into him. Neither of them allowed the memory of Ilsa to dampen their relationship. They had grown very close over the past few months.

The priest waved his hand over the casket giving his benediction. He stood at the altar and gazed down at the congregation. He was a kindly man; his words were soothing, his manner sensitive and comforting, dulling the painful reality of the mass and rosary.

Maureen nodded to her father. He stood up and walked to a corner platform. The dulcet tones of his tenor sax echoed softly through the church in a heart-breaking rendition of John Lennon's *Let it Be*.

CHAPTER THIRTY-SEVEN

LORENZO PEERED OVER THE edge of his newspaper and watched as Rosie poured her morning coffee. She limped slightly.

"I know you're watching me," she said, her back to him and a little smile on her face.

"I can't help it. You've got such a cute little ass. But that flowered nightgown leaves a lot to be desired. I mean, it's a good thing I can see through it or it would be totally useless." The lace was separated from the bodice, the hem hung down in several places and the flowered print had faded into a blur of colors.

"You're the one that's totally useless," she chided. "This is a legacy from my mother. It reminds me of Joey because he always teased me about it."

At Lorenzo's insistence, Rosie had moved into his house when she was released from the hospital. In any event, she could not bear the thought of moving back to Ramon's house. Besides, Ramon had left everything to Alberto and this was the catalyst for Alberto and Annie to get married. As far as Rosie knew the Gringo Palace was closed. Lorenzo would not let her go there until she was ready to face the task of repairing it.

◇◇◇

During Rosie's stay in the hospital, Lorenzo made several trips to the Gringo Palace. He organized a neighborhood meeting in the back room. The damages were not as extensive as first believed. Hector and Danny, skilled with a hammer and nails, were able to repair most of it. Broken glass was cleaned up, hardwood flooring restored and shelving put upright. The neighborhood came together, each providing a skill toward the Palace's restoration. Danny Bracco and Marty Ramirez worked as many hours as necessary to keep the store open, maintaining impeccable receipts of sales and expenses. Marty taught his sister, Hannah, to do the books and ordering. Clara resumed the evening classes.

◇◇◇

Rosie was feeling claustrophobic. "Too much time doing nothing," she complained to Lorenzo. "I need to reopen the Palace."

"Okay, we'll go this coming Saturday." Word spread quickly throughout the neighborhood that Rosie was coming. A sign was ordered for Rosie's benefit:

GRAND RE-OPENING

ROSIE'S GRINGO PALACE

The following week, the neighbors gathered around as she arrived with Lorenzo. The bestowed hugs and kisses and opened a path for her to the front door. Danny stood behind the counter. Everything was as it had been over a month ago.

"Speech, speech," everyone shouted, but Rosie was overwhelmed and not prepared to address the crowd. They would not be discouraged so she stood on the front doorstep until they quieted down.

"My dear friends, how can I thank you?" She looked out at the crowd and waved her hand. "Look how far we've come in trust and friendship. Three years ago we did not know each other. Today we gather as a family because we have learned to open our minds and hearts. Our community has flourished. This would not have been possible if you had not had the courage to rise above old perceptions, to set aside intolerance. This is the American dream you sought when you came to this country. This is the heritage you are bequeathing to your children." Rosie stepped forward and Lorenzo took her arm. He nodded to the crowd.

"She is tired," he said as he led her back to the car for the short ride home.

There was a moment of silence. Then everyone was cheering, applauding, hugging each other.

"Get well soon, Rosie; we are waiting for you."

CHAPTER THIRTY-EIGHT

THE WORLD WAS GETTING ready for the demise of nineteen seventy-five and the promise of nineteen-seventy-six. It had been an interesting year. World population exceeded four billion. Median household income in the United States was $11,800. In the Super Bowl, Pittsburgh defeated Minnesota sixteen to six. *Saturday Night Live* premiered on NBC with George Carlin hosting the first show. The federal debt reached $541.9 billion.

. . . And Lorenzo proposed! They knew they would marry eventually; it was never a matter of 'will we do it,' but 'when will we do it?'

As she did every year since the opening in 1973, Rosie was planning a New Year's Day party at the Gringo Palace and Lorenzo suggested they hire a Justice of the Peace and surprise everyone and get married. Rosie thought it was a great idea. She put a sign in the window.

FRIENDS AND NEIGHBORS
ROSIE'S GRINGO PALACE INVITES YOU
TO A VERY SPECIAL
NEW YEAR'S DAY PARTY
JANUARY 1ST AT 4:00 P.M.

Without revealing the details, Lorenzo spoke with Danny Bracco. "You know, I'd really like this to be a special party and I'm wondering if you know a local band that could entertain? Mariachis, guitars? That sort of thing?"

"Hell, yes, but you should ask Hector about that. He plays a mean guitar."

"Hector? You're kidding!"

"Hell I am," Danny said. "Hector used to play all the time until he got hooked up with Chicory. But now that he's joined the human race he plays gigs every weekend with a local Mexican band."

"Well, I'll be damned. I'll talk to him right away."

"Yeah. By the way, how's he doing at the lumber yard job?" Danny asked.

"He's doing great. He'll probably own the place before you know it. He loves the job."

"You really did a good thing getting him that job, Lorenzo. You changed the kid's life."

"Yeah, I hope so."

◇◇◇

Lorenzo enlisted Maureen's assistance. Together they selected a wedding band for Rosie. When he told her about getting a band, her ears perked up.

"Lorenzo, I can get you the best sax player in the world."

"Oh, yeah? And who would that be?"

"A guy called Harry Lax, the man with the sax," she laughed.

"Harry Lax? Never heard of him."

"Me neither, until a couple months ago. He's my dad."

"Is he the guy who played at Ramon's funeral?"

"Yep, he's the one."

"Maureen, you've been holding out on us. I didn't know you had a dad hereabouts."

Maureen told Lorenzo the story of how she found Harry.

"Jesus, did you tell your Mom and grandmother that you found him?"

"Not my Mom; just my grandmother."

"What did she say," Lorenzo asked.

"Well, she encouraged me to keep in touch with him. It's wonderful. Best thing that ever happened to me."

"You think he'll play for us?"

"Are you kidding? I'm having dinner with him tonight and I'll set it up."

◇◇◇

Everyone turned out for the New Year's Day festivities. Alberto and his wife Annie were there with their infant son whom he had named for his brother, Ramon. Hortencia had flown in for the christening and she proudly held her grandson in her arms. Hector and three of his friends played guitars, mariachis and drums. The children danced to the music as their parents looked on in amusement and pride. Eventually husbands joined in, unable to resist the seductive rhythm, the swaying of hips, the stomping of feet on the pavement.

Rosie had arranged to dress at Clara's. She wore an ankle length pale lavender dress. The circle of white pearls around her neck and small pearl earrings had belonged to her mother. The air around Rosie moved with the spirits of Joey and Ramon. Hannah, sensing a flood of tears, said, "Rosie, if you shed one tear I will kill you because your makeup will be totally destroyed!" Rosie pushed back the memories and tried to smile.

The doorbell rang and Clara opened it wide for Lorenzo. She gasped at how handsome he looked, dashing in a charcoal blazer, white shirt and grey silk tie. He watched as Rosie descended the stairs, her slim body hesitating halfway down, a captivating shy look on her face. He had never seen her more beautiful. He smiled as she approached him, took her hand and escorted her to the car. They drove to the Palace and entered through the back door.

The neighbors, still unaware this was to be a wedding, shouted "Where's Rosie, we want Rosie."

Suddenly the front door of the Palace opened and the Justice of the Peace took his place before the crowd. They stirred and quieted down. *Shhh, shhh. What's happening here?* He faced them, his voice sonorous and distinctive.

"*Senors y Senoras, Ninos, Amigos* . . . friends and neighbors. This is the beginning of a new year, and also the beginning of a new life for Rosie and Lorenzo." The door opened wider and Rosie and Lorenzo stepped out.

It took a moment for the crowd to understand they were there to witness Rosie's marriage. She was so beautiful, they gasped and started to applaud, but the Justice held up his hand for silence. The ceremony was short, adhering to the wishes of bride and groom. They looked into each other's eyes as they said their vows.

"Do you . . ."

"Yes, I do . . ."

He slipped the ring on her finger and they kissed. The crowd burst into cheers and laughter.

The mellow tones of Harry Lax's tenor sax played in the background. "I'll be loving you, *ALWAYS.*"

Joey. Ramon. Are you listening?

Rosie's Gringo Palace

BOOK GROUP DISCUSSION

- Drawing from either your own experience or the book, why do you think Rosie never traveled prior to Joey's death? She couldn't or wouldn't leave her ailing brother? Insufficient financial resources? Fear of leaving the comfort of a nice safe job?

- Discuss whether Hortencia had an ulterior motive when she tried to convince her sons to leave. Was she looking out for herself, or for them?

- What factors would cause an intelligent young woman like Maureen to hook up with someone like Paul? In your personal life, have you, or do you know others, who have made such mistakes? What were the catalysts that enabled a shift or an end to such a relationship?

- On the way to Cleveland, Maureen discarded her cocktail dress and exited the ladies room looking like a *different person*. What did she mean when she told Alberto, 'this is the old me.'

- Do you think Gloria and her husband, Martin, were self-serving when they convinced their parents Clara and Frank to uproot their lives in Manhattan and move to California to look after their teenage children? Were they more interested in their own needs, or were they genuinely concerned for their aging parents?

- What was different about the abuse Maureen withstood from her mother, and the abuse Chicory suffered from Aunt Rita? Why was Chicory unable to rise above the abuse, while Maureen went on to become a successful lawyer?

- Foster children usually have difficulty overcoming abandonment and abuse issues. Given the circumstances of Chicory's life with Aunt Rita, at what age do you think he still could have been "saved?" Could he ever have overcome the damage?

- What was the core of Rosie's success with the Gringo Palace? Her personality? Perseverance? Spanish language skills? Or just plain guts?

- From your own personal experience, do you know many people who made a notable difference in other people's lives?

Breinigsville, PA USA
02 November 2010
248492BV00004B/1/P